Preface

Life in India had a predictable side, as Queen Victoria herself acknowledged. When the Prince of Wales was on tour the Queen noted ". . . such a constant repetition of elephants – trappings – jewels – illuminations and fireworks."

But unexpected and inexplicable events confronted many of the Queen's British subjects (and other "Europeans") who went out in increasing numbers to work, or simply to travel and observe. Indeed, so unpredictable were some of their experiences in India that they did not live to tell their tale, struck down as they were by mortal sickness, wild beast or rebellious hand.

Fortunately, the majority did survive, and they produced a wealth of vivid reportage on what they saw and experienced: graphic eyewitness accounts, candid character studies, revealing anecdotes – all now diffused among a daunting and inaccessible mass of books and papers on dusty library shelves. My objective has been to rescue some of the very best of this material for the enjoyment of modern readers.

The past comes alive with an exhilarating freshness and immediacy through these writings, often suffused with the humour or emotion of the moment. But even more than this, the stories illuminate the essential continuity of past and present in people's attitudes, preferences, and prejudices. There are such enduring qualities about the country and its peoples (and about the British, too) that many of these images of India remain as recognisable today as when they first appeared. In this sense the *True Tales* have as much to say to the present as they do about the past.

Michael Wise

OUR AIM in presenting *True Tales* has been to give voice to a representative band of travellers from the past speaking in their own words about India as they knew it. Some of their material – a small part – contains descriptions of unusual violence and expressions of racialist sentiment. These have been included here to reflect accurately the spirit of their time, and with the intention of conveying a proper sense of the place and period concerned. (Similarly their individual spelling and punctuation have been retained throughout for complete authenticity, even when not conforming to accepted usage.)

All the views expressed in this book, therefore, are those of the original authors and are not necessarily shared by the present publisher or compiler.

TRUE TALES
OF
BRITISH INDIA
&
The Princely States

compiled by
Michael Wise

Foreword by
Alan Campbell-Johnson

In Print
1993

In Print Publishing Ltd is registered with the Publishers Licensing Society in the UK and the Copyright Clearance Center in the USA.

British Library Cataloguing in Publication Data: A catalogue record for this book is available from the British Library.

ISBN 1 873047 06 1

Cover design by Russell Townsend
Typeset by MC Typeset Ltd
Printed by Utopia Press

First published in 1993 by
In Print Publishing Ltd, 9 Beaufort Terrace, Brighton BN2 2SU, UK.
Tel: (0273) 682836. Fax: (0273) 620958

CONTENTS

Journeys and Journey's End

Magic and Mystery

Affairs of State

Dangers and Disasters

Indian Sketches

Travellers and Tourists

Eastern Enigma

War and Freedom

Foreword

by
Alan Campbell-Johnson C.I.E., O.B.E.
Formerly Press Attaché to the Viceroy and Governor-General of
India, Earl Mountbatten of Burma

Across ninety years of British rule in India, from the Mutiny to the Transfer of Power, Michael Wise draws upon the eye-witness records of over eighty writers to amaze and amuse, test and terrify, but above all enlighten a new generation of readers for whom the Raj is already a fading tapestry. Having had the honour to be selected to provide the tail of this anthology – an account of being alone with the last Viceroy, Lord Mountbatten, at the midnight hour when power actually passed – I have been invited to produce a top as well. But it is a risky undertaking to try and "point a moral or adorn a tale" from this formidable sequence of self-contained incidents.

It has been justly observed about the historian's discipline that there is no substitute for a primary source, and the validity of this assertion will be confirmed as the reader's vision is enlarged and stretched from seeing Imperial India through such a diversity of personal experience. The only distinction which should perhaps be made at the outset is between stories recalled in tranquility some years after the event, and those "fly in amber" records caught and retained for ever in the present tense.

Hardened as we have become in our time to the horrors of genocide and holocaust, the traumas of the Indian Mutiny continue to make painful reading. But one cannot fail to be impressed with the contribution of William Howard Russell, correspondent of *The Times*, the pioneer and greatest exponent of so-called investigative journalism, applying to the outcome of the Indian uprising the realism that shocked the world in his previous coverage of the impact of war in the Crimea. No less searching are the perceptions of Rudyard Kipling recalling with the same word-magic how he reached the maturity to produce his saga of Kim's encounters with "The Great Game."

Particularly pertinent, too, are the recollections of Herbert Compton which span the years between 1871 and 1905 and take into account what he calls "pre and post Suez Canal days." While hospitality remains "the shining virtue" of the Anglo-Indian, "his chief difficulty will be the cliques into which society in the East habitually falls." Compton is alive to the emphasis placed on social status in a "select population governed by the strictest laws of precedence," and he asserts that "there have been more quarrels over precedence in Anglo-India than over any other cause. It is regulated by a table edited and issued by Government and which is in effect the charter of Anglo-Indian society."

With the passing of the years a cogent extract from Robert Bernays's brilliant "Naked Fakir", which I first encountered as a schoolboy in 1931, reveals the survival of the same inhibitions and imperatives, by which time it is getting dangerously late in the day to harbour them. I recall with amusement the difficulty the kindly Colonel Douglas Currie, last Military Secretary to the last Viceroy, had in providing a precedence for my unprecedented job as Press Attaché. Identity was finally established and honour satisfied when he settled for placing me 42nd in the élite top 50 alongside the Master in Lunacy.

There is no escaping the hierarchic motif: it appears again and again throughout these excerpts – the hideous birth mark of untouchability, food polluted by the human shadow, death with symbols of purification by fire and water as release from the degradation of life. But this is to paint too dark a picture, for, however strange or alien the customs and behaviour patterns of the native Indian subjects may seem to the self-appointed visiting rulers from Britain, the sense that two historic cultures are addressing each other somehow survives.

On the Indian side, no amount of Imperial Pomp and Circumstance alone could have generated the "spontaneous, genuine and impulsive feelings of the huge mass of the people of all ages" shown at the great Coronation Durbar in Delhi of King George V and Queen Mary – which so surprised General Woodyatt in his account of the historic scene. There was the same outpouring of friendship from the vast concourse when thirty-six tempestuous years later the British flag was lowered for the last time and the King ceased to be Emperor. As Jawaharlal Nehru put it, a morally unacceptable and rough Imperial power-relationship was smoothed over because both parties belonged to what he termed "Mother civilisations."

In the context of these short and sharp commentaries, however, there is no need to pursue such deep reflections. Certainly the authors themselves are not aware of doing so. It is entirely sufficient to enjoy each surprising twist and turn in the journey through their various stories. The dramatis personae make a bizarre fellowship: the young Winston Churchill defying almost certain death that would have deprived him and us of the subsequent glory, and in contrast the unlikely assassination of the popular and enlightened Lord Mayo, Disraeli's Viceroy. There is Mark Twain working out his relationship with his manservant Satan; and his compatriot, Lady Curzon, far from reconciled to the conditions of the Viceregal round. Aldous Huxley is here, too, watching the effect of an eclipse of the sun while sailing down the holy but overcrowded Ganges.

But the fascination of this anthology is more than the impact made by contributions from a catalogue of celebrities. It is to be found as well in the private and informal correspondence of men and women not so famous describing their daily rounds and adventures and resolutely coping with unfamiliar circumstance. Therein, perhaps, is the deepest truth about these tales. They are not just by people about people; they involve coming to terms with an animal kingdom which includes both reptiles and insects, and, in addition, with the whole appointed order of things which seem to have lives of their own.

Reflect, for example, upon the description by Lord Frederic Hamilton of Colonel Barnard who, armed with a camera, definitely saw with his own eyes the Indian rope trick performed – the boy and his master ascending and descending – but whose photographs, when the negatives were developed, showed . . . Well, without further introduction, read on.

THE MUTINY

I KNOW that at the present moment an unusual agitation is pervading the ranks of the entire native army, but what it will exactly result in, I am afraid to say. I can detect the near approach of the storm, I can hear the moaning of the hurricane, but I can't say how, when, or where it will break forth.

CAPT. E.M. MARTINEAU
10th Native Infantry
from a letter dated 5 May 1857

"The Sepoys have Risen"

*The Reverend George Coopland had recently been appointed
Chaplain to the East India Company and posted, with his wife,
to Gwalior – where there were only "native" troops and a few
British officers. They soon realised that trouble was brewing,
and when it did break out the small British community faced a
long night of terror. Mrs Coopland tells what happened.
(June 1857)*

I was much struck with the conduct of our servants – they grew so
impertinent. My ayah evidently looked on all my property as her
share of the plunder. When I opened my dressing-case, she would ask
me questions about the ornaments, and inquire if the tops of the
scent-bottles were real silver; and she always watched where I put my
things. One evening, on returning from our drive, we heard a
tremendous quarrelling going on between the sepoys of our guard and
the ayah and kitmutghar. They were evidently disputing about the
spoil; and it afterwards turned out that the sepoys got quite masters,
and would not let the servants share any of the plunder, but kept them
prisoners, and starved and ill-treated them. They had much better
have remained faithful to us, and have helped us to escape; instead of
which, at the first shot, they vanished, and began to plunder what they
could. My husband overheard the punkah coolies outside talking
about us, and saying that these Feringhis would soon have a different
home, and *they* would then be masters; and that the Feringhis were
quite different in the cool weather, but were now such poor creatures
as to require to be punkahed and kept cool. I could not help fancying
they might have made us punkah and fan *them*, so completely were we
in their power.

During this week the bunian, who supplied us with grain for the
cattle and other things, the church-bearer and the schoolmaster, all
came to be paid at once; they said they were going to take all their
property to the Lushkur. This looked as if mischief was brewing. . . .

My husband now sent for all the servants and gave them each

3

handsome presents in money: to his bearer and my ayah he gave double; he also rewarded the guard of six sepoys, who had come to guard our house . . . We then drove out. We saw scarcely any one about, everything looked as it had done for days past; but as we were returning we passed several parties of sepoys, none of whom saluted us. We met the Brigadier and Major Blake, who were just going to pass a party of sepoys, and I remember saying to my husband, "If the sepoys don't salute the Brigadier the storm is nigh at hand." *They did not.* The Brigadier and Major Blake turned and looked at them. We found our guard still at our house, but they also took no notice of us. We then had tea, and sat reading till gun-fire; and at 9 we retired to rest, as my husband was much exhausted.

I hope no one will think me unfeeling in writing what follows: it *must* be obvious to all that I cannot do so without great pain; but I think that Englishmen ought to know what their own countrywomen have endured at the hands of the sepoys; and what we went through that night and the following week, hundreds of ladies suffered all over India. Only a few survived to tell the tale; which can only be *faithfully* told by one who has experienced the misery. . . .

My husband went into his dressing room, and I, after undressing and dismissing my ayah, arranged my dress for flight, and lay down. A single lamp shed a ghostly glimmer in the room. Soon afterwards the gun fired – instantly the alarm bugle rang out its shrill warning on the still night. Our guard loaded their muskets, and I felt that our death knell had sounded when the butts went down with a muffled sound. My husband opened his door and said, "All is over with us! dress immediately." The ayah and bearer rushed in, calling out, "Fly! the sepoys have risen, and will kill you." The ayah then quickly helped me to dress. I put on a morning wrapper, cloth jacket, and bonnet, and snatched up a bottle of aromatic vinegar and another of opium from the dressing table, but left my watch and rings. My husband then came in, and we opened my bath-room door, which led into the garden, and rushed out. Fortunately it was very dark. I said, "Let us go to the Stuarts, and see what they are doing." We soon reached their house, and found Mrs. Stuart in great distress, as her husband had just ridden off to the lines. . . .

Our syce now appeared with the buggy, accompanied by our kitmutghar; the latter appeared very much excited, and had a tulwah in each hand. He advised us to cross the bridge leading to the Lushkur; but the syce said it was guarded with guns and sentries. . . .

Just as we were going to turn towards the artillery lines, a young sepoy came running from them towards us, weeping and sobbing. He called out, "They have shot the Sahib," and though my husband spoke to him, he ran past without answering. All this time we heard volleys of musketry, bugles, shots, and terrible shrieks, and saw some of the houses burning. We drove to the Blakes' bungalow, where we found Mrs. Blake, Mrs. Raikes, and Dr. and Mrs. Kirke; none of them knowing what to do. Major Blake had ridden off to the lines the instant the alarm bugle had sounded; and things were rather quieter here.

It was now 10 o'clock. Dr. Kirke said the guard had promised to stay by us, and that now it was utterly impossible to escape, as every road was guarded and planted with guns, and cavalry were riding about. After a short time, passed in terrible suspense, the guard of the house suggested that we had better hide in the garden, as the sepoys would soon be coming to "loot" the house, and would kill us. It was only postponing our deaths, as we knew that escape was now hopeless; but as life is dear to all, we did what we could to save it. . . .

Mrs. Blake's kitmutghar, Muza, who remained faithful, now took us to a shady place in the garden, where we lay concealed behind a bank, well covered with trees. He told us to lie down and not to move, and then brought a large dark shawl for my husband, who was in a white suit. It was now about 11. The guard (composed of men of the 1st) still remained faithful; though they took no active part in helping us. They kept coming to us with reports that Mrs. Campbell was lying dead in her compound; that the Brigadier was shot on the bridge, and Dr. MacKeller near one of the hospitals, and (worst of all) that poor Major Blake was killed. This last report was only too true.

At last about a hundred sepoys came to attack Mrs. Campbell's house, which was close to our hiding place. We heard them tearing down the doors and windows, and smashing the glass and furniture; they even brought carts into the garden to carry off the plunder; then they set fire to it, and the flames shot up into the clear night air. They seemed to take pleasure in their mad work, for their wild shouts of laughter mingled with the crackling of the flames. . . .

At last, when the mutineers had wreaked their vengeance on Mrs. Campbell's house, and only a heap of smouldering and blackened ruins remained, they commenced their attack on the Blakes' house. We heard them looking for us; but not finding their victims there, they came into the garden and made a diligent search for us. I saw the moonlight glancing on their bayonets, as they thrust aside the bushes, and they passed so close by us that we might have touched them. But God baffled their malice for a time . . .

Our faithful Muza now crept to us, and said we were no longer safe where we were, but that he might hide us in his house, and perhaps get us some native dresses to disguise ourselves in; and gratefully we hurried after him during a lull in the storm. His house was a low, small hut, close to the garden . . . We crouched down in the hut, not daring to move, and scarcely to breathe. I remember asking Mrs. Blake to take off her silk cape, as it rustled, which she did. In the dark I fell backward over a small bed and hurt myself. Muza then barred the door, and fastened it with a chain. After half an hour the sepoys returned, more furious than before; they evidently knew we were somewhere about. We heard them disputing, and the clang of their guns sounded as though they were loading them.

They entered the kitchen of the house, which was only separated from the room we were in by a thin wooden partition. Muza then went out; we did not know what for. Had he deserted us? The sepoys talked and argued with him; we heard them count over the cooking vessels and dishes . . . After dividing the spoil, we heard them again ask Muza if we were in his house, and say they must search; but he replied that his mother was ill, and that they might frighten her. They asked him, "Have you no Feringhis concealed?" and he swore the most sacred oath on the Koran, that there were none in his house: but this did not appear to satisfy them, and we heard them coming in; they forced open the door with the butts of their muskets, the chain fell with a clang, and as the door burst open, we saw the moon glistening on their fixed bayonets. We thought they were going to charge in upon us: but no; the hut was so dark that they could not see us. They called for a light; but Muza stopped them, and said, "You see they are not here: come, and I will show you where they are." He then shut and fastened the door, and they again went away.

There was again a dead silence, followed by the dying shrieks of a horse, as it rushed past our hiding place; so we supposed they had gone to the stables.

It was now nearly six o'clock, and grew gradually lighter, when the sepoys again returned howling and raging like wild beasts. They came round the hut, the baby cried, and we heard them ask, "Whose child is that?" One of the women replied they did not know; they called "Bring it out;" when Mrs. Raikes exclaimed in an agony of fear, "Oh! they will kill my child!" When the woman carried it out, the sepoys yelled, "Feringhi, hi: Kill them!" and I saw through the doorway a great number of them loading their muskets. . . .

We all stood up close together in a corner of the hut; each of us took up one of the logs of wood that lay on the ground, as some means of defence. I did not know if my husband had his gun, as it was too dark in the hut to see even our faces. The sepoys then began to pull off the roof: the cowardly wretches dared not come in, as they thought we had weapons. When they had unroofed the hut, they fired in upon us. At the first shot we dropped our pieces of wood, and my husband said, "We will not die here, let us go outside." We all rushed out; and Mrs. Blake, Mrs. Raikes, and I, clasped our hands and cried, "Mut maro, mut maro" (do not kill us). The sepoys said, "We will not kill the mem-sahibs, only the Sahib." We were surrounded by a crowd of them, and as soon as they distinguished my husband, they fired at him. . . . I saw no more; but volley after volley soon told me that all was over.

R.M. COOPLAND
A Lady's Escape from Gwalior (1859)

The Chase

*A small party of Europeans, besieged by rebel sepoys in
Fatehgarh fort on the banks of the Ganges, decided to escape
in boats down the river. Gavin Jones, an engineer on the Great
Indian Peninsula Railway, was one of only a handful of
survivors of this desperate venture. (July 1857)*

. . . The sepoys kept up the chase for several hours, which they
eventually abandoned as they could not gain on us, being like
ourselves ill supplied with boatmen. Our progress was by this time
improving as we gained experience and confidence; unfortunately an
accident to Colonel Smith's boat necessitated stoppage for repairs.
The rabble that had followed down at a respectable distance from our
muskets, in a few minutes surrounded us, taking long pots with their
matchlocks, killing one of the two boatmen, who fell shot through the
heart while engaged in the repairs; we were hurriedly, therefore,
forced to push off to escape a worse fate. The precious time thus lost
enabled the sepoys to start after us better equipped. It was not long
after that Major Robertson's boat stranded on a bar, over which
Colonel Smith's lighter boat had passed on ahead, and was much too
far in advance in midchannel to permit of their stopping to help us off.

Thus unintentionally abandoned we were left to our own resources,
every man got into the water and applied their backs and shoulders to
push her into deep water, but both wind and current were against us,
and all our efforts failed to clear the bend which would have floated us
into the channel. The crisis had now come, though we could not
realize it. The rabble which had gained strength as they followed us
down, being reinforced by the villages on the way, swarmed in
hundreds, kept up an unceasing yell, and assailed us from every
available direction with their matchlocks and showers of arrows. At
this time two boats, apparently empty, with their solitary steersman
on each, were seen slowly dropping down with the stream towards us,
their inoffensive exterior disarmed suspicion, and we paid no heed to
them but continued our futile efforts to push off our boat, contending

hopelessly with the current, the wind, and the merciless rabble who were only kept at bay by our muskets. The surprise was complete; at about 20 yards the sepoys unmasked and poured in a volley into us, and, ere we could recover from the suddenness of the attack, the boats were alongside. Resistance was useless, but rather than yield to the savage ruffians, we called to the ladies to follow us into the river. The summons, however, was unnecessary, for the instant the rebels boarded, it became the signal for a general rush to the water, into which they plunged, praying aloud to the Almighty for mercy and succour in their dire extremity. The scene that followed, it is impossible for me to depict, little groups formed in the lea of the boat of wives and children clinging to their husbands and parents, the irresistible current swept past till they disappeared in the deep, either shot down by the sepoys' muskets, or mercifully engulfed by the river. Others driven frantic, rushed madly hither and thither in wild despair in the hope of eluding the fire of the murderers till exhausted or shot, death relieved them of their agony, and the sacred Ganges claimed their mortal frames. In their insatiable thirst for blood and plunder, the rebels pursued the fugitives, breast deep in water . . . At this crisis I was hit on the right shoulder by a musket ball.

For a moment I felt bewildered and helpless, and knew not what to do under the circumstances; death was certain, and the idea of attempting to escape never entered my mind. Some others, like myself, stood hopeless, and resigned by the side of the boat being unarmed, unable to make any resistance. Suddenly my eyes fell on "Bhairo" issuing from the side of the boat, with my poor brother's only child in his arms, imploring the mob to spare her life and that of her mother, who followed, both apparently severely wounded. "God help them," I exclaimed in an agony of grief, and sprung up into the boat, resolved to sell my life. I hastened in for my rifle and revolver which were near the stern, but both were in the possession of the enemy; hurrying back I came upon Captain Fitzgerald whose wife and child were clinging to him weeping bitterly, and besought him to give me the musket he held in his hand, but he was too agonised to attend to my appeals, and I turned round to search elsewhere, when I seized one from the hands of an Eurasian drummer, who was that instant emerging from beneath the floor, and dashed astern, where the sepoys were looting. I appeared just in time to see the thatched roof of the enemies' boat alongside left, and the hairy chest of a powerful sepoy stand displayed before me, a score of muzzles protruded simultaneously at my feet, quick as thought I levelled my piece, without shouldering, and discharged the contents into his breast. He fell with a heavy thud, and the roof dropped with him, leaving me an interval to re-load. I had not, however, time to snatch a percussion cap from the ammunition box, before I was forced to beat a retreat. I rushed from one side to the other in search of a cap, but could find none, nor could I obtain one from any of those who still lingered in the boat; feeling myself helpless and incapable of defending myself, my heart sickened at the sight of the wounded and dying, and a feeling of horror seized me at the thought of the torture and mutilation that awaited them, and of which I too might be a victim. I flung the useless musket aside and hastened to fly from the boat, when my first thought was that, if struck, I should find a peaceable end in the water and escape the terrible possibility of being wounded and captured. On my way out my eyes fell on a gourd which lay in a corner in my path, instinctively I seized it and sprang overboard . . . Casting a last look at the boat, and the struggling groups in the water, I turned my head, sickened at the sight, towards midstream and swam out with all my might to get out of range.

G.S. JONES
"The Story of My Escape from Fatehgarh"
Blackwoods Magazine (1859)

Punishment

These were not times for the irresolute – or the squeamish. Captain Francis Maude, in command of the guns in General Havelock's column, was quickly able to perfect a form of gun-drill not taught at artillery school. (July 1857)

. . . a few days afterwards, Havelock asked me if I "knew how to blow a man from a gun?" Naturally this had not formed part of our *curriculum* at Woolwich; but I had no hesitation in at once answering in the affirmative. For it will be obvious to anyone that three pounds of good powder (the service charge of a brass 9-pounder) would be pretty sure to effect the desired purpose. "Very well, then," replied the General, "I shall send you a man this evening!" I believe the culprit had been taken as a spy. Accordingly, when we halted for the night, I moved one of my guns on to the causeway, unlimbered it, and brought it into "action front."

The evening was just beginning to grow dusk, and the enemy were still in sight, on the crest of some rising ground, a few hundred yards distant. The remainder of my guns were "parked," in a nice mango-tope, to the right of the road. As soon as the news of the intended execution became known among our Force, they crowded on both sides of the ditch, near the causeway. I had them all cleared from anywhere near the front of the gun; but, laterally, the audience was very numerous indeed.

The first man led out was a fine-looking young Sepoy, with good features, and a bold, resolute expression. He begged that he might not be bound, but this could not be allowed, and I had his wrists tied tightly, each to the upper part of a wheel of the gun. Then I depressed the muzzle, until it pointed to the pit of his stomach, just below the *sternum*. We put no shot in, and I only kept one gunner, (besides the "firing" No.) near the gun, standing myself about ten feet to the left rear. The young Sepoy looked undauntedly at us during the whole process of pinioning: indeed, he never flinched for a moment. Then I

11

ordered the port-fire to be lighted, and gave the word "Fire!" There was a considerable recoil from the gun, and a thick cloud of smoke hung over us. As this cleared away, we saw two legs lying in front of the gun; but no other sign of what had, just before, been a human being and a brave man. At this moment, perhaps from six to eight seconds after the explosion (and the same thing happened on the second occasion), down fell the man's head among us, slightly blackened, but otherwise scarcely changed. It must have gone straight up into the air, probably about 200 feet. The pent-up feelings of the bystanders found vent in a sort of loud gasp, like ah-h! Then many of them came across the ditch to inspect the remains of the legs, and the horrible affair was over.

Precisely the same results happened in the case of the next man, who was blown away on another occasion, except that he writhed and struggled violently, doing his utmost to escape from this terrible death, and that, in his case, he was tied with his back to the gun. Havelock's tent was the only one pitched in advance that evening. It lay a little in rear of my gun park. I went over to him to tell him that I had carried out his orders. As I jumped across the ditch, I became aware that I was covered, from head to foot, at least in front, with minute blackened particles of the man's flesh, some of it sticking in my ears and hair. My white silk coat, puggree, belt, etc., were also spotted in this sickening manner. . . .

The "gun number" at the second execution happened to be the same man who had fired the first. He was also dressed for the most part in white, and consequently was in the same "plight" as myself; perhaps even a little worse. So he made a request, which was not unreasonable, namely, that he might be allowed the sum of twelve annas (1s. 6d.) for each execution, as it cost him exactly that amount to get his clothes washed. I believe I succeeded in getting that sum for him. . . .

. . . Just after the gun had been fired, Maxwell Mowatt . . . one of the Sergeants of the 78th (Seaforth) Highlanders, was seen writhing in great pain; holding his hands over his stomach. One of his officers went up to him, and asked him what was the matter. For some time the Sergeant would not answer. At last he admitted that he had been struck in the abdomen by a piece of the man's shoulder, that had been driven across the ditch, with great violence, to the immediate right of the gun, which was the extreme point of limit of the crowd. Probably there would have been more such accidents if the audience had stood farther in front.

. . . these were the only two occasions on which this truly fearful punishment was inflicted by Havelock; although, at Meerut, Delhi, and other places, there were many more.

FRANCIS CORNWALLIS MAUDE
Memories of the Mutiny (1894)

Siege

The siege of Lucknow Residency is justly famous in the annals of war. Captain Anderson of the 25th Regiment, Native Infantry, was placed in command of a particularly exposed outpost with only one subaltern and eighteen men. Against all odds this truly gallant band held their position for an incredible four and a half months *before final relief arrived. (August 1857)*

. . . A great many men were killed by standing incautiously at the loopholes; some would fire, and then look out to see if their shot had taken effect, when a return bullet would kill them on the spot. I saw one poor fellow, of Her Majesty's 32nd, who was killed in this way, but he was not the only man; I was close beside him at the time, and warned him to be careful, and not to stand opposite the loophole after firing; however, he forgot what I said, and in a few seconds after, he fell back, with a groan, quite dead – a musket ball had entered his eye, and passed through his brain; poor fellow! we soon picked him up, only to find that the pool of blood under his head plainly indicated that his life had left him; horrid to relate, there we saw bits of brain amidst the gory flood, about the spot where he fell.

We are now in the month of August, and no signs of relief; the heat, too, is intense, and we have no servants to fill our punkahs. Dead bodies are decomposing in all directions outside the entrenchments, and the graves in our churchyards are so shallow, that the whole air is tainted with putrid smells; now our torments commence in real earnest. We are pestered to death by swarms of great, *cold*, clammy flies, which have probably been feeding off festering corpses in the vicinity; we cannot read, sleep, or eat our food, with any degree of comfort. We had only one Madras boy between five of us to do all the work, and he fell ill with fever; we had, therefore, to chop our own wood, prepare the fire, cook the food, &c., &c.; besides this, we had to wash our own clothes, and perform (each in our turn), the lowest menial duties. A nice state of affairs for folks who are generally

14

termed officers and gentlemen? but so it was, and there was no help for it; our little garrison was so exposed, that not a servant would stay there whilst other people in the place had as many as six and seven servants throughout the siege!!

In the midst of all these miseries (when, perhaps, in the very act of cooking!) you would hear the cry of "turn out," and then you had to seize your musket, and rush to your post. Then there was a constant state of anxiety as to whether we were *mined* or not; and we were not quite sure, whilst we were at a loophole, that we might not suddenly see the ground open, or observe the whole materials of the house fly into the air by the explosion of a mine!! Shells came smashing right into our rooms, and dashed our property to pieces; then followed round shot, and down tumbled huge pieces of masonry, and bits of wood and bricks flew in all directions. I have seen beds literally blown to atoms, and trunks and boxes were completely smashed into little bits. When an inch shell exploded in the room, you could not see anything for several minutes, and all we heard after was the cry of individuals, asking each other from opposite directions, if it was "all right?" and now and then a poor fellow would be seen to creep out of a heap of lime and bricks, and say, "I'm not hurt, thank God."

I recollect, one day, after the bursting of a shell, Signor Barsottelli looked for his trunk, and found that it had been *blown up* completely. He now wished to have a little fun, so he called his Madras boy, and said, "Where is my trunk?" The boy went off, and looked in the corner, where the trunk always stood, but found it not; he could not understand this, so he came with a face of astonishment to his master, and said, "Trunk not got, sir." Signor pretended to be angry, and said, "Not got a trunk, you rascal, where is it?" In the meantime, some one drew the lad's attention to some bits of wood in the corner, which were all that remained of Signor's trunk, and the boy's face brightened up, as he said to his master, "Before trunk got, sir – *now*, not got – shell break him." . . .

These are simply the day occurrences, which were followed by the long, dreary nights. We would sit for hours, expecting every moment to be attacked. Officers would come round, and say, in a solemn manner, "The brigadier requests you will be *particularly* on the alert." Here and there, by the glimmer of a miserable lamp, you observed the pale, careworn faces of half a dozen volunteers. One man loading his musket, another looking at his pistol, and a third filling his cartridge-box. One of the party would presently shoulder his musket, and go off to stand on sentry, whilst another dived down into our mine, to see that the enemy were not getting *under* our house. . . . Every now and then we *fancied* we saw the figure of a man, and then it seemed as suddenly to disappear. Sometimes the moon, shining on the leaves of the castor-oil tree, used to look like men's turbans, and more than once we were induced to fire at them. . . .

Throughout the siege the mutineers lost no opportunity to try and make our Sepoys desert, by telling them that they would starve us all to death, if they could not take the place; and they tried to make them believe that the English were beaten all over India, and that there was not the least hope of our obtaining any relief; and there was so much delay in our reinforcement arriving, that many began to believe what they said; and had the relieving force been much longer in coming to our assistance, I am afraid that even the fidelity of our brave native troops might have been shaken; I feel sure that every man felt fearfully disappointed at the delay in obtaining relief, and the poor natives would have probably been more tortured than the Europeans, had the enemy carried our position.

CAPTAIN R.P. ANDERSON
A Personal Journal of the Siege of Lucknow (1858)

The Indian Army

Failing to get himself posted to India for the mutiny, Captain Oliver Jones (Royal Navy) obtained a year's leave and came out as a volunteer. Meeting Lieutenant Colonel English of the 53rd Regiment on his way up to "the front", Jones attached himself to the 53rd for some five months of action. Although a Navy man he quickly adapted to Army life.
(January/February 1858)

My days used to be spent at this time one very like the other. I used to get up about six, and saunter over to English's tent, and squat down on a box or chair, if there was one, and chat with him till it was warm enough (for the mornings in January and February are very cold) to have my musshack, and then perform my toilet.

A musshack is called so after the skin in which the bheestie carries the water. The operation is usually performed *al fresco* at one's tent door. Having reduced one's apparel to bathing costume, consisting of a very short pair of thick drawers, one squats down on a bit of board, and the bheestie proceeds to squirt the contents of his musshack or skin, which holds about two pailfuls of water, all over one; and a wonderful luxury and comfort it is, and marvellously refreshing. One's servants are all ready around to dry one and wash one's feet, &c. &c. . . .

After breakfast, which was a substantial one, curries, stews, ragouts, cold meat, &c., being handsomely performed upon, I used to stroll over to the Naval Brigade camp and watch their parade . . .

When the parade was over, Peel and I and some of the officers usually rode to the fort to see the progress of the gun-carriages, or sometimes to Walpole's camp at the Ramgunga, then home to dinner, and about ten o'clock to bed, so that the time passed very pleasantly, especially that the weather was most charming; but we still wished and hoped for a move, for everybody felt that India was not to be reconquered by sitting still . . .

The encampment around Onoa was a very large one . . . and the enormous quantity of ground covered by the army and its belongings is incredible, and would not be believed out of India.

A division of the army, and that not a very large one, moved from one side to the other of Onoa, a distance of two miles, and it took eight hours from the time the advanced guard left the old ground till the rear-guard arrived at the new encampment . . .

Besides bullocks there are elephants, camels, horses, ponies, "tats" (a miserable kind of pony), goats, fowls, geese, &c., and camp-followers innumerable, and yet not a quarter of what there used to be before Sir Charles Napier commenced his reforms of the establishments which formerly accompanied a force of the Indian army in the field.

Even now every officer has from four to twelve servants, and the men also have several attached to each company, for a private in India cannot draw his own water, nor cook his own victuals, nor could he, till lately, clean his own boots, nor shave his own chin, but shoe-cleaners and barbers were attached to each regiment.

There is a bazaar also which follows every corps, and which is under the control of the commanding officer. It supplies all the things which are required by soldiers on a campaign, such as soap, tobacco, &c.; also gram for the horses, a kind of vetch, which is their principal food, and which they much prefer to oats; and many other things which it would be very inconvenient to carry about with one.

Officers, even the Commander-in-Chief, who in this, as in everything else, sets a good example to his army, now live in what is called a staff-sergeant's tent, which is not more than 12 feet square, and these, in the junior ranks, are tenanted by two, and sometimes three officers. They can be carried by one large, or two small camels, whereas formerly every officer had a large tent, which required four or five camels to carry it, and those of the field-officers were almost as large and luxurious as a good house, and of course required a proportionate number of elephants or camels, and their attendants.

The number of servants every officer is obliged to keep in India is a great addition to the impediments of an army . . . No one tried to do with fewer than I did, but I had got up to nine, and had I remained in India much longer, I should have been obliged to have two or three more.

True that five of them belonged to my horses, for usually every horse has its groom and grass-cutter; I made two syces do for three horses; but for myself, I had Mr. Malakoff, who was as good as two or three, for he was cook, butler, valet, and first-lieutenant; a coolie, a bheestie, or water-carrier, and a dhobie, or washerman, and a camel-driver, who had two camels in charge. The grass-cutter sallies out at early day-light, provided with an instrument not unlike a brick-layer's trowel in shape, though one edge is very sharp, with which he scrapes up the grass close to the earth; and it is marvellous what a quantity he will collect from ground as brown and burnt-up and apparently as innocent of any herbage as the bare palm of one's hand.

The grass which the horses prefer, and, indeed, which is best for keeping them in condition, is very dry, short, and crispy, almost resembling moss, which he shaves off the ground, roots and all. Should the grass-cutter bring any of a coarser or longer description, or any with the slightest appearance of green-ness, the syce – who would not himself cut a blade of grass for your horse were it starving – would most certainly reject it, and send the grass-cutter for more, and very likely give him a good licking into the bargain.

There certainly is a good deal of club-law among the natives; and every one of them thinks he has a right to *wop* any other who is the least beneath him in caste, situation, or service; but I can truly say that I saw very little, if any of that kind of thing from officers to their servants . . . All these servants are not so serious an expense as it might be thought, for their wages vary from twelve to four rupees a month, for which they have to feed and clothe themselves. I found that my nine servants and three horses did not cost me more than one fine young gentleman, who did me the honour to call himself my groom and valet, and one horse did in England.

Besides my horses and camels, I had a goat and half a dozen fowls, which gave me a plentiful supply of milk and eggs; it was a curious fact, that these beasts and birds always knew their own tents and belongings, and never strayed to any one else's domains, nor did other people's, and some had pigeons besides the fowls and goats; but they always kept to their own master's tent. The hens were very particular when and where they chose to lay their eggs. Sir William Peel had one which selected a corner of his tent, behind a particular portmanteau, and used to produce its daily *ovation* soon after the march was over and the tent pitched, but never would do so until the portmanteau was placed in the proper corner . . .

The servants are generally of different castes, and will neither cook nor eat together; nor indeed will they let one another, still less their masters, approach their cooking-places. One day, while my syce was cooking his dinner, one of the officers took a bit of burning wood from the fire to light his cigar; of course the dinner was defiled, much to the grief of the syce, and to the benefit of the Matey, who, being the lowest of the low, eats after anybody, and, I believe, after everything, and who was soon demolishing the savoury currie which the indignant syce turned over to him. . . .

In addition to the servants, &c., belonging to the officers and regiments, there are ten dhoolies attached to each hundred men; each dhoolie having five (four and a spare one) bearers, so that a regiment has from four to five hundred of these people with it. Also, the field-hospital of the force has a small army of dhoolies and dhoolie-bearers. And moreover, and above all these, there is the commissariat, who have to carry provisions and necessaries innumerable for the forces, and whose beasts, servants, &c. &c., nearly double the "impedimenta" of the army . . .

It can be easily conceived what difficulties these armies of camp-followers, and servants, and multitudes of animals add to those of the movements of troops, and how much they increase the cares of the Commander-in-Chief, and hinder his movements and operations.

CAPT. OLIVER J. JONES, R.N.
Recollections of a Winter Campaign in India (1859)

Drunk with Plunder

The capture of Lucknow itself came several months after the relief of the Residency and in effect marked the final crushing of the sepoy revolt. William Howard Russell, special correspondent of the London Times, *was on the spot when the British plundered the Kaisarbagh Palace complex at Lucknow. (March 1858)*

It was one of the strangest and most distressing sights that could be seen . . . Here and there the invaders have forced their way into the long corridors, and you hear the musketry rattling inside; the crash of glass, the shouts and yells of the combatants, and little jets of smoke curl out of the closed lattices. Lying amid the orange-groves are dead and dying sepoys; and the white statues are reddened with blood. Leaning against a smiling Venus is a British soldier shot through the neck, gasping, and at every gasp bleeding to death! Here and there officers are running to and fro after their men, persuading or threatening in vain. From the broken portals issue soldiers laden with loot or plunder. Shawls, rich tapestry, gold and silver brocade, caskets of jewels, arms, splendid dresses. The men are wild with fury and lust of gold – literally drunk with plunder. Some come out with china vases or mirrors, dash them to pieces on the ground, and return to seek more valuable booty. Others are busy gouging out the precious stones from the stems of pipes, from saddle-cloths, or the hilts of swords, or butts of pistols and fire-arms. Some swathe their bodies in stuffs crusted with precious metals and gems; others carry off useless lumber, brass pots, pictures, or vases of jade and china.

Court after court the scene is still the same. These courts open one to the other by lofty gateways, ornamented with the double fish of the royal family of Oude, or by arched passages, in which lie the dead sepoys, their clothes smouldering on their flesh.

The court we had now reached was exceedingly narrow . . . Just where we turned into the court, there was a stone-topped well somewhat in the shade, and close to it was one store-room, the door of which had been left open or forced in by a marauder. On going in we found it literally filled with wooden cases, which were each crammed with nicely-packed china or enormous vases, bowls, goblets, cups of the finest jade. Others contained nothing but spoons, hookah mouth-pieces, and small drinking vessels, and saucers of the same valuable material. I do not in the least exaggerate, when I say there must have been at least a camel-load of these curiosities, of which Stewart and myself, and one or two other officers, selected a few pieces, and put them aside . . . Enter three or four banditti of H.M.'s ——— Regiment. Faces black with powder; cross-belts specked with blood; coats stuffed out with all sorts of valuables. And now commenced the work of plunder under our very eyes. The first door resisted every sort of violence till the rifle-muzzle was placed to the lock, which was sent flying by the discharge of the piece. The men rushed in with a shout, and soon they came out with caskets of jewels, iron boxes and safes, and wooden boxes full of arms crusted with gold

18003 Kaiser Bagh, Lucknow.

Kaiser Bagh, Lucknow

and precious stones! One fellow, having burst open a leaden-looking lid, which was in reality of solid silver, drew out an armlet of emeralds, and diamonds, and pearls, so large, that I really believed they were not real stones, and that they formed part of a chandelier chain. "What will your honour give me for these?" said he. "I'll take a hundred rupees on chance."

Oh, wretched fate! I had not a penny in my pocket, nor had any of us. No one has in India. His servant keeps his money. My Simon was far away in the quiet camp. He hunted through my clothes every morning, and neither gold mohur nor silver rupee was permitted to remain in any of my pockets; and so I said –

"I will give you a hundred rupees; but it is right to tell you if the stones are real they are worth a great deal more."

"Bedad, I won't grudge them to your honour, and you're welcome to them for the hundred rupees. Here, take them!"

"Well, then, you must come to me at the Head-Quarters' camp to-night, or give me your name and company, and I'll send the money to you."

"Oh! faith an' your honour, how do I know where I'd be this blissed night? It's may be dead I'd be, wid a bullet in me body. I'll take two gold mores" (mohurs at 32*s*. each) "and a bottle of rum, on the spot. But shure it's not safe to have any but reddy money transactions these times."

There was no arguing against the propriety of the views entertained by our friend, and he put the chain of great nobbly emeralds, and diamonds, and pearls, into the casket, and I saw my fortune vanish.

As the man turned to leave the place, as if struck by compunction at his own severity, he took two trinkets from a tray in the casket, and said, "There, gentlemen, I'd not like to lave you without a little keepsake. Take whichever you like, and you can give me something another time."

That which fell to my share was a nose-ring of small rubies and pearls, with a single stone diamond drop. My friend was made happy with a very handsome brooch, consisting of a large butterfly, with opal and diamond wings. . . .

By this time, twenty men – mostly English, but some Sikhs – were in the court. The explosion of their rifles, as they burst open locks and doors, had attracted stray marauders. More than one quarrel, which came nigh to blood-letting, had already arisen: things looked threatening: we could do no good: and, as a musbee sapper just happened to look in, we laid hold of him to carry our jade bowls, and got into the outer court, in which there was, on a larger scale, a repetition of the same scene as we had just left. . . .

At last I got to camp. Simon was busy in his little tent weighing gold and silver for natives who had already returned with or got plunder from the soldiers. For days the chink, chink of his scales never ceased. He had a percentage for weighing, and he must have driven a roaring trade. Done up beyond expression, I threw myself on a charpoy, and for an hour slept a sleep of dreams almost as bad as the realities I had just witnessed.

WILLIAM HOWARD RUSSELL
My Diary in India in the Year 1858-9 (1860)

SAHIBS AND MEMSAHIBS

LIFE IN a small Mofussil station is often considered wearisome, there are no concerts or
theatres, no dances, no shops, and very little
society. . . . but there is a kind of camaraderie
and good fellowship amongst a small community
of Anglo-Indians, such as one rarely finds in
England, which makes life very pleasant, and I
cannot say I found time hang heavily on my hands.
"The daily round, the common task," furnished
me with plenty of varied occupation, and, in
addition to my ordinary home duties, I held the
responsible post of Secretary to the Mutton Club
. . . (1865)

MRS HERBERT REYNOLDS
At Home in India (1903)

With the Viceroy

It was less than ten years since Simla had become the regular summer capital of India, and facilities on the Ridge were still fairly primitive even for senior officials. Lord Northbrook had just been made Viceroy and Arthur Hobhouse was the recently appointed Legal Member of the Viceroy's Council. His wife, Mary, wrote home every week to tell her sister about their new life at the top.

SIMLA, May 8, 1872.

I fear this will be a short letter, for though I have much to *tell* I have still more to *do*. I wish you could see my numerous occupations, though I cannot wish for you here, at any rate in our house. Fancy the dirtiest London lodging, every article (those very few in number) buried in dust and dirt, paper hanging from walls, no doors that fasten, no five inches of consecutive paint, no article of furniture with four legs, leaks visible on all ceilings, rags of carpet on every floor, and you will have some idea of a good *house*.

. . . It is a large house, which makes matters worse. I really felt too miserable to write on arrival, and have only cheered up since Arthur became unhappy, chiefly on my account. The house is buried in deodars, one very fine specimen in front. There is no garden, only potsherds, slates, and a few weeds. Nevertheless I am much happier to-day, as we have been unpacking some English boxes, and I find divers things which remind me of home, and will cheer our dingy house. We have persuaded our landlord to repaper three of our rooms; some of his furniture, filthy mattresses, and carpet-rags I am going to return to him.

Eight tailors are now sitting cross-legged in the verandah making mattresses something like eider-down quilts, pillows, curtains, etc. I stand over them watching the cutting out, then I go and superintend the cleaning – two water-carriers pour water over the floors, one or two sweepers push it about with brooms, while eight jhampannies (the

27

people who carry me) dabble their feet in the water and look on. Elizabeth says, "How I long to go down on my knees with a scrubbing-brush!" Twenty live ducks and ditto fowls have appeared on the premises to-day with a fowlman. Two cows and a cowkeeper are coming, and I am to look after these as well as after house and garden, for no one is to be trusted. Each day I am to look over accounts of previous day, a long column, and must "just see," as my acquaintance tell me, that the saucepans are well tinned once a fortnight. This is the easy, lazy Indian life. . . .

Yesterday we dined with the Viceroy, and as dining out in India is new to you, I will tell you all about it. The invariable hour is 8 P.M., and at 7 I started in my chair on poles – four men carrying, with a relief of four to take their places, a mate directing and carrying the lantern – Arthur on horseback, and so in slow procession we go along the Simla Mall, where fashion congregates about 6 P.M. – the Mall being the road, one mile long, between little Simla where we live and the larger town. I modestly draw my curtain, but many ladies go bareheaded through the crowd and dust. Some A.-D.-C.'s passed us at a gallop, and had ample time to get home and dress to receive us in the verandah at Peterhoff and escort us to the drawing-room, gaudily papered by Lady Mayo, and where a deodar fire was blazing. Presently Lord Northbrook came in, grumbling at the variations of Simla clocks. There is a midday gun, fired when the artilleryman has finished his morning pipe, says General Earle. I went in to dinner with Lord Northbrook, and his private secretary, Evelyn Baring, took in the other lady present, Mrs. Aitcheson – her husband is Foreign Secretary. Six or seven A.D.C.'s filled up the table, but I can't fit their names and faces together as yet. Lord Northbrook is quite ignorant of Hindustanee, not knowing my two expressions "saf karo" and "tik karo," "make clean" and "make straight," but then he has not had the same necessity for using them. We both abused King, the tardy agent, and presently moved altogether into the drawing-room. Lord Northbrook soon slid into a chair by Mr. Aitcheson and remained talking till 10 P.M., when he wished us "Good night" and vanished, and I had a weary three-quarters of an hour's jolting ere getting home to bed. . . .

Arthur is amused at the intrepidity of my Hindustanee, but I must and will talk to the wretched gardener, who is treated as the dirt beneath their feet by the Madrassee and Mussulman servants. I despair of giving any idea of the life here, which yet is becoming quite commonplace to us, *e.g.* I never ring a bell, but shout "Qui hi," and a voice answers "Mem Sahib," and its owner appears. This is generally one of the chuprassees, four of whom with their chief the jemadar wait in the verandah for no object but to answer calls and take messages. There are eight of them altogether, and to-day the four on duty with the jemadar startled me when alone, surrounding me, and the leader uttering a long oration, of which the gist was one rupee extra per man per month in addition to Government wages. Arthur came in and said he should inquire what was the usual thing to do, when they made answer that all the good gentlemen who gave this had gone home, and the newcomers would not adopt the practice. I hope the poor creatures will get it, for six rupees a month, and a suit of clothes once in two years, does not seem extravagant pay.

SIMLA, June 8, 1872

. . . Here is a history of my days. Tea at 6 A.M., then get up, and come down about 7. At 8 a moonshee appears, a queer old man, fond of a joke and not at all bad company. Arthur and I stumble through a Hindu lesson, which ends at 9.30, when we breakfast, then I look over the khansomah's account. He charges every day for the previous day's consumption and has no stores, so the account runs:-

Meat	for soup	. . . .	8 annas
Pepper	"	. . . .	1 pice
Salt	"	. . . .	1 pice
Vegetables	"	. . . .	4 annas
Eggs	"	. . . .	1 anna

and so forth, the ingredients for each dish being charged separately; then I write notes, read the paper, give a look to gardeners, workmen, tailor, etc., till 12, when if visitors come I talk, if they don't I draw or work. Tiffin is at 2, and afterwards I read, sometimes I sleep, and sometimes I shop, as shops come to you and not you to them, till 4.30, when tea appears, then I often loiter about verandah and garden till 6, when I go out either on horseback or in my dandy. A quiet pony has been procured for me, and I hope to get up my pluck again, but precipices on one side and sharp corners every few yards don't prove encouraging. Lord N. nearly impaled himself on my jhampan the other day, and good rider as he is, could not get his horse quite up to it afterwards to speak to me, and no one can have a fight with his horse when there is a precipice of any depth on one side; happily the horses are mostly very quiet. . . .

. . . I have not yet had courage to look at my finery, but must next week, when the Viceroy has asked us for three successive evenings. I have had framed the little sketch of Westminster I made from the India Office, partly because I like to look at the familiar towers, and partly because our walls are so bare. To-day we have put up coloured glass lights in the verandah – very casinoish – but one gives up good taste, and looks only for cheerfulness and habitableness here. . . .

MARY HOBHOUSE
Letters from India 1872-1877 (1906)

"Following the Drum"

For the wives coming out fresh from the British Isles, army life in India seemed a world apart. A.M.C., wife of an infantry officer, was impressed by the sheer scale of her first march with the Regiment. (c. 1875)

For the last three months we knew we were to march in the coming cold weather; vague and wild rumour was at work as to our destination; and the whole Regiment had an unsettled feel, at least that portion which mostly frequented our "*Chota hazari*" (little breakfast).

On this particular morning, as I sat in the verandah, after my drive, waiting for my husband's return from parade, I, too, was busy conjecturing and wondering how we would manage to move, self and three children, – one of them a baby.

My husband did not count, he marched with his Company, he had his horse to carry him; and, for that matter, I had my buggy, but that would not hold us all comfortably; in fact, everything was looking very *blue*, when my husband and three or four of his familiars, rode up to the verandah, looking very jubilant, all exclaiming in a breath: "Hurrah! The route has come! we march on the 1st November for Saugor, and Nowgong, Central India." . . .

"Well, on these conditions, I will give you your tea," I said.

Whereupon our *Khansamah*, with his attendant sprite the *Khitmutgar*, appeared with the said tea, poached and buttered eggs, and sundry other delicacies, of which *Chota hazari* generally consists.

It is a pleasant, sociable meal, and is always done ample justice to by the warriors who have been at parade and barrack routine since 5 o'clock. We laughed and chatted till 8, when the sun, which even in October on the plains becomes too strong to be pleasant, drove us in, and the gentlemen off.

I had never had such a nice house as the one we were about to leave in Ferozpore, and I looked sadly round my pretty shaded rooms, and dismally thought *not of to-morrow* – but of the 1st of November.

31

I was interrupted by my husband, who came to tell me to make out a "*List of property for Sale*," as is the custom (and a very excellent one it is), in these parts.

Every article of furniture, stock, poultry, everything in fact that you wish to dispose of, is written down with the prices attached, and sent round the Station; and ten to one before the week is out, you have sold all your belongings – (though I've known some queer things happen "about the bargains" bought from some lists. A confiding purchaser puts down his name opposite, say, a table, chair, anything you will, in the full expectation that it is sound. When, lo! on the delivery of the article, the deluded purchaser finds his table, or chair standing, perhaps, *on three legs*, the fourth carefully bandaged up by the cunning bearer, who broke it long ago!). . .

. . . by the dreaded 1st our pretty home was thoroughly dismantled, the proceeds in my pocket "against the road" – as we say in Ireland; and we in "*light marching order*," possessors of a few chairs, a couple of camp tables and carpets, a small dinner service and kitchen utensils, etc.

Our wardrobe was stowed away in sundry camel trunks, chests of drawers, and boxes handy for camel transit.

Then came "*big lists*," "indents for carriage," and then also began grumbling from wives and husbands; the former wanting an extra bullock-cart or camel for the conveyance of her poor reduced belongings; the husband *storming* at the heap of rubbish the *Mem-Sahib* will take with her.

I silenced my lord by showing, *vide* the indent, that I asked for less carriage than any of the ladies with the same number of bairns as myself.

The carriage is expensive – you pay five rupees per mensem for each camel or bullock-gharry. The tents and boxes usually go on camels, the kitchen utensils and a dozen or so of women and children, the families of the servants, travel in the gharrys.

With the best intentions to economise, your carriage amounts to as much as your house-rent in the Station.

My husband got us "a bullock carriage" to travel in; the bullocks were a pair of beauties, milk white, and they came from Neemuch, a place celebrated for "Bhillies." The carriage was "a cut" between a little omnibus and a bathing machine, on two wheels! Every one said it was just the thing, and very cheap for two hundred rupees.

All our servants were paid up, no joke where there were thirteen or fourteen of these creatures expecting "*tallop*," and otherwise made comfortable, with a suit of warm clothes for the march – and every thing was in readiness.

Every one was jolly, it seemed, but me; I was truly sorry to leave our Station, where we had made many kind friends. And now began a round of farewell dinners and parties of all sorts, and at last many touching leave-takings; and on the morning, i.e., about 3 o'clock A.M. of the 1st of November, we started on our first march, the ayah, self, and three children (one of them a baby) in the "machine." The children were frightened, and so was *I*. We seemed to be in the ruck of the march, jolting along amongst camels, elephants, bullock-carts, baggage waggons, and doolies; confusion of all sorts – all in the dark. The coachman came from Neemuch with the bullocks, and whether he spoke a different language to what ayah and I were accustomed to roar at the servants in, I don't know, but he either did not, or would not, pay the least attention to our repeated cries of *Khabadar; aste jao*: – which means in Punjabee – take care, go quietly . . .

Oh! how glad I was when we at last pulled up at our camping-ground, and I found myself in our tent. I saw, to my amazement, our breakfast laid out as neatly and temptingly as in cantonments, the servants in attendance, our baths ready, and everything *"ship shape,"* or, rather, *"tent shape."*

I had never marched before, and could not make out how it was all managed yet. . . .

I had given no order for breakfast, fancying it would be impossible to get anything more substantial than tea and bread and butter.

Fancy, then, my astonishment to find the usual half-dozen nice little hot dishes, which "they say" you require to give an appetite in India!

Before breakfast was over a host of people dropped in to hear, and tell, their adventures of the morning. . . .

After ordering dinner, etc., I went out with my husband to see the camp. It was such a pretty sight; we were encamped in a lovely green park, with magnificent topes and avenues of banyan and tamarind trees; the branches of the former bend down, take root, and form arch after arch round the giant parent stem. The tamarind trees were full of fruit, on which the natives were already making a raid.

I suppose all camps of Her Majesty's Infantry are laid out alike; but to me it was all new; such regular streets, such even squares, would put many a more substantial town to shame. There was not a tent-peg out of place; the tents snowy white, each line marked out by a bright red flag; the Doctor and his Hospital, a little apart from the rest of the camp; as well the travelling bazaar, Commissariat, etc.

We walked about sight-seeing, and then visiting; there were eight of us ladies *"following the drum;"* each of us as fresh and merry as if we had not travelled our ten miles that morning.

We dined early to allow the baggage to leave for the next camping-ground at about 5 o'clock P.M. . . .

All the world *"turn in"* early, so as to be able to rise at *reveille*, which is really a trying moment; – no *"forty winks"* to be had after the inexorable "taps" go. And if you don't jump up out of bed, and after swallowing a cup of scalding tea (which our ayah presented to us) and start off into the carriage post haste, you are liable to be smothered in the folds of your tent, which the *Khalassies* have been striking ever since the bugle went.

We had been jogging along for about a week, and I was getting accustomed to the jolting of the *machine* and the bolting of the bullocks, when all my confidence in both was seriously damaged.

We were nearing the Coffee Shop, a half-way halt. The blazing fire for boiling the cauldrons of tea and coffee frightened the bullocks; they made a furious dash forward, and then down they went on their knees – the effect of the *"Gharryman"* pulling them up too violently.

The result was that I, with my baby in my arms, was pitched to the roof of the machine, and cut my eye severely, baby escaped quite unhurt. We were soon got out of the carriage. The Assistant-Surgeon was disturbed from toasting his buns on the point of his sword at the Coffee Shop fire to dress my wounds, and I was comfortably ensconced near the blazing fire on a pile of cloaks and rugs, and soon *"came to"* by the aid of tea and buns!

By the way, this was the only time I ever saw swords *"actively engaged"* and really useful, when they were used as toasting-forks!

A.M.C.
On the March (1904)

At Dinapore

Looking back on his postings to India as a subaltern, Colonel Callwell of the Royal Artillery chiefly remembered Dinapore where life could be eventful for a young officer. (1879 & 1882)

People who have not travelled far afield are under the impression that out in India one is perpetually discovering serpents under one's pillow and scorpions in one's boots. These creatures, of course, exist in quantities; but, throughout the whole of two tours of service in that sunny land spent in a number of different localities, I do not remember seeing a single scorpion at large, nor did I come across more than a score of snakes – and nearly all of those were met with within the space of a couple of hours on one day. It was during my first hot weather and at Dinapore that the Ganges rose day by day alongside the shady "bund" where the regimental bands sometimes played of an evening, until one forenoon the great river came creeping up the surface-drains, spread itself out over the maidan and the roads, and began lapping against the verandah of our mess bungalow. We were watching the rising of the sacred waters, somewhat disturbed lest they should bring a corpse to violate our privacy, when something was descried struggling along the surface towards us, and presently a cobra dragged itself wearily out of the turgid flood and paused an instant to recuperate ere seeking out a hiding-place. The intruder was dealt with speedily and effectually. But others followed, and deadly little mercurial cheraits came wriggling along, so that the bungalow for a while underwent a species of siege, and the whole of the servant establishment had to be formed up to keep close watch and to announce each fresh arrival. When the native lights upon a snake there is a tremendous shouting, and if there is a "Sahib" about he is summoned to come and conquer the reptile; but once the enemy has received the *coup de grâce* by a shrewd stroke from a riding-whip or polo-stick, the native will stamp passionately on the remains, accompanying the process with a torrent of opprobrious remarks . . .

The fates decreed that I should find myself again at Dinapore in another battery, two or three years later, on another tour of Indian service; and as there happened to be no captain, and as the other subalterns were even younger, I was left in command when the major went off to the Hills on leave. All went merry as a marriage-bell during this brief term of early responsibility, but for one unfortunate incident connected with the battery horses. The veterinary surgeon came to me one morning with an anxious air. He announced that a steed which had for some days been segregated and kept under observation, now displayed unmistakable symptoms of glanders; he declared that the animal must be slain forthwith, and he gave it as his professional opinion that the carcass ought to be utterly destroyed for fear of contagion. Shooting the horse was a simple matter; but making away with the remains obviously offered a more formidable problem. There was, however, a scientifically constructed "cinerator" in the lines – a circular mud platform, standing about six feet above ground-level, and furnished with ventilating-shafts coming up from below to ensure an abundant draught. The virtues of this erection had never been put to the test, and the opportunity which now offered itself for trying how the device would act was too good a one not to be taken advantage of. So faggots and hampers and straw were piled up on the altar, and then, to the accompaniment of much grunting and chatter on the part of the battery native establishment, the carcass was hoisted up and perched on the top of the combustibles like the remains of a defunct Brahman. The torch was duly applied, and the hearts of the spectators were gladdened by the sight of a blaze which appeared to herald a speedy triumph.

But nothing would induce that horse to burn properly. Fresh fuel was sent for and applied. A native very nearly immolated himself in trying to pour on kerosene oil, – the scantiness of his raiment proved his salvation, for there was so little of it that he was able to shed it in a moment. In the meantime a column of dense smoke rose up from the funeral-pyre, and as the wind was blowing from the most inconvenient quarter, a cloud soon hung over the cantonment like a pall. Zeal and fertility of resource were alike of no avail. The horse merely went on cooking slowly, in defiance of our most strenuous efforts, and a scent of roast meat pervaded the entire station. The Cantonment Magistrate wrote out a peremptory – indeed an almost intemperate – ukase, ordaining that the nuisance was instantly to cease. The Principal Medical Officer declared that the artillery were jeopardising the health of the community. It was a day of stress and anxiety, and years afterwards . . . I often recalled that early episode of the glandered horse at Dinapore. The object to be consumed could scarcely have shown itself more fire-proof had it been made of asbestos. . . .

One time when the general commanding the district came to inspect the troops at Dinapore – he was a very distinguished soldier, long since gone over to the great majority – he expressed a wish to see the subalterns of the Line battalion ride, seeing that he had to report on their capacity in this respect. He arranged that they should all mount their ponies (or other people's ponies), should proceed to the end of the "straight" of the local race-course, should there form up in line across the course and draw their swords, and should then, on word of command given by the Adjutant, advance down the course at a nice steady trot with their swords at the "carry," keeping their dressing as they passed him, and should pull up a hundred yards beyond the winning-post, where he intimated that he was going to take up his position. Now, the straight was about half a mile in length, a good many of the ponies were not wholly unused to engaging in competitions along this stretch, and all of them had their heads turned towards home. Moreover, although several of the subalterns were capital horsemen and good polo-players, their ranks included certain weaker vessels who were none too secure in the saddle. What the spectators, grouped respectfully two horses' lengths in rear of the general, witnessed was this.

The subalterns were seen afar off, formed up in line across the course as for a race. Then there suddenly was a violent commotion and the whole party came tearing along like a hurricane, *ventre à terre*, in a cloud of dust. Many lengths ahead of the ruck a chesnut mare had singled herself out, galloping like one possessed. Her rider had abandoned his stirrups and had thrown away his sword, his helmet was on one side of his head, and he was holding on grimly to the pommel of his saddle; but even in that awful moment he never lost his presence of mind, for as he flashed past the general he made a dab at the side of his head with his outer hand by way of salute, and then the pair of them disappeared out into the road, and he was not seen again until he was found on a long chair in the mess verandah, with an empty "peg" tumbler by his side, after the inspection had concluded. The rest of the troop came rushing past the general in a wild, irregular swarm. A few of the riders were endeavouring frantically to keep some sort of control over their sabres and their steeds. Others sat in correct military pose, their swords at the carry, the stirrup on the ball of the foot and the heel down on the side that was visible – but it seemed not improbable that heels on the far side were hard at work.

As an illustration of the military manoeuvre, carried out with a rigid steadiness and precision, the experiment could hardly be called an unqualified success; but the general was much pleased, and he laughed till the tears ran down his cheeks.

COLONEL C.E. CALLWELL
Service Yarns and Memories (1912)

A Roving Correspondent

Born in Bombay but schooled in England, Rudyard Kipling returned to India at the age of 16. His family were living at Lahore where his father worked at the Museum and School of Art. Rudyard began his career as "fifty per cent of the 'editorial staff' of the one daily paper of the Punjab" - The Civil and Military Gazette. (1883–1885)

So soon as my paper could trust me a little, and I had behaved well at routine work, I was sent out, first for local reporting; then to race-meetings which included curious nights in the lottery-tent. . . . Later I described openings of big bridges and such-like, which meant a night or two with the engineers; floods on railways – more nights in the wet with wretched heads of repair gangs; village festivals and consequent outbreaks of cholera or small-pox; communal riots under the shadow of the Mosque of Wazir Khan, where the patient waiting troops lay in timber-yards or side-alleys till the order came to go in and hit the crowds on the feet with the gun-butt (killing in Civil Administration was then reckoned confession of failure), and the growling, flaring, creed-drunk city would be brought to hand without effusion of blood, or the appearance of any agitated Viceroy; visits of Viceroys to neighbouring Princes on the edge of the great Indian Desert, where a man might have to wash his raw hands and face in soda-water; reviews of Armies expecting to move against Russia next week; receptions of an Afghan Potentate, with whom the Indian Government wished to stand well (this included a walk into the Khyber, where I was shot at, but without malice, by a rapparee who disapproved of his ruler's foreign policy); murder and divorce trials, and (a really filthy job) an inquiry into the percentage of lepers among the butchers who supplied beef and mutton to the European community of Lahore. . . . It was Squeers' method of instruction, but how could I fail to be equipped with more than all I might need? I was saturated with it, and if I tripped over detail, the Club attended to me.

My first bribe was offered to me at the age of nineteen when I was

Mosque of Wazir Khan

in a Native State where, naturally, one concern of the Administration was to get more guns of honour added to the Ruler's official salute when he visited British India, and even a roving correspondent's good word might be useful. Hence in the basket of fruits (*dali* is its name) laid at my tent door each morning, a five-hundred-rupee note and a Cashmere shawl. As the sender was of high caste I returned the gift at the hands of the camp-sweeper, who was not. Upon this my servant, responsible to his father, and mine, for my well-being, said without emotion: "Till we get home you eat and drink from my hands." This I did.

On return to work I found my Chief had fever, and I was in sole charge. Among his editorial correspondence was a letter from this Native State setting forth the record during a few days' visit of "your reporter, a person called Kipling"; who had broken, it seemed, the Decalogue in every detail from rape to theft. I wrote back that as Acting Editor I had received the complaints and would investigate, but they must expect me to be biassed because I was the person complained of.

I visited the State more than once later, and there was not a cloud on our relations. I had dealt with the insult *more Asiatico* – which *they* understood; the ball had been returned *more Asiatico* – which *I* understood; and the incident had been closed. . . .

My Mother and Sister would go up to the Hills for the hot weather, and in due course my Father too. My own holiday came when I could be spared. Thus I often lived alone in the big house, where I commanded by choice native food, as less revolting than meat-cookery, and so added indigestion to my more intimate possessions.

In those months – mid-April to mid-October – one took up one's bed and walked about with it from room to room, seeking for less heated air; or slept on the flat roof with the waterman to throw half-skinfuls of water on one's parched carcase. This brought on fever but saved heat-stroke.

Often the night got into my head . . . and I would wander till dawn in all manner of odd places – liquor-shops, gambling- and opium-dens, which are not a bit mysterious, wayside entertainments such as puppet-shows, native dances; or in and about the narrow gullies under the Mosque of Wazir Khan for the sheer sake of looking. Sometimes, the Police would challenge, but I knew most of their officers, and many folk in some quarters knew me for the son of my Father, which in the East more than anywhere else is useful. Otherwise, the word "Newspaper" sufficed; though I did not supply my paper with many accounts of these prowls. One would come home, just as the light broke, in some night-hawk of a hired carriage which stank of hookah-fumes, jasmine-flowers, and sandalwood; and if the driver were moved to talk, he told one a good deal. Much of real Indian life goes on in the hot weather nights. That is why the native staff of the offices are not much use next morning. All native offices aestivate from May at least till September. Files and correspondence are then as a matter of course pitched unopened into corners, to be written up or faked when the weather gets cooler. But the English who go Home on leave, having imposed the set hours of a northern working day upon the children of children, are surprised that India does not work as they do. This is one of the reasons why autonomous India will be interesting.

And there were "wet" nights too at The Club or one's Mess, when a tableful of boys, half-crazed with discomfort, but with just sense enough to stick to beer and bones which seldom betray, tried to rejoice and somehow succeeded. I remember one night when we ate tinned haggis with cholera in the cantonments "to see what would happen," and another when a savage stallion in harness was presented with a very hot leg of roast mutton, as he snapped. Theoretically this is a cure for biting, but it only made him more of a cannibal.

I got to meet the soldiery of those days in visits to Fort Lahore and, in a less degree, at Mian Mir Cantonments. My first and best beloved Battalion was the 2nd Fifth Fusiliers, with whom I dined in awed silence a few weeks after I came out. . . . There were ghostly dinners too with Subalterns in charge of the Infantry Detachment at Fort Lahore, where, all among marble-inlaid, empty apartments of dead Queens, or under the domes of old tombs, meals began with the regulation thirty grains of quinine in the sherry, and ended – as Allah pleased! . . .

Having no position to consider, and my trade enforcing it, I could move at will in the fourth dimension. I came to realise the bare horrors of the private's life, and the unnecessary torments he endured on account of the Christian doctrine which lays down that "the wages of sin is death." It was counted impious that bazaar prostitutes should be inspected; or that the men should be taught elementary precautions in their dealings with them. This official virtue cost our Army in India nine thousand expensive white men a year always laid up from venereal disease. . . .

Heaven knows the men died fast enough from typhoid, which seemed to have something to do with water, but we were not sure; or from cholera, which was manifestly a breath of the Devil that could kill all on one side of a barrack-room and spare the others; from seasonal fever; or from what was described as "blood-poisoning."

Lord Roberts, at that time Commander-in-Chief in India, who knew my people, was interested in the men, and – I had by then written one or two stories about soldiers – the proudest moment of my young life was when I rode up Simla Mall beside him on his usual explosive red Arab, while he asked me what the men thought about their accommodation, entertainment-rooms and the like. I told him, and he thanked me as gravely as though I had been a full Colonel.

RUDYARD KIPLING
Something of Myself (1937)

Under the Punkah

During the months she spent travelling and visiting friends, Christina Bremner gradually reached some practical recommendations about adapting to life in India. (1890)

Twice you may get the better of the mosquito plague. The first occasion is under mosquito curtains. Your enemy has gorged himself on your blood; unfit for the slightest exertion, suffering from repletion, you slaughter him with his feet caught in the meshes.

But mosquito curtains prevent the circulation of air, they are equal to a heavy blanket, and must be discarded when April and May approach. By an evilly-designed coincidence . . . it is at this time the mosquito grows more vigorous and numerous. He is as the sand on the sea shore for multitude. Beds must all be placed under the punkah, and here the ingenuity of the Saheb comes in. He pins a towel on the punkah frill so that it clears his nose by one inch. The flicking of the towel and creaking of the punkah-rope are fatal to the repose of the normally constituted individual for two or three nights, but soon it is the stoppage of what a week ago harassed him, that breaks his sleep and rouses his anger. If the punkah-wallah do but cease from his labours for forty brief winks, the Presence awakes gaspingly hot, a crowd of mosquitoes on his person. He must be more than a man who can forbear flinging his boots or any other convenient missile at the offending coolie. . . .

. . . What would the unhappy Saheb do in this trying heat, were it not for the imperturbable serenity and equanimity of Indian servants? The more irritable he is, the more gently sympathetic do they appear to be, watchful to anticipate his slightest wish, wishful to alleviate his sufferings. In their white garments and bare feet, they noiselessly minister to his wants, not even remarking that it is hot. I often felt grateful to a black-handed bearer who incited the punkah-coolie to renewed exertions, warned the bhisti to pour more water on the kus-kus tattie, and silently placed an iced drink near my hand without bothering me with questions, when the afternoon sun grew unendurable. My first experience of Indian hot weather was valuable and more amusing to those to whom I related it than to myself . . . . It was the end of March, and every day the thermometer was rising, till early in April it stood at ninety-four degrees, an absurdly high figure for the time of year. I began to calculate that by June we should have reached the boiling point at the present rate of increase, and mentioned my fears to a lady who was dining with us. "It really *does* feel hot here," remarked she, "and we have not yet begun with punkahs. What time do you shut the house up?" I gazed at her. "We never shut it up. All the doors are open on every side, but for all that, the heat is frightful." A hearty laugh was all the answer I obtained for a minute, in which the whole company joined. It was then explained to me that every day the house should be closed at eight o'clock till sunset, that chinks should all be filled up, and no breath from the outer furnace blast be permitted to enter our dwelling except through the kus-kus tatties, which must be fixed in the doorways on the side towards which the wind is blowing, and water poured on them.

The following day these directions were carried out, and our house never registered much more than ninety-two degrees in April, though the heat was growing daily. . . . I then had minutely explained to me a favourite Anglo-Indian theory touching ability to endure heat, which I heard asserted on every side. It is said that people, English people of course, feel the heat least during the first year of exile, that every succeeding year finds them less able to support it, more open to the maladies that are brought in its train. I could not help thinking, that if this is true, and many are to be found who assert it, it points to some errors in diet that could be avoided with a certain amount of care. Take for instance the eating of flesh. It is fully recognized that meat is a diet suitable for a cold climate, and that even then it should be partaken of in moderation. The vast majority of English people of the middle classes in England only eat fresh meat once a day. Yet with one exception I never was in an Anglo-Indian household where people did not have fresh meat twice a day at least, and at dinner several kinds of it. In many ordinary households of no pretension the evening meal has half a dozen courses. Usually the cooking is good, undertaken by Muhammadans who serve out of a miserable little den a far better cooked meal than is placed on an average English table by a cook who has all kinds of ingenious appliances to assist her. . . . Many intelligent persons hold the opinion that the poverty of Indian meat, its lean, tasteless flabbiness requires redoubled effort on the part of the English exile in order to make up in quantity for wretched quality, and many persons do actually eat far more meat in India than they would consider advisable in England. I cannot help thinking that to throw additional burdens on the digestive organs in a hot climate is false animal economy, tending probably to develop that thirst that is so deadly an enemy of appetite. How often have I seen an Englishman, how often have I not myself, come in out of the hot sun and quenched appetite for hours by drinking first an immense tumblerful of iced aerated water. It is what you *want*, and when did a thirsty man ever listen to reason? It is believable that the stomach can stand such refrigerating treatment for a year or two, but it is difficult to believe that it can be endured for many consecutive years without working harm.

CHRISTINA S. BREMNER
A Month in a Dandi (1891)

A Bachelor's Bungalow

When young Julia Curtis came out to visit her coffee-planter brother on an outlying estate in the hill country of south west India she encountered a change of climate which related to morals as much as to monsoons. (c. 1895)

When the monsoon gets into its stride and torrential rain falls day after day, some of its disadvantages soon become apparent to the doraisanny. The dorai is too much engrossed in his planting to be conscious of any shortcomings in his life. Mildew begins to cover one's shoes, and ruin one's books; fishtail insects feed on the pictures, and white ants devour the bamboo matting on floors. The chimneys smoke and the roof leaks, and always there's a selection of wet estate clothes drying in front of a fire. And the soft roads become cut up into morasses of mud, and one feels cut off from one's kind. And, to crown the doraisanny's depression, this happens to be the time when she gets tantalizing letters from home bringing whiffs of a gay world wherein her friends frivolously disport themselves – letters that enlarge upon the glories of a London June and the riot of colour in the parks. And, ah me! most alluring of all, those that dwell upon the prospective joys of August and September in the Highlands. At the very thought, moments of discontent would assail me, and visions haunted me of breezy moorlands fragrant with the scent of bog myrtle . . .

But such dazzling dreams would soon be dispelled by the hoarse croaking of frogs and the maddening, unnerving whir of cicada beetles, reminding me of the fact that from the Highlands "Mountains divided me and a waste of seas" . . .

And then, ah! then there would come a morning when one gazed upon a transformation scene. The rain had ceased, the mist in the valley had dispersed, revealing the distant hills, clear against a sky of turquoise blue. This miracle was called a "Break", and its advent made an astonishing difference to one's outlook upon life.

The bungalow resumed normal conditions. Windows and doors were flung open to the sunshine which soon dispelled the pervading atmosphere of wood smoke, of charcoal fumes, and of damp mustiness. And the mournful procession of crockery on the floors to catch the leaks disappeared.

Smart clothes, odorous of camphor and naphthalene were dragged out of tin-lined boxes and donned to go breakfasting or dining, and once more one felt civilized. And all the gardens under the influence of sunshine soon blossomed out into a riot of colour, and the perfume of many-scented flowers filled the air.

Although a "Break" is of but short duration, rarely exceeding ten days or a fortnight, it comes as a foretaste of the lovely days of September, October, November and December, those enchanting months, which, in the hills of South India, are the most perfect throughout the year.

In a short time I became independent in the matter of getting about, and was able to dispense with my brother's company when riding round the district to visit people. There was always a *syce* in attendance, and he showed me all the short cuts through jungle and across paddy fields, which saved time if I happened to be in a hurry to get to my destination.

One morning, I was due for breakfast at an estate ten miles away. Being late, I requested Hussein to take me the shortest way. He agreed to take me past a certain planter's bungalow, which saved half an hour, and got me to my destination up to time.

When, on my return, I mentioned casually to my brother about the new route which Hussein showed me, he displayed great annoyance, and said I was on no account to repeat such a brazen crime as to ride past a bachelor's bungalow. I was stung into retorting icily: "May I ask if the coffee-coloured children playing on the front verandah explains why I should not pass through a bachelor's garden?" He flushed angrily and said nothing. . . .

My readers must remember that it was the Victorian age, and girls were expected to be very genteel in their conversation.

As regards the above subject, it was generally understood by Englishwomen, that most unmarried men "kept" a native woman, and they usually got their knowledge from gossiping ayahs, if not from their husbands. But the subject was rarely discussed even among themselves, because, in the 'nineties, it was considered too indelicate a matter to dwell upon. It was shortly after I went out that such a thing came under my notice. A few months before, a planter had brought out an English bride. Some weeks later, a malicious ayah, who had been dismissed for theft, divulged to the lady the fact that her husband had half a dozen half-caste children, and that they and the mother lived in a house nearby.

Result, the bride, shocked and disgusted, took the next boat home, and it was currently reported that the bridegroom had become a confirmed drunkard and reverted to his former life. The scandal was still fresh in the public mind by the time I arrived, and it was reported that, at the Club, men roundly condemned the bride for her foolish, and quite unnecessary, action. One day at a breakfast party, when we had retired to the coolness of a bedroom, I was privileged to hear the views of three women on the subject – and after all, since Englishwomen, sooner or later, become involved in those pre-marriage arrangements, they have every right to their views.

Mrs. A. said she didn't blame her at all. Why should any decent Englishwoman inflict upon any possible children she might have, the indignity of half-caste brothers and sisters? Men had no right to bring wives out to face that sort of thing. And, if they were content with a *ménage* of that kind, and the companionship of a common black woman (the one in question had been his cook's sister), why the devil should they wish to associate with Englishwomen at all? . . . He should have told her beforehand, and given her the chance of choosing whether she should come out or not.

Mrs. B., a chaste Victorian matron, said, how could a man possibly discuss such a subject with a young and innocent girl? And besides, she added sapiently, they would never come out if they were told beforehand.

Mrs. C., bringing a little more charity to bear upon the matter, said that for her own part, she was sorry for the poor things – that it all started when they were sent out as young boys and stuck down on outlying estates where they never saw a white face for weeks on end – that when the country was opened up and more Englishwomen came out, she was sure Such Goings On would cease.

Mrs. A. told her to tell that to the Horse Marines – that men would go on until the Day of Judgement filling India with their half-caste progeny. And what could be more pitiable than the lot of that crushed race, regarded with contempt and scorn not only by Indians but by the Europeans responsible for their existence.

JULIA CURTIS
Mists and Monsoons (1935)

The Indian Day

*With so many young Englishmen going out each year to begin
a career in India, there was a steady demand for information
about the way of life they would find on arrival. Herbert
Compton, a writer, could advise them on what to do – and
what to avoid. (c. 1905)*

In small up-country stations there are generally one or two "Europe
shops", kept more often than not by Parsees, where you can purchase
the most miscellaneous assortment of articles, ranging from patent
medicines and Scotch whisky to composite candles and Christmas
cards. But for your other tradesmen, such as the tailor, bootmaker,
draper, and barber, you send for them to attend you. Your tailor,
indeed, you often keep on the premises, for the Indian *derzie*, or
knight of the needle, squats in the verandah, and can adapt his art to
either sex, turning out hot-weather suits of white drill, or tea-gowns,
or summer frocks with a sort of ambidexterity. The hat is another
affair; in the land of the turban you will do well not to rely on the
vernacular hatter. It is well to obtain your *topee* from a reliable
source, for the native-made head-gear of the Muffassil, a monstrous
"mushroom" made out of pith an inch in thickness, is the sort of thing
to provide novelty and amusement in a pantomime. Your washerman
is your private property, and resides on the premises; if you are a
bachelor you pay him four or five shillings a month, and he does all
your washing; even if it runs to seven suits of white drill clothes and
fourteen shirts a week there is no extra charge. The Anglo-Indian
changes his linen very frequently, and when he returns to England the
first thing he curses is the laundry bill. . . .

One of the luxuries of England is the daily morning paper to be
purchased everywhere and in endless variety. Off the line of rail in
India you cannot buy a paper . . . The *Pioneer*, or *Englishman* or
Times of India is always received by post, and imparts a peculiar sense
of welcome to the man in scarlet, the distinctive uniform of the Indian
postman. The craving for home news is very marked and the London

Dhobi

cablegrams are the first things glanced at or inquired about. They not unfrequently constitute the one excitement of the Indian day. After them the advertisement columns attract as much attention as any other, for here you shall glean much personal information that is vastly interesting. You do your shopping from them as a matter of course, but more edifying than this is to learn who is selling-off and going home. For the first thing an Anglo-Indian does who premeditates a trip to England is to advertise his household goods in the Press. If you want to buy a piano, horse, dog, tent, dinner service, or anything substantial in value, your first course is to scan the advertisement columns of your paper, wherein from March to June, the season when every one desires to leave India, you can rely on a plethora of bargains offered to you; but prices go up from October to December, when all who are on leave, and can fix their own time, return to the country, and are on the buy.

The Indian daily paper is far more to the Anglo-Indian than you would suppose; it is his living link with England, and its meagre cablegrams – for they are miserly meagre – bring delight to thousands of exiles. That feeling of being "in touch with home" cannot be understood by any one who has not left it. There are men parted from those they hold most dear who keep account of the approximate speed of the various mail steamers, and will tell you at a moment's notice whether the week's mail may be expected a day earlier or a day later than the average, or on the contract date. . . .

The food in India, whilst far inferior in the raw material to England is rendered much more tasty by the excellence of the cooking. No one ever sits down to a dinner of less than four courses, and the native *chef* is peculiarly skilful at *entrees*, or "side dishes", as they are called. The country itself provides some excellent appetizers, and *pillaos, ketcheries*, and curries will tempt the most jaded palate when English cooking would nauseate it. For tiffin in the hottest weather there is nothing like currie. Joints are at a discount in a country where all the meat is bad, and people who turn up their noses at Australian mutton would find it convenient to be born snub-nosed for a residence in the East. Chicken is the standard dish of India, and beef the least consumed. Eggs enter very largely into the dietary, but are small, scarce bigger than bantam's; and, in the season, game can be shot or purchased almost everywhere.

There is no difficulty in making acquaintances in India, for the first call is the prerogative of the last arrival. Every Anglo-Indian's bungalow stands in its own garden, and at the gate hangs suspended a board with his name painted on it. Each station is a directory in itself, and all the new-comer requires is a sheaf of visiting-cards. Having delivered these he enters society, and his subsequent experience depends upon himself. Hospitality, though behind the standard of the pre-Suez-Canal days, is still a shining virtue of the Anglo-Indian, and a stranger who is able to make himself agreeable is never a stranger long. His chief difficulty will be to avoid the cliques into which society in the East habitually falls; this is perhaps a natural result in a community where every one knows every one, and a splitting up into groups of affinities is the corollary; and not only knows every one else, but his income, his prospects and his particular social status in a select population governed by the strictest laws of precedence. There have been more quarrels over precedence in Anglo-India than over any other cause; it is regulated by a table edited and issued by Government, which is, in effect, the Charter of Anglo-Indian society. Ladies are pedantically jealous, and woe betide the unhappy hostess who makes some quite unintentional error in the order in which she sends her guests in to dinner. It often leads to a row royal. When it becomes very acute, some one pitches the Table of Precedence at the parties, as Moses did the Tables of the Law, and that settles it.

And talking of Anglo-Indian ladies, their position in the East is not what it was. The fatal Canal supplied them in such legions that the difficulty of the modern hostess is to get dancing men, not spinsters. In the "good old days" a ball was often put off when it was known that an unmarried girl or two – "spins", as they are called in Anglo-Indian phrase – were *daking* up to the station, consequent on the arrival of a ship from England; nowadays it is deferred until a polo match or *gymkhana* (a gathering for sports) is due, to bring the men into headquarters. When I went out to India in 1871, there were nine "spins" in a passenger-list of forty, and all were married within the year; returning in 1896 in a P. and O. mail steamer, there were more blighted ambitions on board than I counted. The modern Anglo-Indian is prone to marriage, but he goes home to get him a wife in the majority of cases. And if there is one thing he avoids, it is the "country-bred".

"Country" is a peculiar adjective in Anglo-Indianism that at once diminishes the value of anything. It is a sneer and a condemnation. A "country-bred" individual is at once stigmatized by the appellation. "Country-made" goods are a synonym for inferiority. On the other hand, anything "English" or "imported" at once acquires a special value, and an imported dog, iron bedstead, carpet or article of furniture stamps the owner as a man of taste and means, and sheds dignity over him. "What is she?" a man asks, nodding towards a pretty brunette in a ballroom. "Oh, only a C.B." That suffices. But you must know your audience in using the initials. There is a story told of a gentleman who was extolling the merits of a certain handsome young official, already a Companion of the Bath, to a young lady of the country, and observed he was a "C.B." "What is that?" she inquired, half daring, half doubting, for she could not believe the individual in question was not "imported". "A Companion of the Bath", came the explanation. "Oh, you must not speak to me like that!" was the protest of the coy creature.

HERBERT COMPTON
Indian Life in Town and Country (1905)

SPORT AND SPORTSMEN

THE NEWCOMER still stood motionless, looking at me; and I smiled at my men's alarm. Still I thought it advisable to put the camera down and take up my rifle. It was unloaded; so I slipped in a couple of solid bullets instead of the "soft-nosed" ones used for animals less hard to pierce than elephants or bison. But I had no intention of firing; for the forest regulations impose penalties up to six months' imprisonment or a fine of five hundred rupees for killing an elephant. I looked regretfully at the fine tusks; they would have been a splendid trophy. Still smoking my pipe I walked towards the animal which had not moved but was regarding me with a fixed stare. I halted and, taking off my big sun-helmet, waved it in the air and shouted:

"Shoo! you brute. Be off!"

My voice seemed to enrage the elephant. Up went its head, it curled its trunk, uttered a slight squeal and charged at me. I dropped on one knee and aimed at its forehead. With the fear of the forestry department before my eyes, I hesitated to press the trigger until the huge bulk seemed almost towering over me. Then I fired. As if struck by a thunderbolt the elephant stopped dead in its furious rush and sank on its knees only fifteen paces from me. But even then I did not realise what an escape I had had. My first thought, as I picked up my pipe and stood erect was: "How can I hide the body . . ." (1909)

MAJOR GORDON CASSERLY
Life in an Indian Outpost (1914)

Elephants' Arena

The court of the Gaekwar, king of Baroda, still preserved the customs of the Middle Ages in all their primitive splendour. When Louis Rousselet, the accomplished French author who resided in India for a number of years, visited the court he witnessed scenes redolent of ancient times and barbarous ways. (1865)

The contests of athletes and animals are what the Guicowar prefers to all other entertainments; and he spends enormous sums upon them. . . . The elephant, which is in general an animal of a most gentle disposition, can be brought by a system of exciting nourishment to a state of rage which the Indians call *musth*. He then becomes furious, and attacks whatever comes in his way, men or animals. The males alone are capable of becoming *musthi*, and, to bring them to this state, it is usually necessary to feed them with sugar and butter for three months. . . .

Next morning, Harybadada, the grand-huntsman, came in a carriage to the Motibaugh, to take me to the Haghuroo, or elephants' arena. . . . On an elevated mound are placed the female elephants, and these, it appears, have a decided taste for such sights. In the arena itself are the two males, each chained to one of the extremities; expressing their wrath by trumpetings, and fiercely digging their tusks into the sand. By instinct the elephant always recognises his *mahout*, or driver, and allows him to approach him even while in this condition. Gracefully formed young men, nearly naked, are walking about in groups. These are the *satmari-wallahs*, who play the same part here as the *toreadors* at bull-fights in Spain, and whom I may be allowed to call *elephantadors*. They wear nothing but a light, coloured turban, and a scanty, tight-fitting pair of drawers, which give the elephant nothing to lay hold of. The most active carry only a horsewhip and a veil of red silk; others are armed with long lances; and, lastly a small number have only a fuse fastened to the end of a stick, and a lighted match. These last have the least showy but the most important functions to perform. They must post themselves at different points of the arena, and run to the rescue of the elephantador, when in danger. Rushing in front of the infuriated animal, they flash their fuses in his face, when he recoils in terror, and they succour the wounded. . . .

A few minutes after our arrival, the Guicowar entered the box and took his seat between us. At a given signal the arena is cleared for the contest. Each mahout seats himself on the neck of his elephant, the chains are cast loose, and the two animals are in full view. After an instant's hesitation, they approach one another, with their trunks raised, and trumpeting fiercely: their pace increases, and they meet in the centre of the arena. Their foreheads strike together, and the violence of the shock is so great that their fore feet give way, and they remain leaning against each other. They wrestle with their trunks, which they entwine like arms, and the mahouts have sometimes to defend themselves with their goads. For some minutes the elephants remain head to head, until one of them, finding himself growing gradually weak, feels that he is going to be conquered. It is a critical moment, for the creature well knows that in taking flight he must present his flank to the enemy, who may pierce him with his tusks or throw him prostrate. The worsted one, therefore, summoning up all his strength, pushes his adversary back by one desperate thrust, and takes flight. The combat is decided; shouts re-echo on all sides, and the spectators are occupied more with their wagers than with the elephants. The vanquished one has now to be taken away, and the field left free to the conqueror. A party of men come with great iron pincers, indented, with long handles united by a spring. They skilfully fix a pair on one of the hind legs of each elephant, where, through the operation of the spring, they remain tight. The long handles get entangled with the other three legs, and, as the teeth of the pincers at every step bite a little into the skin, the elephant stops short. He is forthwith surrounded, chained, bound with cords, and, if vanquished is led by a band of armed men behind the arena. The victor remains alone; his mahout dismounts, the pincers and fetters are removed, and the *satmari* commences. This is the second act – a combat between the elephant and men. The arena is invaded by elephanta-dors and fuse-bearers, this brilliant troop, with loud cries, approaching the elephant from every side. The latter, taken aback by this sudden onslaught, stands undecided at first; but soon he receives a stroke of the whip on the trunk, the lances prick him all over, and he rushes with fury on one or other of his assailants. One comes in front and waves his red veil; the elephant pursues him, but, constantly plagued in this way, he repeatedly changes his course, and never catches any one. After a short time spent in useless effort, he at length perceives his mistake, and changes his tactics: he waits. Then one of the best elephantadors advances, gives him a vigorous stroke with his whip, and springs on one side just as the trunk is on the point of seizing him. But the elephant does not let him go in safety. This time he has fixed on his enemy, and nothing will make him abandon him: all that remains for the fugitive is to reach one of the small doors, and so make his escape out of the arena. The animal, blind with rage, strikes the wall, and, fancying he has at last got hold of his assailant, furiously tramples the soil. . . . In the first combat at which I was present the elephant resolutely pursued a young man, who was a very good runner, and, in spite of the thrusts of lances with which he was assailed, never lost sight of him for an instant. The unhappy man made desperate efforts to gain one of the outlets; but, just as he reached it, the creature's trunk seized him by the wrist, lifted him into the air, and dashed him violently to the earth. A moment more and the enormous foot, already raised, would have crushed his skull, when one of the fuse-bearers sprang in front of the elephant and covered him with flames, and the terrified animal fled bellowing away.

At last the trumpets sound, and I see the elephantadors disappear through the small doors. The elephant does not understand the meaning of this sudden flight, and appears to be on the lookout for some unexpected attack. A door opens, and a Mahratta horseman, lance in hand, and mounted on a beautiful steed, enters the arena. Prancing up to our balcony, he gracefully salutes the king. I remark that the horse has his tail cut very short, and I am told that this is to prevent the elephant laying hold of him. The latter runs towards him with his trunk raised aloft, in order to annihilate the creature whom he hates most of all. He has, in fact, a peculiar aversion for the horse, which he manifests even in his gentlest moments. This third act of the combat is the most attractive. The horse, admirably trained, does not stir, save by order of his rider; so that the latter allows the elephant almost to touch him with his trunk before getting out of his way. He attacks the enormous beast with his lance, sometimes in front, sometimes in flank, driving him into a paroxysm of rage. But even at this moment the elephant displays his extraordinary intelligence. Pretending to take no notice of the horseman, he allows him to approach behind; and, suddenly turning round with astounding rapidity, he is on the point of seizing the horse, who only saves himself by a desperate bound. At length the combat terminates; the horseman again salutes us and withdraws, and the pincer-bearers enter, welcomed by the shouts of the crowd, to secure the elephant. These poor fellows have hard work of it, for the elephant charges them, and they have great difficulty in bringing it to a stand-still. The king calls before him the fuse-bearer who saved the life of the *satmari-wallah*, and rewards him with a piece of figured stuff and a purse of five hundred rupees.

LOUIS ROUSSELET
India and its Native Princes (1876)

The Tigress

*With over twenty years' experience in the Imperial Forest
Service of India, Frederick Hicks was well aware of the danger
which a wounded tiger represented. The trouble was, he did
not know for certain if this one was wounded or already dead –
until too late. (1890)*

The tigress was evidently a very shy and cunning beast, for the
moment the beat started she appeared at a gallop, giving me an
awkward right-hand shot . . .

I was shooting with my .450 Express rifle, a very accurate weapon –
though how I wished afterwards it had been a larger bore – and
succeeded in getting in one barrel, to which she spoke and tumbled
over. But recovering herself immediately she plunged into the water
behind me and rushed across to the opposite bank, where she
disappeared into the cover, before I could get another shot. However,
I felt certain that my shot had been a crippling one and that she would
not go far; so when the beaters came up, I at once sent some of them
to camp to fetch up my dogs. In the meanwhile I sat and smoked and
weighed my chances. But the more I considered the matter the more
convinced I became that she must be dead within perhaps, a couple of
hundred yards, and that I was making a fuss and delaying needlessly.
The only reason that I delayed at all was that I had promised my wife,
after my last adventure, that I would follow up no more wounded
tigers on foot without dogs or buffs [buffaloes]. But now in my
impatience I persuaded myself that the present was not a case of
following a wounded tiger, but the picking up of a dead one lying
dead, "just beyond that bush!"

Thus did I break my promise, did follow, and was punished for it.
Giving my spare gun loaded to my orderly, an ex-constable, I took up
the blood-trail, which was copious, just as if the blood had been
poured out of a jug.

I pushed on slowly and quietly across the river-bed, through a lot of
dense grass (a foolish act), and on to the top of the bank above, which

I found covered with a lot of stunted palm bushes called by the native *cheen*. The fronds of these dwarf palms hung over touching the ground so as to form regular kind of dog-kennels.

I was poking about in among these, when suddenly there was a rush from under one of these kennels, and a terrific roar, and I was conscious that the wounded tigress was in mid-air, coming straight at my head. I had only time to throw up my rifle and pull both barrels simultaneously into her chest, when I was knocked flat on the ground with the tigress on top of me. My shot, however, had for the moment knocked her senseless; and as soon as I realized this I shook myself free of her weight and jumped to my feet and tried to reload my empty rifle. But alas! my pockets had been ripped open by the claws of the tigress and were lying, unknown to me, on the grass at my feet, and before I discovered the fact, the tigress recovered her senses and rose to her feet. I had no time to pick up even one of the precious cartridges, which were so near and yet so far, for she at once reared herself up against me with a fierce gurgling snarl, while I ground my heel into the ground and for just a moment held her off by her throat, while I frantically searched with the other hand the corners of my pocket in the despairing hope of perhaps finding in them just one cartridge; but the next moment I was down with the terrible brute on top of me.

What happened after that, I am not quite certain, for far from feeling painless and placid contentment recorded by some other sportsmen under similar circumstances, I never felt more in a rage in my life, and had I even a knife in my hand I would have ripped her from end to end. As it was I could only beat her with my fists as she seized me by my hip and shook me like a terrier would a rat. Suddenly she dropped my hip, and seized my left hand in her mouth and commenced chewing it up. Then everything seemed to go round and round, and the last thing that I remember is the tigress with her head raised in a listening attitude with a far-away look in her eyes, with the tendon of my wrist hanging hooked on her eye-tooth, jerking it from time to time and sending excruciating shocks of pain up my arm – and then blank!

How long I lay like that I do not know; it may have been only a few minutes, or it may have been an hour. But when I came to, my first sensation was that of being suffocated by some heavy weight on top of me, which I found to be the dead body of the tigress which was lying partially across my body.

My left hand was a pulp of raw flesh and broken or crushed bones;

my coat and trousers were in shreds; a portion of my left hip had been torn out by the tiger's jaws; my leggings were torn off by the claws of the tiger, which had also deeply lacerated my legs, besides some, fortunately minor, scratches on the stomach. There was not a single human being within sight. My boots were full of blood; in fact I was covered with blood from head to foot, mostly my own and partly that of the tiger. In this state I dragged myself to the water in the river, in which I wallowed and tried to wash out all my wounds in order to try and get rid of as much of the poison as possible. I may have again fainted here; I do not quite recollect, for the whole of that time seems like a far-away dream.

At any rate I remember I finally made an attempt to bind some of my wounds with portions of my shirt in order to staunch the flow of blood, for I feared I might bleed to death before I could reach help. I then started to totter as best I could towards camp, which lay over three miles away. I believe some of my men joined me on my way, two of whom then supported me, one on each side as I walked. It seems that when the tigress attacked me, all the men bolted, most of them straight to camp, where the orderly was the first to arrive and inform my wife that I had been killed. That brave woman at once snatched the still loaded gun from the orderly's hands, and telling the men to follow her, started off to my rescue. Apparently my conscience pricked me, for I am told, that when I saw my wife on the way coming towards me through the jungles, I at once made my supporters stand off, while I lit a cigar and putting my left hand behind my back, met her jauntily whistling a tune as if nothing had happened, though my boots, by squelching with blood, gave the show away rather.

F.C. HICKS
Forty Years among the Wild Animals of India (1910)

Hotch-Potch

A satisfactory day's sport depends as much on making the right preparations as on the availability of suitable game. Sir Frederick Price was invited to contribute an expert chapter on sport to the new railway guide for southern India, and he included some well-researched advice on what the sportsman should consume when in the field. (1900)

There is no doubt, I consider, that it is desirable, before starting out in the morning for a day's shooting, to have a good, solid meal, the best drink at which is unsweetened cocoa (Van Houten's being a particularly good one): this has a very sustaining effect when taking hard exercise, can be prepared in a minute or two, does not require absolutely boiling water, and can be drunk without milk. Whilst out, however, it is a mistake to eat meat of any kind. The best meal for one person is a half pound tin of preserved soup, of one of the thick varieties, with half an ordinary pound loaf of bread and, perhaps, where the appetite is large, a cuddy biscuit and cheese, with plantains, or a cold milk pudding of some sort or the other after it. The only drink that can safely be taken, is a very weak whisky, brandy, or gin, and soda water. Wine and beer are both, to my mind, absolutely pernicious. A pound tin of soup is quite enough for two persons. It should be diluted with half the tin full of water; salt, pepper, and a little sugar, which last takes all taste of tin off, should be added, and the mixture then heated up to the verge of boiling, which can be done either in a small enamelled saucepan, or, what is very much better, in the very handy cooking tin, used by the German soldiers, which stows into a very small space and can be made of brass or aluminium. The beaters can always pick up the few sticks necessary to boil the soup. Whether the weather is warm, or cold, hot soup, fairly thick (hotch-potch is one of the best) pulls one together in a most wonderful way, and the effect of it lasts for a considerable time. Whilst actually shooting, the best drink is, I believe, water, and drinking it, freely, is good, as it makes the skin act. I have tried pretty nearly everything, weak tea, with and without milk or sugar, tea, with a slice of lime in it, weak cocoa and weak coffee – the former of which produces a consuming thirst whilst the latter does not allay it – lime juice and water, lime cordial and water, and divers other concoctions including, once, when I knew no better, weak claret and water, and I have finally returned, and adhered to water. It is often difficult to get this good, on the spot, but, wherever obtained, it is always desirable to have it boiled before drinking. Filtered water is popularly supposed to be quite safe, but with the filters generally in use, this is, by no means, the case. The water should be procured from the best source available and the sportsman should *make sure* that, before being put into his bottle, it has been thoroughly boiled. He should, in this respect, take nothing on trust; wherever natives have anything to do with the supply, boiled water means safety, and unboiled, the reverse. The best bottle to use is a half gallon vulcanite one, with a cup of the same material fitting on top of it . . . This is secured by an eyelet to a hasp in front, and the whole thing can thus be padlocked so as to prevent a cooly helping himself to a drink, when other water is not handy. The bottle is covered with thick felt and if this is well soaked before starting and wetted at intervals during the day, the water will remain agreeably cool during the hottest weather. It is desirable to have a stout rattan tiffin basket, which, unless the sportsman is prepared . . . to find that the whisky has evaporated, "God knows how," as the tiffin cooly will tell him, should be kept fastened with a good padlock. Ice is a very pleasant adjunct to a day's shooting, and if one is within what an up-country friend of mine used to call "the glacial circle," it is as well to have it. It fully repays the cost of the extra cooly, necessary to carry it.

SIR FREDERICK PRICE
contrib. *Illustrated Guide to the South Indian Railway (1900)*

Deed of Daring

Based at Shahjehanpur in northern India, William Prescott-
Westcar and his fellow subalterns were able to enjoy some first
class sport. He particularly recalled the time when, out
pig-sticking with his chum Hamlet Riley and one or two others,
they encountered a really magnificent boar; but it could only be
despatched after a most unconventional attack. (1907)

The boar had gained a good start, but he'd a long way to go to reach
the jungle he was heading for. I felt sure we would catch him. There
was no need to say anything, we all knew what to do; opening out,
fanwise, to give each spear room to avoid obstacles, we settled down
to ride for all we were worth.

Being all well mounted we kept a very fair line, and before long
began to get on terms with the boar. Hamlet had a slight lead as we
closed in the race for first spear, and dropped his point as he drew
level with the boar.

However, the boar, seeing the flash out of the corner of his eye,
jinked at right-angles and went into a small clump of trees.

The trees were not very thickly clumped together, so we formed
line again and rode forward slowly to drive the boar out of their cover.
However, there was a patch of cactus in the middle of the clump. The
boar took refuge in this.

We could see his fierce eyes glaring at us through the spear-like
leaves, but our ponies could not face their sharp points, so we could
not ride in to drive him out. Our spears were too short to reach him. It
would have been both risky and difficult to force our way in on foot.
Moreover, none of us hankered to do so. It must have led to one of us,
at least, getting damaged.

While we were racking our brains for some device to make the boar
bolt, several villagers came up. They had been busy scooping water
out of a well into an irrigation ditch, but, no doubt glad of an excuse to
stop work, now came to watch us. Behind them toddled a very old

man, who had been sitting in the sun babbling to them while they worked. He was blind in his left eye.

We could have shot the boar with the revolvers we carried on our saddles, to finish off a pony in case it broke its leg or was too badly wounded to recover, but that was not the game. We wanted to kill the boar, but to kill him fairly with our spears while he fought for his life. He was too brave a beast to murder with a pistol.

One of the villagers came up to me. "I can make the boar come out of the cactus, Sahib. If you will give me five rupees," said he.

I looked him over. He was a sturdy fellow, middle-aged. He had cruel, mean eyes and did not strike me as looking particularly brave, but one never knows.

"How?" I demanded.

"That old man is very clever," he replied, pointing to the old fellow as he toddled up.

I looked at the others. They nodded, so I gave him his five rupees.

He beckoned to the old man, and said something to him in a low voice, pointing to the cactus. All I could hear was five annas, so the old chap was not going to get much of a cut out of the five rupees. However, the old man nodded. The two then walked towards the cactus. I noticed that they went in such a way that the old man's blind eye was towards the cactus. When they came to it the younger man suddenly seized the other round the waist and, in place of the deed of daring I had expected, threw him into the cactus, right on top of the boar.

That boar would have faced anything in reason, but the sight of that old man, spreadeagled in the air, flying at his head was too much even for his dauntless courage. He panicked, swung about and came out of the cactus like a bullet out of a gun.

We were so taken aback by the man's brutal action that the boar took us unawares. Hamlet was in his line of flight and had barely time to drop the point of his spear before the boar was on him. It jinked at the last instant, as the spear came down, passed like a tornado, laying open the flank of Hamlet's pony with a flick of his head.

I swung my pony round on his haunches and clapped in my spurs. This unaccustomed violence sent him forward with two mighty bounds. I leant out, as my pony's hoofs touched the ground for the second time, and just managed to cut a gash along the boar's flank with the point of my spear.

"First blood!" I yelled triumphantly, waving the spear to show the red on its point.

The boar, smarting from the sharp pain of the cut, tried to turn, but he was bowled over by the others, their spears clashing together in his body.

So that was the end of him!

Then we went back to deal out a little primitive justice to the heartless ruffian, who had thrown the old man into the cactus, literally to the swine. That is to say, if so gallant an animal as a wild boar can be called a swine.

When we got back to the clump of trees, we found the poor old man still lying, like a pin-cushion, on the sharp prickles of the cactus bushes. He did not appear to be very badly hurt, judging from the loudness of his complaints, voiced in shrill, cracked tones, but he certainly was not comfortable.

I looked round for the ruffian who had thrown the old man in and saw him trying to slink away. However, we very soon rounded him up and brought him back. Then we forced him to retrieve the old man from his prickly bed.

It was much harder work forcing a way into the cactus than being flung there, so by the time the younger man emerged carrying the old chap on his shoulders, like some modern Aeneas, he was bleeding liberally from countless scratches.

The old man, wonderful to relate, was practically undamaged. The cactus points had given him a few useful pricks, but, considering all things, he had a marvellous escape.

The only excuse the young man could offer was that the old man was his father! That he was too old to work, so no longer any use. He added that the five rupees would pay the family land tax.

We took the five rupees from him and gave them to his father. Then we picked up the son and flung him into the middle of the cactus. The old chap chortled for joy!

The howls of the undutiful son followed us, like music to our ears, as we rode away.

LT.-COL. W.V. PRESCOTT-WESTCAR
Big Game, Boers and Boches (1937)

"Panther, Sir"

R.E. Vernède was visiting his friend the Collector and accompanying him on his administrative rounds in up-country Bengal. One evening, while staying near a remote village, they heard about a local big-game hunter called T.B. Webb – more usually known as Tibi Ou-opp Sahib – and arranged by note to go hunting with him next morning at eight. (c. 1911)

Punctually at that hour Ou-opp Sahib presented himself before the bungalow, and as though resolved to elude all ordinary formulas turned out to be an entirely brown young man. At least, his colour was brown, and he had the small features of a slim Bengali. In dress, on the other hand, he was English. He wore a solar topi, knickerbockers, puttees, and a white jacket. Indeed all his things had once been white, but that was some time before, and the dhobie had not seen them for many weeks. . . . He saluted slightly, and in reply to the Collector's inquiries showed himself truly laconic.

"Ah," said the Collector, "you're the Mr. Webb who sent me the letter last night."

"Yes, sir."

"I suppose you've done a good deal of shikar round here? What sort?"

"All sort," said Ou-opp Sahib.

"Including panthers," said the Collector.

"Yes," said Ou-opp Sahib. He had not waved his hand, but he gave me the impression of having waved his hand as though to signify that panthers were of very small account indeed.

"Tigers too?" asked the Collector.

"I have shooted the tigers. No tigers here now."

There was nothing boastful in his speech, even though it suggested that Ou-opp Sahib had rid the district of tigers . . .

"All right; I leave it to you," said the Collector.

"You have the elephants?"

69

"Two," said the Collector. "You will go on our second elephant with my chuprassie? You've brought a gun?"

"Yes," said Ou-opp Sahib, and called to the small boy who had brought the note the evening before. With much pride the boy handed to him a muzzle-loading gun, and with much nonchalance Ou-opp received it.

"The elephants are ready?" he inquired.

The Collector supposed they were. . . . But it seemed there was to be a hitch. One of the mahouts was in waiting to say that his elephant had strained herself, and would be unable to go hunting.

"I don't believe it," said the Collector, and we all went over to where the elephants stood. "Now let's see this strain," he went on, – "off fore leg is it? Let's see it walking."

The mahout salaamed and called to the great creature to lift him up. Then he made it walk towards us. On it came, walking on three legs, with the third held up pathetically like a hurt dog's. Also it rolled its trunk as a man rolls his eyes in anguish. There seemed to me no doubt that it was badly strained.

But Ou-opp Sahib had drawn the Collector aside and was whispering to him, and after a moment the Collector said – "Let the mahout get down."

The mahout got down somewhat unwillingly.

"Now let the mahout call to the elephant to come towards us."

A little crowd had collected from nowhere in particular, as it always does in India if there is anything of interest to be seen, and with genial faces waited for the experiment. The mahout called in the elephant language, and calmly and steadily, without the least sign of lameness, the elephant walked towards us. Judging from the native faces, one might have supposed that a somewhat commonplace miracle had taken place. But judging from the Collector's voice as he spoke a few warm words to the mahout, one realised that a somewhat ordinary trick had been tried on. It is not always easy to detect them. In this case the mahout had no doubt for some private reason wanted a day off, and by some simple pressure of the hand or foot had induced the elephant to walk lame. . . .

. . . Ou-opp steered the elephants as a captain his ship, pausing at various spots as if they were ports of call for the picking up of panthers. I was too interested in his woodcraft to mind that no panthers as a matter of fact showed themselves at these points, but the Collector did not wholly approve.

"It's all very well," he said; "they're just the sort of places you would find panthers in, but they're not going to wait for us to come up. And they can hide themselves anywhere in this thickness. What's he up to now?". . .

A little later, after we had just crossed a dry tangled gully in Ou-opp's wake, we came up to find that he had descended from his elephant, and was making a reconnaissance on foot. The chuprassie murmured to us that they had just come on fresh leavings, and that there was a sort of hole in the bank hard by.

"But where is Ou-opp Sahib?" demanded the Collector.

"He look in, your Honour, to see if panther is there," said the chuprassie; and following the direction of his finger, we perceived in among the undergrowth, with his gun held carelessly in one hand, Ou-opp down on his knees peering into a hole in the bank.

"Here, I say," began the Collector in tones of remonstrance, "supposing there is a leopard inside."

Ou-opp had already got quietly to his feet again. "Otter," he said, and slung himself up the tail of the elephant. I thought to myself that it would take a good deal to persuade me to go on all fours in front of a leopard's possible lair and decide it was only an otter's.

Another quarter of an hour's thorny going, such as the elephants hate, brought us out of the wooded area on to the edge of the river. Crossing it, we got at once into a great grass waste, and the Collector was about to stop Ou-opp and ask him what his plan of campaign now was, when Ou-opp himself called a halt. His own elephant was at the time close to what might be described as a dense tussock of grass, some ten feet high and the same in diameter, and as ours came up Ou-opp held up his hand warningly.

"What is it?" asked the Collector, expecting, as he told me, to see a pig break away.

"Panther, sir," said Ou-opp, and pointed into the tussock. His gun lay carelessly across his knee and his legs swung idly down. It is not a position in which I have ever seen an English gamekeeper, but somehow a smart young English gamekeeper was what Ou-opp reminded me of at that moment. I fancy it was the respectful air of patronage with which he offered something irreproachable in the way of sport to the gentlemen amateurs before him. He as good as said, "It will amuse you, but I have seen so much of it"; and while I was being amused, and just beginning to wonder vaguely whether it was usual to shoot at leopards before you saw them, the Collector had let fly into the tussock, there was a snarling hiss, and something had bounded out on the side away from us and was leaving behind it a wake of shivering jungle-grass. After that we were in the thick of the chase. The mahouts had become yelling fiends, the elephants were going at a floundering gallop, the jungle was like a sea swept by a violent squall. Then, as I was wondering how much practice it required to be able to be in an upright position on the pad at the critical moment, we had all, so to speak, pulled up on our haunches, and Ou-opp's mahout was pointing excitedly at a patch of grass. Ou-opp evidently had his eye on it, but his gun still lay across his lap idle. He did not lift it even when, a second later, the leopard, with another sudden snarl, leapt at his dangling legs. The elephant wheeled right round trumpeting.

"Look out," I said involuntarily, and Ou-opp smiled slightly.

"Panther leg broken," he said, and it was so. Owing to that fact it had missed its spring by inches and dropped back in the grass, a bunch of snarling, crouching yellow. Another bullet and it turned over on its side dead, and Ou-opp had dismounted to measure it.

We went on afterwards for two or three hours, but we got nothing else, and there was no particular reason why we should. Panthers do not herd together, and there is not much beating to be done with two elephants. Only I had the fanciful impression that Ou-opp was not interested in producing another bagh for us. His preserves, so to speak, had been shot over sufficiently for the day. . . .

We learnt a little about him that evening from one of the chuprassies, who had got it from the schoolmaster; and it appeared from this source that Tibi Ou-opp Sahib was son to yet another Tibi Ou-opp Sahib, who had settled in the village many many years before. What had this original Ou-opp Sahib been? Nothing less than an English Tommy. No wonder that our Tibi had jaunty legs and a devil-may-care bearing that was not of Bengal. . . .

. . . Thomas Bertram? Timothy Benjamin? His father must have known, but I doubt if Tibi himself remembered or had known himself to bear any name but Tibi Ou-opp for many years. It was twenty, the schoolmaster said, since the old man died; and all that survived of him – besides Tibi – was the topi and the puttees and the jacket that Tibi wore, and the muzzle-loading gun which he carried so professionally.

R.E. VERNÈDE
An Ignorant in India (1911)

The Thrill of the Chase

Maharajah Dhiraj of Patiala liked cars. He had forty two Rolls Royces, and there were some two hundred and fifty other assorted cars in the royal garage. American travel writer, Alexander Powell, and his cousin, Colonel Gallowhur, stayed as guests of the Maharajah and were soon being taken for a ride. (1928)

Learning that we were fond of shooting, the maharajah gave orders that a hunt should be arranged for the following day, for roaming the plains in the vicinity of the capital are vast herds of nilghai, sambhur and black buck. I had expected that we would shoot from blinds, and that a vast number of beaters would be employed to round up the game, and I had hoped we might even get a glimpse of a form of sport peculiar to India – hunting with trained cheetahs. I was mildly disappointed, therefore, when, early the following afternoon, there drew up before the guest-house a light American touring car, of a type noted for its speed, stripped of running-boards, top and wind-shield, with a pair of Mannlicher sporting rifles resting in the tonneau. At the wheel was the maharajah's principal A.D.C., a most companionable and amusing colonel of cavalry, who was also captain of the Patiala polo team.

"We always shoot from cars here in Patiala," he explained. "It's much more sporting than using beaters, because the game has a better chance, and, as I think you will agree with me after you have had a taste of it, it is much more exciting."

It certainly was. The only wonder was that we came back alive, for the colonel drove the car as recklessly as he rides his polo ponies.

The game herds, comprising thousands of animals, range over vast and comparatively level plains, which, however, are by no means as free from obstructions as the plains of the American Southwest. On the contrary, they are dotted with clumps of thorn-scrub and mimosa, broken at frequent intervals by stony watercourses, irrigation ditches, groves of trees, patches of dense jungle, and occasionally by the low

73

Maharajah of Patiala

mud walls surrounding the fields of peasant farmers.

We had driven scarcely half-a-dozen miles along the Simla highroad before we spied, some distance to the right, a large herd of black buck. There must have been several hundred in all. As long as we kept to the highway the beautiful animals, the color of dark Jersey cows with white markings, paid no attention to us, but the moment the colonel swung the car on to the open prairie they took alarm.

Long ere we could get within range they were off in a mad stampede. I did not know that any animal could cover ground at such speed, could jump so high or far. They progressed, indeed, in a series of amazing bounds, some of the bucks seeming to go fully ten feet into the air. A beautiful and thrilling sight.

"Are your rifles loaded?" called the colonel. "All ready? Hang on, then. Here we go!"

He jammed his foot hard upon the accelerator and the speedy little car leaped forward, almost from under us, like a race-horse at the rise of the starting-gate. Straight across the plain we tore, our pilot shaping a course which would eventually converge with the line taken by the fleeing game. Our speed was increasing with every revolution of the wheels. I glanced at the speedometer needle. We were doing fifty-five miles an hour.

Suddenly a low wall of sun-dried bricks rose squarely athwart our course. "Look out!" I cried instinctively, my fingers dug deep into the leather cushion. But our pilot, forgetful of everything save the thrill of the chase, paid no heed to my warning. *Crash!* We went through the flimsy wall as though it were made of cardboard. We wallowed across a plowed field, the car rocking and rolling like a motor-boat in a heavy sea, threatening at every instant to go over. Then out upon the open plain again, with smoother going before us. Now we were abreast of the thundering herd, though the panic-stricken animals were still beyond the effective range of our rifles. The speedometer needle was hovering between sixty and sixty-five. And that's going some even on a paved highway, let me tell you.

We splashed through the shallow bed of a stream amid a smother of spray; took an irrigation ditch in our stride as a hunter takes a fence, all four wheels of the car leaving the ground; plunged into a patch of forest, our hubs missing the trees by fractions of inches; burst through a screen of thorn-bush, one of the spines laying open the back of my hand, though I failed to notice the wound in the excitement, and emerged into the open again to find ourselves racing parallel to the leader of the herd. The animal, a magnificent buck with a splendid pair of spiral horns, was perhaps a hundred yards distant.

"Now's your chance!" the colonel shouted over his shoulder.

"Go ahead! Shoot!" I urged my cousin.

"Shoot yourself," he shouted. "Don't waste time being polite."

The terrain was for the moment comparatively smooth and the car was traveling at the pace of the Twentieth Century Limited when it is making up time. The buck, which the colonel had skilfully cut out from the herd as a cow-puncher cuts out a steer, was covering the ground in thirty-foot leaps, bounding across my field of vision like an animal target in a shooting gallery.

I braced myself as well as I could in the swaying tonneau, brought the Mannlicher to my shoulder, caught a glimpse between the sights of a slender pair of horns, a straining neck, a sleek black shoulder . . . and pressed the trigger. *Whang!* With the crash of the rifle the buck gave a convulsive bound and crumpled in its tracks with my bullet through its heart. It was a magnificent head – even the old shikari who shared the front seat with the colonel admitted that – and one of these days, I hope, it will fill the space over my great fireplace at Journey's End.

A little later my cousin brought down another fine buck and our hunt in Patiala was over, for I have no patience with those game-hogs who turn shooting parties into massacres. When we drew up before the guest-house, our trophies lashed to the fenders, I stepped in front of the little car and gravely raised my topée.

"What are you doing?" my cousin asked curiously.

"I'm lifting my hat to the car," I answered. "I'm proud of its being an American."

E. ALEXANDER POWELL
The Last Home of Mystery (1929)

ORIENTALS OBSERVED

TO A stranger landing in India for the first time, knowing nothing of the language or the customs of the people . . . there were many minor personal perplexities, especially about servants. Their very titles were embarrassing. Bearers, kitmagars, dhobies, durzees, bheesties, chuprassies, punkah-wallahs, hookahbadars, syces, and others. What were their duties? That was the point. Because in India, as we soon found, one man will only do his own mite of work, and scorns the idea of making himself generally useful. Any attempt to enlarge the sphere of their duties would lead, so we were told, to loss of caste. There were, of course, exceptional cases, such as that of the native servant who, on being asked by a new-comer as to his caste, replied, "Same caste as master, drink brandy sahib." (1857)

GENERAL SIR JOHN ADYE
Recollections of a Military Life (1895)

The Opium Trade

As the wife of a missionary, Mrs Murray Mitchell watched with an unhappy eye the crowds at the official Government auction in Calcutta. (c. 1870)

Mrs. S. and I have just returned from one of the most singular scenes I have ever witnessed – namely, an opium sale. A strange place for ladies to go to, I dare say you will think; but my friend and I are equal to a good deal together, and we were properly escorted by Mr. M., who is the Government inspector of opium, and obliged to be present at the sales. Besides this, we kept strictly "behind the purdah;" a screen having been placed on purpose for us, and so well placed, that, though entirely unseen, we saw and heard perfectly. The sale takes place once a month. It is a sort of auction, when the chests are put up in lots, and disposed of to the highest bidder. Government, as you know, has a monopoly of the opium trade, making as much gain as possible on the deadly export as it passes from its own hands into those of the dealers; who bid for it, and buy it, and send it on to do its work on unhappy China. The purchase, of course, is a pure speculation, depending for the return on the state of the market when the consignment reaches China; and hence the extraordinary nature of the scene we witnessed. The huge hall was one sea of faces. Men were congregated there from every part of the country – Hindus, Musulmans, Jews, Parsees, Europeans, and Indo Europeans. . . . The keen restless eyes were all turned on the seller, who stood in a thing like a school-desk, or small pulpit, with a little hammer in his hand. There was a subdued buzz in the room, as of many eager hushed voices, while the street below was a perfect Babel of deafening tongues. A great crowd of the same sort of men as those in the hall, had assembled below the windows. These were not buyers; their object was to bet on the results of every purchase; and in this they showed the same terrible eagerness as the actual buyers did within. As each lot was knocked down, and the little hammer had given its tap,

tap, some one rushed out to make known the result to the crowd below. . . .

After watching the scene within for a while . . . we went to a little balcony overhanging the street to survey the crowd of gamblers without; and I think the spectacle was even more curious than the one we had left. The men were a rather lower-looking set; certainly the most disreputable company of natives I have seen. . . . The Babu element was small. There were some shabby Jews, low Parsees, wily Marwarrees, overgrown Banyans, and, lowest-looking of all, some loafer-like Europeans. . . .

I must say I came off with a blush of shame on my cheek. This sale is conducted by our Christian Government! A most important item in its revenue is drawn from this vile opium trade, so ruinous both to the bodies and souls of the poor Chinese. Nay, we forced the use of it upon them at the bayonet's point.

MRS. MURRAY MITCHELL
In India (1876)

Success in Business

John Russell Young, a journalist on the New York Herald, *accompanied General Ulysses S. Grant's party round the world and published an account of their experiences. Here, at Agra, they shopped for souvenirs, and the General's friend Edward Borie – a merchant and financier who was almost seventy – found he still had something to learn about business methods. (1879)*

. . . If you are skilled in Indian bartering, the moment a price is named your true tone is one of astonishment, anger, grief; and if you have a cane raise it, as though your indignation was roused to such a pitch that it was with difficulty you could be persuaded from taking summary vengeance on a peddler who would presume to insult your understanding by asking such a price for garnets or shawls. When a trade opens in this way the sport is sure to be fine, and the bazaars are hopeful of a good day. But none of us were up to this, and our purchases began in a slow, plaintive way, until Kassim was called in as interpreter, and then the trade took a poetic turn. Kassim's cue was despair, and from despair to anger. He began with a remonstrance to the dealers upon the sin and madness of such a charge. Then he appealed to their religion. Taking out a silver rupee, and pointing to the head of the Queen and the imperial superscription, he asked the dealer whether he would swear that his wares were worth what was asked. This suggestion led to loud clamors, in which both parties took part, the voices rising higher and higher, and the spectators coming in to swell the chorus, until all that was left was to sit in patience until the chorus ended. I never saw any trader swear on the rupee. I am told that there is some spell attached to the oath on the rupee . . . As a matter of observation the merchant seems to really ask about thirty per cent. more than he will take eventually. I have seen a good many abatements in the course of those small trades, but rarely more than thirty per cent.

Mr. Borie's well-ordered mercantile mind was so disturbed by these violations of sound business maxims in his purchases of bangles, garnets, jewels, cloths, laces, and shawls that it was with a sense of relief he discovered one honest merchant, who lived on the main street, and who bid us welcome to his bazaar with the assurance that he always charged one price, and had sold rampose chuddahs to Lord Lytton and the Prince of Wales. . . . Signals of our coming had been sent, for we found the establishment in a fluttering state, Hindoos in various stages of delight meeting us as we came. The proprietor was a smooth-faced Brahmin, in a blue, flowing robe, with a bland, smiling face, who spoke English enough for us not to understand him. By dint of pantomime, and now and then a noun asserting itself, and the aid of one or two clerks who knew English, we managed to open negotiations. The merchant sat on a cushion on the floor . . . Taking from his breast a packet of papers, we found them letters from various exalted people commending his merchandise. . . . All this while servants were bringing in stuffs and throwing them around the floor. Other servants brought in trays laden with sweetmeats, among which I recall a candied mango, which was pleasant and new. Then champagne came in, and we began to feel as if we were at a fancy ball or some public entertainment, and not an afternoon visit to a shop. Mr. Borie commended the merchant for the sound business principles he had enunciated, which, he continued, were the fundamental elements of all success in business, and without which there could be no real prosperity. Looking over the various treasures strewn around, he intimated a fear that he might not be able to buy them. Then the merchant, with captivating tact, offered to sell Mr. Borie all the goods he wanted on credit, and if our friend was in need of money he would give him ten or twenty thousand rupees until he reached Calcutta or New York. To these courtesies and assurances Mr. Borie listened with beaming eyes, rejoiced to see sound business principles in India, and to know that his name was one which even in the farthest East was a spell to conjure up rupees.

Then the merchant told us of his family life, his wife and his children, sitting on his cushion all the time and looking at us with his smooth, bland smiling face. . . . Then, when the conversation lulled, our merchant would tell us how honest he was, and never sold but at one price, in which resolution Mr. Borie confirmed him, from the results of his own ample and notable experience. Now and then, if a suggestion was made that something was too dear, the merchant would fold his hands and bow, and say he would have other articles opened at lesser value, but he had only one price. So our afternoon passed away, and when we returned home Mr. Borie expressed himself pleased with his day's visit, that it was really one of the most satisfactory days he had known in India, and that no one but a merchant could know the comfort it was to buy and sell at fixed prices. It did not change Mr. Borie's opinions in the least, but gave him a more extended view of the Indian character when he learned, a few days later, that there was no merchant in India more disposed to dicker than this tradesman, and that if he had bought his goods on Indian principles the afternoon would have passed just as pleasantly, and they would have cost him at least twenty per cent. less than was paid for them.

JOHN RUSSELL YOUNG
Around the World with General Grant (1879)

Raging Thirst

*While on leave from his parish in Oxfordshire, The Reverend
Allen found material for a sermon on an Indian train. (1883)*

From Seringapatam I took the train back to Bangalore, and on this
journey I had a curious experience of the rigid way in which the law of
"caste" rules the Hindu population of India. I was travelling in a
second-class carriage, and in the next compartment there were three
natives, only separated from me by a low partition. One of them was a
boy suffering from a fever, and parched with thirst. They were all
high-caste Brahmins from Gujerat, and were on a pilgrimage to the
holy places in the South of India. One of the men with this sick lad was
an intelligent, courteous person, speaking good English. I could not
help being attracted by the moans of the poor lad, and I heard him
asking for water. I knew it would be useless to offer my water-bottle
to them, as they would not drink from any vessel which I had used.
Still as it was a case of emergency, I ventured to make the offer as
politely as I could. I was not surprised at its being courteously refused;
but the younger of the two men asked me to call the station master at
the next station, and get him to obtain a drink of water for them. He
thought as I was an Englishman, my request would be more likely to
be attended to. When the train stopped, I called the station master
and told him what they wanted. But as soon as he saw them, he shook
his head. He explained that he had no "bhisti" (water-carrier) at that
station of high enough caste to give these gentlemen water. They were
superior to ordinary people, and though the bhisti at most stations is
chosen from a high caste, in order that he may be able to minister to
everyone's wants, yet my fellow-travellers were of a higher caste than
the bhisti at that station, and therefore could not have their drinking
vessels filled by him without suffering contamination. So we were no
further forward, and the poor sick lad had to go on enduring his raging

thirst without alleviation. Yet there was no hint on his part of a wish to break through the rules of his religion, and he seemed ready to endure any suffering rather than do what he felt to be wrong. It was an example of consistency and rectitude, which many a Christian might imitate with advantage. However, at the next station his sufferings were relieved. As soon as we stopped, one of the men got out with his drinking vessel, and soon came back radiant with joy. He explained that he had found a well from which he had drawn the water himself, and as no one else had touched it, this water was lawful for them to drink. So the sick lad got his sufferings relieved, and I learnt a lesson of the heaviness of the yoke which "caste" puts on the necks of the Hindu population.

W. OSBORN B. ALLEN
A Parson's Holiday (1885)

Professional Duties

The Ghorawalla or Syce was a vital member of an Anglo-Indian's household: he looked after the horse. As observed by E.H. Aitken - originally writing in the Times of India *- the relationship between employer, employee, and, apparently, the horse, was essentially competitive. (c. 1889)*

A boy for yourself, a boy for your dog, then a man for your horse; that is the usual order of trouble. Of course the horse itself precedes the horse-keeper, but then I do not reckon the buying of a horse among life's troubles, rather among its luxuries. . . . Then the *Ghorawalla* supervenes.

The first symptom of him is an indent for certain articles which he asserts to be absolutely necessary before he can enter on his professional duties . . . It is not very rational to be angry, for most of the articles, if not all, are really required. Several of them, indeed, are only ropes, for the *Ghorawalla*, or syce, as they call him on the other side of India, gives every bit of cordage about his beast a separate name, as a sailor describes the rigging of a ship. . . . You think you have fitted him out with everything the heart of syce can desire, and he goes away seemingly happy . . . but his happiness needs constant sustenance. Next morning he is at the door with a request for an anna to buy oil. Horses in this country cannot sleep without a night-light. They are afraid of rats, I suppose, like ladies. However, it is a small demand; all the syce's demands are small, so are mosquitoes. Next day he again wants an anna for oil but this has nothing to do with the other. Yesterday's was one sort of oil for burning, this is another sort of oil for cleaning the bits. To-morrow he will require a third sort of oil for softening the leather nose-bag, and the oils of the country will not be exhausted then. . . . I suppose a time will come when he will have got every article he can possibly use, and it is natural to hope that he will then be obliged to leave you. But this also is a delusion. On the contrary, his resources only begin to develop themselves when he has got all his wants. First one of the leather things on the horse's hind feet gives way and has to be cobbled, then a rope wears out and must be replaced, then a buckle gets loose and wants a stitch. But his chief reliance is on the headstall and the nose-bag. When these have got well into use, one or other of them may be counted on to give way about every other day, and when nothing of the original article is left, the patches of which it is composed keep on giving way. Each repair costs from one to three pice, and it puzzles one to conceive what benefit a well-paid groom can derive from being the broker in such petty transactions. But all the details of life in this country are microscopical, not only among the poor, but among those whose business is conducted in lakhs. I have been told of a certain well-known, wealthy mill-owner who, when a water Brahmin at a railway station had supplied him and all his attendants with drinking-water, was seen to fumble in his waistband, and reward the useful man with one copper pie. A pie at present rates of exchange is worth about $^{47}/_{128}$ of a farthing, and it is instructive to note that emergency, when it came, found this Croesus provided with such a coin.

Now it is evident that if the syce can extort two pice [six pies] from you for repairs and get the work done for five pies, one clear pie will adhere to his glutinous palm. I do not assert that this is what happens, for I know nothing about it. All I maintain is that there is no hypothesis which will satisfactorily explain all the facts, unless you admit the general principle that the syce derives advantage of some kind from the manipulation of the smallest copper coin. One notable phenomenon which this principle helps to explain is the syce's anxiety to have his horse shod on the due date every month. If the shoes are put on so atrociously that they stick for more than a month, I suspect he considers it professional to help them off.

Horses in this country are fed mostly on "gram," *cicer arietinum,* a kind of pea, which, when split, forms *dall*, and can be made into a most nutritious and palatable curry. The Ghorawalla recognises this fact. If he is modest, you may be none the wiser, perhaps none the worse; but if he is not, then his horse will grow lean, while he grows stout. How to obviate this result is indeed the main problem which the syce presents, and many are the ways in vogue of trying to solve it. One way is to have the horse fed in your presence, you doing butler and watching him feed. Another is to play upon the caste feelings of the syce, defiling the horse's food in some way. I believe the editor of the *Aryan Trumpet* considers this a violation of the Queen's proclamation, and, in any case, it is a futile device. It may work with

An Indian bungalow

the haughty *Purdaisee*, but suppose your *Ghorawalla* is a Mahar, whose caste is a good way below that of his horse? I have nothing to do with any of these devices. I establish a compact with my man, the unwritten conditions of which are, that I pay him his wages, and supply a proper quantity of provender, while he, on his part, must see that his horse is always fat enough to work, and himself lean enough to run. If he cannot do this, I propose to find someone who can. Once he comes to a clear understanding of this treaty, and especially of its last clause, he will give little trouble. As some atonement for worrying you so much about the accoutrements, the *Ghorawalla* is very careful not to disturb you about the horse. If the saddle galls it, or its hoof cracks, he suppresses the fact, and experiments upon the ailment with his own "vernacular medicines," as the Baboo called them. When those fail, and the case is almost past cure, he mentions it casually, as an unfortunate circumstance which has come to his notice. There are a few things, only a few, which make me feel homicidal, and this is one of them.

EHA
Behind the Bungalow (1889)

Asiatic Servants

Civil Engineer A.C. Newcombe spent nearly thirty years in India with the Public Works Department. He was a man who took his food and drink very seriously, sometimes dieting or turning vegetarian, and always trying to ensure that what he consumed was absolutely wholesome. In this his domestic staff were not completely supportive. (c. 1890)

There are certain propensities of the Asiatic servants for which they should not be unduly blamed, but which must be watched and checked. For instance, a cook will curry very bad meat which he gets cheap in the bazaar because it is too bad for ordinary use. When curried, of course its bad and perhaps poisonous character is hidden by the strong pungent flavour of the curry powder, and it is a source of danger which the cook had no idea of causing. . . . Very dirty dusters are occasionally used for cleaning plates and dishes for the table, and a black streak may be left across a plate from the much-used cloth passed over it in cleaning. The ends of the white flowing garment or *puggree* a man is wearing come in useful for him to wipe a plate clean when the usual dish-cloths are not at once forthcoming and the plate is wanted quickly for the table. Little things like these have to be stopped, as they are important to one's health and in other ways; but they frequently recur if supervision is relaxed. . . .

An illustration of the kind of detail and the real necessity of attending to it may be given in the filtering of the drinking-water. A good native servant, one would think, could well be trusted to look after such matters. One of my servants in the Punjaub had to see to the boiling and filtering of water for the table as one of his daily duties. I inspected the filter now and then to see that it was in order and clean. But one day the water was discoloured and tasted bad. On inquiry the servant assured me that it had been filtered, but it turned out that he had forgotten to put the water into the filter in time to get a good supply for dinner. Annoyed at the slowness of the filtering, he had taken out the nasty black lump (the carbon block) to make the water run through more quickly. It was done no doubt in my interests according to his own lights, and it was hardly an error I could foresee he was likely to fall into.

The same peculiar danger exists in the fact that most of the cooking utensils are of copper. Of course, if no precautions were taken, the copper would at times corrode and poison the food. To prevent this an amalgam of tin is laid over the inside of the copper pots and pans. This has to be done once a-month to prevent exposure of any part of the copper through wearing away of the tinning. When properly done, and often enough, it is convenient and safe; but there is lurking in the system a danger not readily suspected. After some years of satisfactory working I found in the Madras Presidency that the men whose business it is to do the tinning were using a mixture in which lead was a component part. This was easier to lay on, and probably cheaper, but of course it was likely to injure and even poison the food. To obviate such risks I tried using block tin (and lately aluminium) instead of copper utensils, so that no tinning would be required. When, however, the cook's monthly accounts came to be paid, "tinning" was charged for as usual. It being the custom to tin the cooking-pots, the servants saw no reason why tin ones should not be tinned as well as copper ones, especially as a certain percentage on all charges for work done is pocketed by the cook in his department and by the bearer in his. My next experiment was to discard the pots and pans altogether and introduce instead a Warren's cooking apparatus made of block tin. In this there are several compartments through which steam passes, and we get what is called "conservative" cooking, by which, the food being steamed instead of boiled, the nutritious salts which Nature provides are not dissolved out into the cooking-water and lost. I explained to my cook, and with the customary native politeness he expressed his strong approval of the change. The meals were satisfactory for some weeks, until it was discovered that he was not using the Warren's cooking apparatus at all. He had borrowed some old copper utensils, for they were what he was used to, it was the custom to use them, and therefore they were, in his opinion, the proper things to use in spite of the cranky ideas of his master.

A.C. NEWCOMBE
Village, Town, and Jungle Life in India (1905)

Satan

When he was sixty, and penniless following an unlucky investment, Mark Twain embarked on a world lecture tour to pay off his debts. While spending several weeks in India, the creator of Tom Sawyer and Huck Finn met Satan, who became his personal servant. (1896)

. . . He was an astonishing creature to fly around and do things. He didn't always do them quite right, but he *did* them, and did them suddenly. There was no time wasted. You would say:

"Pack the trunks and bags, Satan."

"Wair good" (very good).

Then there would be a brief sound of thrashing and slashing and humming and buzzing, and a spectacle as of a whirlwind spinning gowns and jackets and coats and boots and things through the air, and then – with bow and touch –

"Awready, master."

It was wonderful. It made one dizzy. He crumpled dresses a good deal, and he had no particular plan about the work – at first – except to put each article into the trunk it didn't belong in. But he soon reformed, in this matter. Not entirely; for, to the last, he would cram into the satchel sacred to literature any odds and ends of rubbish that he couldn't find a handy place for elsewhere. When threatened with death for this, it did not trouble him; he only looked pleasant, saluted with soldierly grace, said "Wair good," and did it again next day.

He was always busy; kept the rooms tidied up, the boots polished, the clothes brushed, the wash-basin full of clean water, my dress clothes laid out and ready for the lecture-hall an hour ahead of time; and he dressed me from head to heel in spite of my determination to do it myself, according to my lifelong custom.

He was a born boss, and loved to command, and to jaw and dispute with inferiors and harry them and bullyrag them. He was fine at the railway station – yes, he was at his finest there. He would shoulder and plunge and paw his violent way through the packed multitude of

91

natives with nineteen coolies at his tail, each bearing a trifle of luggage
– one a trunk, another a parasol, another a shawl, another a fan, and
so on; one article to each, and the longer the procession, the better he
was suited – and he was sure to make for some engaged sleeper and
begin to hurl the owner's things out of it, swearing that it was ours and
that there had been a mistake. Arrived at our own sleeper, he would
undo the bedding-bundles and make the beds and put everything to
rights and shipshape in two minutes; then put his head out at a
window and have a restful good time abusing his gang of coolies and
disputing their bill until we arrived and made him pay them and stop
his noise.

Speaking of noise, he certainly was the noisiest little devil in India –
and that is saying much, very much, indeed. I loved him for his noise,
but the family detested him for it. They could not abide it; they could
not get reconciled to it. It humiliated them. As a rule, when we got
within six hundred yards of one of those big railway stations, a mighty
racket of screaming and shrieking and shouting and storming would
break upon us, and I would be happy to myself, and the family would
say, with shame:

"There – that's Satan. Why *do* you keep him?"

And, sure enough, there in the whirling midst of fifteen hundred
wondering people we would find that little scrap of a creature
gesticulating like a spider with the colic, his black eyes snapping, his
fez-tassel dancing, his jaws pouring out floods of billingsgate upon his
gang of beseeching and astonished coolies.

I loved him; I couldn't help it; but the family – why, they could
hardly speak of him with patience. To this day I regret his loss . . . I
loved Satan. This latter's real name was intensely Indian. I could not
quite get the hang of it, but it sounded like Bunder Rao Ram Chunder
Clam Chowder. It was too long for handy use, anyway; so I reduced
it.

When he had been with us two or three weeks, he began to make
mistakes which I had difficulty in patching up for him. Approaching
Benares one day, he got out of the train to see if he could get up a
misunderstanding with somebody, for it had been a weary, long
journey and he wanted to freshen up. He found what he was after, but
kept up his pow-wow a shade too long and got left. So there we were
in a strange city and no chambermaid. It was awkward for us, and we
told him he must not do so anymore. He saluted and said in his dear,
pleasant way, "Wair good." Then at Lucknow he got drunk. I said it
was a fever, and got the family's compassion and solicitude aroused;

so they gave him a teaspoonful of liquid quinine and it set his vitals on fire. He made several grimaces which gave me a better idea of the Lisbon earthquake than any I have ever got of it from paintings and descriptions. His drunk was still portentously solid next morning, but I could have pulled him through with the family if he would only have taken another spoonful of that remedy; but no, although he was stupefied, his memory still had flickerings of life; so he smiled a divinely dull smile and said, fumblingly saluting:

"Scoose me, Mem Saheb, scoose me, Missy Saheb; Satan not prefer it, please."

Then some instinct revealed to them that he was drunk. They gave him prompt notice that next time this happened he must go. He got out a maudlin and most gentle "Wair good," and saluted indefinitely.

Only one short week later he fell again. And oh, sorrow! not in a hotel this time, but in an English gentleman's private house. And in Agra, of all places. So he had to go. When I told him, he said patiently, "Wair good," and made his parting salute, and went out from us to return no more forever. Dear me! I would rather have lost a hundred angels than that one poor lovely devil.

MARK TWAIN
Following the Equator (1897)

A College Education

The "cram system" in Bengal was recognised by Bowles Daly as "old-fashioned, obsolete and absolutely worthless". Having reached this conclusion from his personal experience, Dr Daly went on to do what he could to bring about reform. As a start he wrote this exposé for the local press. (c. 1896)

It was with a distinct feeling of satisfaction . . . that I accepted the offer of the Professorship of English Literature in the Metropolitan College, made me by the Hon'ble Surendra Nath Bannerjee, the popular tribune and educational broker of Bengal. . . . The recent demand for education has called into existence a large number of such training schools, which are extensively patronised by the youth of the town, and also those of the country, who crowd the lanes and slums of Calcutta. The fees usually range from six to twelve rupees a month; but the Metropolitan valorously offers a university education, with choice of professors, for the ridiculous sum of three rupees all round! Here the cram system is conducted on entirely commercial principles, and can be seen in all its naked deformity. The teaching establishments of Calcutta form a mushroom growth of formidable character. My observations are strictly confined to those of the natives, among whom a strong rivalry exists, not for the acquisition of knowledge, but for getting "passes" and procuring fees. The college authorities are compelled to supply the exact kind of information the students want, and not what is beneficial. . . .

The advantages of a college education I give in its correct order. First, it enables a youth to win good matrimonial stakes for himself; for in India it is the son, and not the daughter, who is put up in the market: the M.A., the B.A., and even the plucked B.A., possess a certain monetary value, rising in grades. Next, the degree gratifies personal vanity, serves as a feather in the cap; praise to the Bengalee Baboo is as sweet as blubber to the Esquimaux . . . The third object of education is the chance of getting a post under the Government. The smallness of the pay is no drawback; the post is everything, for it means authority, and the ingenious methods of exacting indirect taxation are known to every *chuprassie* in the town. . . .

My duties in the college were to teach for nineteen hours a week. All the subjects were prescribed, and the clerk of the establishment supplied a time-table on which they were entered. An hour was devoted to each subject. The students were nearly all young men, few under nineteen and many over twenty-three. Their conduct was characterised by a species of independence which bordered on insolence. My experience of student life in England, France, and Germany presented me with no parallels. They strode into the class-room at all hours and went out as they liked, making noise and seriously interrupting the work of the class, while during the lecture they held conversations with each other which made the business of speaking a labour. The number in the classes ranged from one hundred and twenty to a hundred and seventy. There was no attempt at order or discipline, and the business of signing the roll presented the appearance of a free fight, the clerk's voice being hardly audible.

The books for study comprised Shakespeare, Landor, Spenser's Faerie Queene, Sir Philip Sidney's Apology for Poetry, and Frederick Harrison's admirable Life of Cromwell – a fine selection, but very much beyond the comprehension of men unacquainted with the simplest words of English. The ignorance of the students was petrifying; a slight glimmering of mind within just served to render internal darkness visible; their faces did not express any kind of activity beyond that of perspiring. It was my custom to read a sentence or short paragraph out of any of the books which formed the subject of the lecture. Then give the sense, using the simplest Saxon words, and, having finished the explanation, before going to the next sentence, request the students to ask questions.

The inquiries propounded revealed the qualities of their mind and the extent of their comprehension, which was appalling. Here is a sample – "Ulvir crimwell brought his wife to Huntingdan: meaning of 'to' in sin-tance explain." The whole passage was run together without inflection, uttered with jaws set as tight as a rat-trap, and expressed in a villainous cacking tone which sounded like the rinsing of a bottle. As there are no marks for pronunciation or enunciation, the Indian students regard such accessories to the language as beneath contempt. . . .

The soul-stirring words of Shakespeare, the cameo-cut sentences of Landor, the organ tones of Milton, and the manly sentiments of Tennyson make about as much impression on the Bengalee mind as the taps of an auctioneer's hammer on a block of granite. . . . To make the silk purse out of this bristly raw material would task the efforts of the wisest. The most glaring defect was the absence of any thirst for knowledge; they evidently regarded words merely as a wheel-barrow to convey thoughts, and not the becoming dress of ideas. . . .

The main idea of the student under the cram system is to get a "pass", so he wants his information boiled down and carefully chewed. He cares no more for the quality of the grub given him than a young crow who clamours for sustenance with open beak. Like the bird in question, he does not care to look for his food himself; this he wants the Professor to do for him. The information must be made up in pellets which can be swallowed with as little trouble as possible. The very words must be dictated that he may enter them in his note-book. The only faculty of his mind exercised is that of memory. He objects to be questioned, and makes answers in noises which sound like words bitten in two and swallowed before they are half out. That venerable divine and eminent scholar, The Rev. Father Lafont told me that in an examination in physiology, a student gave so complete an answer to a paper that the examiners suspected the boy of copying. The youth was summoned to appear before the examiners. He denied the charge and boldly challenged them to set him then and there any question on the subject. A question on the brain was given him, which he answered on paper with great accuracy. The examiners were astounded, but one of the number tested his knowledge by calling the servant to bring up a brain from the museum. As the man was leaving the room to execute the order, the examiner said, "Stop, I'll write down what I want." Instead of brain he wrote, "Send up a heart." When the latter was placed before the student, he could not distinguish between a heart and a brain!

J. BOWLES DALY
Indian Sketches and Rambles (1896)

The Concession

The Oxford University Authentics Cricket Club got up a team to play in India at the time of the Coronation Durbar. Cecil Headlam, who played for Middlesex, came on the tour as both player and team secretary. The latter role appears to have been the more demanding. (1903)

All Jacks-in-office, in fact, are alike; the thing to do is to treat them according to their breed. The Babu requires to be dealt with in a tone of authority. The lower class, though excellent in doing his absolutely ordinary routine of clerical work, is frightened out of his wits at the idea of doing anything outside it. To think for himself or act on his own responsibility is completely beyond him. As I, in a weak moment, undertook to do the secretarial work of our tour, to act as the *Bundobast-wallah* of the team, I had frequent opportunities of observing the workings of the Babu's mind. At each place where we stopped I had to pay at least two visits of an hour or two, and sometimes a good deal more, in order to arrive at the simple result of having two first-class carriages reserved on a particular train and of purchasing some two dozen tickets. The railway companies . . . had been good enough to grant our party a concession by which we were enabled to travel at reduced rates; a concession which, when you come to journey some seven thousand miles by rail, amounts to a very welcome sum of money saved. The method employed was that I was given at each starting point a concession-letter, by which the stationmaster or clerk was authorised to grant me first-class tickets, up to a certain number, at second-class fares. The letter was explicit, but there was something unusual in the concession to the mind of a Babu. It was thus that the game used to be played. As I was busy playing cricket all day, my only chance of getting the job done was to ride down to the station before breakfast. On arriving there I usually found no Babu. He was away, at home or at a funeral, and would not be down till ten o'clock. I used to say sweetly that I thought he would come before that, and Babu used to be pulled out of bed and brought.

When he came he would read the letter aloud, in an unintelligent manner, and then ask what I wanted. Internally he had already shied at the responsibility of doing this strange thing, and he was gaining time whilst he searched about for an excuse to put me off. Then I would explain to him the purport of the letter and my desires. He would then say, "Come and get the tickets just before the train starts; they will be issued then." This, of course, was absolutely out of the question, and he knew it. Apart from the hubbub and flurry of an Indian railway station just before a train goes, it was absolutely necessary for me to have the tickets a day beforehand in order to distribute them, so that our servants might get our luggage registered, our beds ready, and that we might come down to our carriages when we liked. So I used to say, "No. The tickets will be issued now." Babu would plead piteously, "But the accounts will get mixed. How can I take money to-day for to-morrow's tickets?" Then I used to explain to him, what he knew already, how to work the ticket-stamp. "But the accounts!" he used to cry, "the accounts! What can do?" Then I would speak sharply, and he would begin to get out the tickets. But we had only just begun. His next move would be to make out the fare. This would sometimes take twenty minutes. I never yet struck a single booking-clerk in India who knew the price of a ticket from any one station to any other. Each time he must consult his book. Next came the great question of the concession. All he had to do, as bidden in the general manager's letter, was to charge second-class fares. But he did not like the look of it. His first gambit would be to look doubtfully at me, and remark in his staccato monotone, "There-is-no-re-duc-tion-on-re-turn-tick-ets." As I did not ask for return tickets or a reduction on them, I would explain the irrelevancy of his remarks. Then he would take the concession-letter and begin to read it again, unintelligently, aloud. I would stamp suddenly, jingle my spurs, and bang my fist on the desk. He would jump off his stool like a scared rabbit and seize a printed book of directions. There was one paragraph in this book of instructions to railway officials which became a positive nightmare to me. It was to the effect that there was no reduction allowed on return tickets! Babu would now solemnly turn up this paragraph and read it out to his brother Babu who was sitting behind him. (No Babu ever seems to trust himself alone. He always has a supernumerary idiot sitting in the background to whom he can appeal.) The assistant would nod approvingly. Then would my Babu turn to me triumphantly. He had said so. There *was* no reduction on return tickets!

Remember that this was all happening before breakfast – a time when, in a hot country, you are inclined to be rather peppery. Can you wonder if I fell back occasionally on the limited resources of my Hindi? It was like falling back on a bed of roses! For, however limited be your resources, if you have any Hindi at all, you will know some terms of abuse so powerful, resonant, and searching . . . that they are an actual intellectual relief. . . . Can you wonder, too, if I used to seize that hateful book of instructions and throw it away, and bring the reluctant Babu back to the point?

The point, by this time, was to multiply, say, 65 rupees, 12 annas, and three pie by 15. Babu would take a piece of paper, a dirty scrap of yellow paper, and begin. I would take another piece of paper and begin also. Later on – a good deal later on – we would announce our various results. For the results always varied. This did not mean that I was always right. Far from it. Years ago I went to a phrenologist. He felt my head and looked serious – wise almost. "You can scarcely count," he said gravely, "much less calculate." And ever since I have had a sneaking inclination to believe in phrenology.

Babu would now hand his account to brother Babu to be checked, and I would go over my sum. I do not think he usually tried to swindle me, as an Italian booking-clerk nearly always does, and an English one often. On the contrary he occasionally nearly succeeded in rushing himself, and, in one case, having rushed me to the extent of several rupees, ran after me and gave me back the excess. So, at last, the tickets safe in my pocket, I would hurry off to breakfast and the cricket field. But do not suppose that Babu was content. He would think the matter out, this way and that turning his swift mind all day. And the more he thought of it, the less would he like it. In the peaceful solitude of his office he would begin to finger again, very lovingly, the leaves of his printed instructions. He would come across a paragraph therein which stated distinctly that there was no reduction allowed on return tickets. And he would remember – cunningly would he thus put two and two together – that the sahib, when shown this rule, had called him a Sua and a Bahnshut, and thrown the book on the floor. Now Babu would begin to lose his nerve. He would begin to imagine vain things – the docking of his monthly pay, the loss of his billet. For had he not issued tickets at a reduction contrary to the printed law? Therefore in the early hours of the morning, when, after a dinner and dance, I would come down to the station to turn into my bunk in our carriages which would be placed on a siding waiting to be attached to the mail, on the platform I would find a very piteous

Babu, shivering with cold and fear. He was a poor man, he would inform me, and there was a Printed Rule. I was his father and his mother, he would add, and I would not willingly see him starve. I used to deny both statements. Then he would hand me a much-thumbed copy of Instructions to Railway Officials, and he would begin to read aloud, "There-is-no-re-duc-tion-all-owed-on ------"!

CECIL HEADLAM
Ten Thousand Miles through India & Burma (1903)

JOURNEYS AND JOURNEY'S END

WE HAD ridden out under the awakening sky of the early morning hours, and as the pale lustrous dawn graduated into perfect day, and the sun rose glorious from behind the snows like an "avenging fire-god," causing the death-white Himalayas to kindle and glow in the light of his presence, a vision which made one speechless and almost breathless, our Transatlantic cousin remarked in a tone of calm finality, "Wall, that's what *I* call vurry neat." To have such a remark hurled at you in an agressively "Yankee" accent, when you are in a state of great mental exaltation and excitement, is like receiving a cold douche with your pulse beating at fever height. (c. 1898)

SARA H. DUNN
Sunny Memories of an Indian Winter (1898)

Deep in the Wilds

*Edwin Arnold planned to ride from Poona – where he was
Principal of the Government Deccan College – up to the hill
station of Mahabaleshwar (a journey of approximately a
hundred miles by way of Wai). As was customary he had
organised a succession of* dâk *horses posted at intervals along
the way, and expected to obtain necessary provisions en route.
After riding all night his plans began to go awry. (1860)*

By this time, fairly hungry and thirsty, I could see in the distance the
gleam of the river Krishna [Kistna], and the pinnacles of the temples
in the town of Waee. Here, no doubt, I should get milk, eggs, at the
worst, water to drink, for the night's riding had made me thirsty. It
was perhaps nine o'clock when I rode down to the river and into the
main street of this very sacred place. But alas! it was a season when
cholera had been very prevalent, and the disease was positively raging
in this holy but extremely dirty town. The Hindoos as a race live
happily and die placidly, but the spectacle presented by that
plague-stricken centre was none the less very painful. All along the
river banks, hastily erected funeral pyres were flaming and smoking.
At many a door bamboos were being lashed together to bear the
newly dead to the burning. In the temples priests were praying, and
citizens and peasants bringing their small pathetic offerings of
propitiation. I was asked by a dozen voices if I was a *hakim*, a *vaidya*,
a doctor; but I had neither skill nor medicines, and rode sorrowfully
through this scene of death and suffering across the river-ford to the
travellers' bungalow on the slope of the opposite hill. Here, in
dismounting, my Deccan pony jibbed and drove me against a post,
which, unluckily, broke the bottle of soda-water which I had thus far
carried. The attendant at the bungalow had died of cholera. Nobody
was in his place. There was nothing to be got, and nobody to get it. I
did not dare to touch water from the river, every ripple of which must
have been full of cholera-germ, and there was nothing, therefore, for
it but to lie down on the cane charpoy and try to sleep away the hot

103

Hindu cremation

hours of the day, with the hope in the early afternoon of riding quickly up the hills and into the station, where friends and comforts were awaiting me. It is a curious fact that, as I lay half asleep that day in Waee, hearing at intervals the funeral cry of the poor townsfolk . . . what with the great heat of the day and the dampness of my clothing from a light rain, the figures of my watch-dial . . . were melted off and nearly obliterated. It may be judged by this that the season was warm as well as sickly. I remember how the sight of the river, sparkling under the steps and porticoes of the marble temples, made me long to go down among the dead and dying, and plunge into it. But I was not yet quite thirsty enough for this rashness, and, at starting again, set my fresh steed at the quickest pace he could command along the slope of the hills leading to the station. I quite expected, in the uplands and glens in front of me, to come across some stream or pool, the water of which would be safe to drink; for it was now getting on for twenty-four hours since I had taken any liquid whatever, and I was beginning to feel that second phase of thirst, when to drink is no longer a desire but a passion and a pain. The horse I was riding was the last of the *dâk*, and the best, his duty being to carry me the eighteen or twenty miles

remaining. Although already suffering, I though'
distance, since, being in good health, nothing was ye'
me except a parched throat; but in the confidence tha...
be safe at the station, I asked a Mahratta peasant whom I me...
knew where there was any water or milk, and when he answered in
the negative, I inquired which of the two turnings before me in the
forest-road led to Mahabuleshwar. That question, too carelessly put,
cost me dear. Mahabuleshwar, which means "the place of the great
Lord of Strength," is really the name merely of a temple and of a
sacred peak deep in the hills. The station, although known generally
by that appellation, is locally called Malcolm-Peth, and it was this for
which I ought to have inquired. The peasant, ignorant of my plight,
and thinking I wanted to visit the shrine, pointed me along the steep
way to the right, which I rashly followed for more than two hours and
a half, until the sun was near setting, and then the utter absence of any
signs of a large station told me too plainly that I had lost my way, and
was deep in the wilds of the Ghauts, thirty hours by this time without
any liquid, and perhaps eighteen or twenty miles away from my home.

Twilight is brief in India, and before long the road became invisible.
My horse was tired, and proceeding now at only a foot pace. The
night-cries began to rise from the jungle, and I heard much too plainly
for my comfort upon the left the sharp quick cough that a tiger gives
when he is calling to his mate. I had, of course, no weapon with me,
but my chief thought was for water, and I listened intently amid the
forest noises for any sound of a running or falling rivulet, towards
which I would have gone at any hazard. But until the rains come in
earnest these Western Ghauts are very dry, and there was no such
welcome sign. On the side of the path, however, I could just make out
a native hut, to the entrance of which I guided my horse. I pushed
open the door, which was unfastened, and, the interior being quite
dark, I struck a light. In the gleam of the lucifer-match I saw
something very unpleasant – the naked body of a man lying upon a
charpoy, evidently dead. I am not very nervous about such things; but
with cholera in the district, and every token that this poor fellow had
been suddenly overtaken by it, it was better to be in the open air,
though I was by this time so bitterly thirsty that I looked into the
chatties by the wall of his hut to see if there was anything to drink.
Luckily, perhaps, for me they were empty. The water-pot, its contents
spilt, lay upon its side by the bed; and I was glad to get into the forest
again. But by this time, though the night fell cool, I was really
beginning to feel the true pangs of a mortal drought. Had there been a

moon, I might, perhaps, have searched for some jungle fruit; but all was gloom. You could just descry the opening in the trees where the road passed, but it seemed out of the question to retrace my steps. When thirst reaches this point you begin to get fever and sharp headache. The lips are dry and crack, and the back of your throat becomes like blistered parchment. I really at that juncture had a wild idea of opening a vein in my horse's neck and sucking it. But he had been a good little beast, and a better inspiration took me. I caressed him, pulled a handful of grass and gave it him to eat, and then, mounting again, laid the bridle on his neck and let him take his own way. He turned round and went down the path by which we had come, now and then quickening his pace. In this way we perhaps traversed five or six miles, till I was beginning to feel too sick to keep the saddle. Just at that moment, in an open place where a little light entered, my horse stopped and pricked up his ears. For a time I could not guess the reason, but presently I heard, in a hollow below our road, the noise of something rustling through the thicket, and suddenly there emerged into the path a couple of hill-men with their axes and sticks. If they had been angels from Heaven I should have been less glad to meet them. I had not much voice left, but soon managed to explain my situation, and, well assured of a reward, they undertook to guide me to Malcolm-Peth, which by a short cut was not very distant. The faithful fellows plunged into the jungle with me – one leading the horse, the other with his arm round me, supporting me in the saddle. Renewed confidence is in itself, meanwhile, a cordial, and I began to allow myself to think of drinking, which before had been a fancy that only increased the fever and the headache. Presently one cried, "Dekho, dekho – Sahib! butti hai." (Look, sir, look! There is a lamp!) And through the dark leaves I did really see a light gleaming. I rode straight up to it. It was a moderator lamp, placed upon a table in the veranda of a bungalow, and two officers were sitting at the table with glasses and beer-bottles before them. I should be ashamed to say what the sight of that beer was to me at that moment. I did not speak to them nor salute them, but sliding from my saddle pointed to my mouth and throat, and to the unopened bottle. One of the good fellows, grasping the situation, drew the cork and poured out a foaming glass of that to me then absolutely divine beverage. I hope he forgave me for clutching the glass from him before he had half filled it, and though to this day I do not know his name, he lives in memory as one of my dearest and truest friends. Do not ask me to describe the passage of that reviving draught into my grateful frame. Every drop seemed a veritable elixir of life, and the odd thing was that I was not so far gone but that the drink brought me round as if by magic. I almost think it must have hissed in my throat as it went down, but I blessed the name of Bass as I shook hands with my unknown benefactors and turned into the well-lighted lane, where I soon found my quarters and the pleasant welcome of anxious friends. Once in a lifetime to be as thirsty as that is quite enough for anybody!

SIR EDWIN ARNOLD
East and West (1896)

House of Refuge

The dâk bungalow was one of the most familiar features encountered by travellers in India. John Matheson, on a visit from Britain, was travelling on business into north west India when he first enjoyed its hospitality. (1862)

At Doomree we made our first acquaintance with that celebrated tenement a *dâk* bungalow – house of refuge, restaurant, and dormitory of the Indian plains. This is simply a low square cottage, roofed with tiles or thatch, and comprising several small apartments surrounded by a wide verandah. Like other hostelries it professes to be thrice-blessed to the traveller in its aids to comfort, providing service, refreshment, and repose. The first of these requisites is rendered by a *khansuma* and a *khitmagar* (cook and waiter), usually a pair of obsequious fellows of most melancholy visage, who either in pretence or reality do not understand a single sentence of English, notwithstanding that their lives are spent in the service of those whose only language it is. The refreshment consists frequently of nothing more than brown bread (musty almost of necessity) and *mourghy*, or chicken, which the people of these parts, with a dash of sanguinary pleasantry, style "sudden death." But not without reason, for the biped may be seen, as visitors enter the house, gaily promenading the compound, and the interval between the shriek that signalizes its capture and its presence on the table, metamorphosed into a smoking dish of curry, may be estimated at thirty-five minutes on the average.

When the traveller is overcome with fatigue, sleep may be courted on a bare *charpoy*, which, with a table and two or three chairs, constitutes the furniture of the room. Altogether the little chamber, with its blank white walls and plain scanty accessories, might be likened to one of our model prison cells, but for the atmospheric brightness in which it is enveloped. Certainly, however, no cell could be drearier when at night a feeble lamp scarcely serves to pierce the darkness, emitting along with its mournful flicker a strong rancid smell. . . . and during the long evening, from sunset till bedtime, not a sound disturbs the utter solitude of this "sweet home," unless it be the sturdy drone of the mosquitoes which usually frequent it in strong force, and thus make known by bugle-call their own presence and their victim's coming fate. . . . But the most agreeable and earliest sought provision of the *dâk* bungalow, as each gharry-crumpled, hair-tangled, dust-sprinkled "arrival" shuffles within its precincts, is the bath . . . a place where the bather crouches on an inclined brick floor, while the *khitmagar*, or his own servant, standing over him administers a thorough "sousing" from *chatties* (earthen pots) filled with cold water, the deluge thus created gravitating to an aperture in the wall, and thence anywhere into the sunshine without.

At the time of which I speak the impression left by the terrible scenes of the Mutiny was still sufficiently fresh to influence some minds with a feeling of apprehension. No doubt public order had been long restored. . . . Yet it was only reasonable to imagine, that in the secret depths of many fanatical breasts, the embers of disaffection still smouldered, ready to blaze up in isolated acts of vengeance as a victim came quietly in the way. And thus it happened, no doubt, that while we were preparing for this North-West journey, several good friends in Calcutta cheered my mind with hints of possible danger. One of these, however, somewhat more practical in his sympathy than the rest, suggested that I should provide myself with a revolver, making me at the same time a present of one with which, he said, I would be able to "blow up" any scoundrel who might venture to assail me. The terrible weapon was accompanied by two bags containing a supply of powder and lead sufficient to exterminate a whole band of *dacoits*.

Well, we were now fairly in the depths of the Mofussil. The hour of peril, if such existed, had arrived; it behoved me to inspect the revolver and ascertain that all was in order. This, I may as well confess, was a most needful procedure in my case, seeing that I had never in my life once handled that celebrated firearm, and might not be able to use it without some observation of the mechanism. But any difficulty on this score was immediately dispelled by the condition in which I found the implement itself. It was rusty, dislocated, hopelessly unfitted to harm a fly! My friend had trusted in his servant; his servant had trusted in him; and my folly in trusting either was visible in the thing before me.

Reparation of the injury being now impossible, I was about to cast the gift away as lumber when a happy thought struck me – there is a moral influence in the mere symbol of power. This weapon certainly could not injure the most vulnerable of rascals, but might it not rouse his fears? . . . Thus, its existence indicated and its impotency concealed, a place among our baggage was reserved for the innocent firearm, which became, to successive dusky attendants an object of special regard when jauntily dandled in the hand, or laid down with just an audible clank beside the rugs and shawls on the bungalow table at night. Although, therefore, I never felt nor saw danger, who will make bold to say that my excellent friend in Calcutta did not provide me after all with a needful weapon of defence?

JOHN MATHESON
England to Delhi (1870)

Towers of Silence

A journalist on the Melbourne Argus, *James Hingston was on
a trip round the world when he visited Bombay. He could not
leave without examining the Parsee's unusual cult of "sky
burials". (1877)*

The Parsees have a walled enclosure sacred to their dead, near the
town, which is called The Towers of Silence. . . . I drive out to these
"towers," and find my way stopped at the foot of the hill on which
they stand, by a gate having on it this inscription, –
"THE TOWERS OF SILENCE.
This place is for Parsees only, and the entrance of all others is
strictly prohibited."
I could see that the notice was meant for my curious race, because it
was in English, and in no other language. Looking at it in that light, I
took it as offensive in so singling out one nationality for exclusion.
Being of Danish descent I resolved not to understand it; and so –
leaving the gharry in waiting – unlatched the gate, and toiled up a
steep path, which in the heat of the day was punishment enough for
any amount of misdoing. Arrived at the top, I found a stone wall of
eight feet high all around, in which was a gateway having a similar
inscription to that seen at the foot of the winding ascent. A native
guardian was standing there, having a staff of office or stick in his
hand. Passing him I walked onwards round the wall, going further up
the hill meanwhile. On the outer side there is a fringe of palm-trees,
and the landscape is worth coming to see, independently of the
walled-in mystery. I endeavoured to look as not wanting to see inside
the walls, but as coming up merely to admire the splendid views from
the height . . . .
   Having got out of the sight of the gate-keeper, I stopped to consider
the position. I had not come to see a stone wall and return so
unsatisfied. Other folks had seen these towers, as I recalled reading
accounts of them. Thinking that folks who go wandering about the
world should be as fertile of resource as was Marshal Ney himself, I

Parsee priest

wandered on until the smooth stone wall broke into a rough rubble one. Further on I noticed a stump of a tree near to it. With the help of that, and the irregularities of the stones, I scrambled to the top, at the expense of a broken finger-nail or two.

A noise in the trees outside makes me look that way before looking inwards. In the tops of these trees, cocoanut palms, all around are congregated groups of ugly-looking vultures. These villainous carrion-eating birds seem to croak at my intrusion among them – so much so that I feel glad that I have a stout umbrella with me that I had used as a sunshade. I think that I will put up this protection against the sun while I sit on the wall, and in doing so, I clumsily knock off my hat which falls within the enclosure. It was a new purchase made that day, cost a power of money, and a lot of hunting up, and was a hat not to be easily matched. Without a second thought I jumped after it, and stood there and then in company with the many towers of silence.

I wonder now that the vultures did not make a sudden onslaught on me, as all flesh within those walls was theirs by right – or rather by custom and usage. It is conscience that makes us cowards, and I had a clear one in that matter of the hat, as to my right to be there. I nevertheless folded up the umbrella, and grabbed it tightly as I went to look around. The "towers" are low circular buildings of stone, like to small gasometers. They stood at equal distances apart, and at one end, near to the gate, stood a plain-looking one-story building, differently shaped. To each tower there was a door, that was closed in all cases but one. As it stood partly open I looked up the steps that led from it, and saw at the top a grating, on which lay a human skeleton with clean-picked bones, which the birds on the surrounding trees had been lately at work upon. It is as well perhaps to be eaten by birds above ground as by worms below, and such is all a matter of taste and fashion, but I felt very uneasy now, and wished myself out of the place. It would be so simple an operation to knock one on the head, hoist one's carcase on to that grating, and let the birds have half an hour at one, when one's identity, even as man or woman, would puzzle a college of surgeons.

Of those birds in the trees I now felt really in awe. Considering the nature of their daily dietary, such was no wonder. I had seen quite enough. Curiosity was satisfied . . . My only thought now was how to get out. Climbing the rubble wall quite foiled me. I got the umbrella handle to catch on the top, and so thought to pull myself up. The ribs and covering, however, slipped off the stick, leaving the handle hanging on the wall, and myself stretched on the ground, in which position two vultures flew down from the trees to look at me. I threw stones at these sacred birds, so driving them back to their roosting-places. I was not going to be eaten alive unresistingly.

The matter was getting desperate. Remorse came also to nag me, as it always does to those in trouble. What business had I here – poking my nose into other people's burials? We are much too curious. What mattered it to me how the defunct Parsees were disposed of? . . .

Desperate cases suggest strange remedies, as necessity breeds invention. I took the now naked umbrella stick from the wall and walked on towards the gate. I had various cards in a pocket-case, one of which was written in Cingalese character, and looked eastern and unintelligible enough for anything. The guardian of the gate soon saw my approach, and came towards me. I held out the card, and said loudly, "Jamserjee Jeejeebhoy," a name that I had learnt was all powerful with the Parsees. It appeased at once the mixture of surprise and anger I had seen in his face. He seemed to take the card and explanation as satisfactory, and so showed me to the gate. Looking again at the inscription on it, I now noticed that Sir Jamserjee's name was mentioned as the donor of the ground. On going down the hill I took care to walk painfully and slowly to avoid any appearance of a run, which I nevertheless felt greatly inclined to break into. That gatekeeper was, I feared, looking after me, with an undecided mind.

JAMES HINGSTON
The Australian Abroad (1880)

Wolf-Child

Major Hobbs had been connected with the indigo business when he first came out to India in the '80s. This meant he had to travel up country from time to time, and sometimes to suffer the consequences. (c. 1885)

One hot and dusty morning in the month of May I crossed the Ganges at Monghyr . . . and for five weeks rode from one indigo factory to another, roasted in the sun, and withered in the West wind. Then the rains set in making a forty-mile ride into Chapra a nightmare of thunder and lightning, pouring rain and breached roads. . . .

I fetched up at Chapra in time to jump into a mixed train. Done to the world, soaking wet, with muddy water squelching out of my boots, my hands like a washer-woman's, it was delightful beyond words to be done with long rides and to feel at peace. Before putting on dry clothes it was worth something to lie flat for a few minutes to take a few kinks out of my back. A cool breeze came through the open windows. After those weeks of glare, dust and thirst, life was worth living. It was a good world.

When I awoke my clothes were dry. Stiff and ill, with an agonizing stitch in my right side, I began to throw up quarts of liquid that looked like ink. When the train pulled up at Gorakhpore I could barely stand. . . . A ticca gharry took me to the Dâk Bungalow, a wretched, dilapidated wreck of a place. I threw myself on the string bed, not caring whether I lived or died.

The *khansamah*, seeing a stranger in such a state, appears to have thrown my red blanket over me before bolting. Not without experience, he sensed that the police might squeeze him under the pretext of holding an inquiry into the death of a stranger. It was safer to be out of the way.

For time without end I seemed to be hopelessly striving to grope my way through the pitch darkness of a black velvet tent. About midnight on the third day the fever broke. For many hours I lay still wondering

115

where I was; what had happened. Jackals howled on the verandah like all the banshees in Ireland. A civet cat at a gallop chased rats and other squeaking things across the ceiling cloth over my head. As morning dawned I saw that profuse perspiration had taken the colour out of the blanket for my khaki suit was dyed pink; it reeked with fever sweat and the carrion odour of the bats that swarmed in the thatched roof.

Free from pain but unable to move, I lay wondering, when an extraordinary creature with open mouth, hands hanging limply in front of his legs, louped into the room like a huge ape and leaned over to grin and breathe in my face.

Going through the motions of firing a gun, he breathed a "Whoop" and went through the contortions of a dying animal.

His next effort with bent wrist and forearm depicted a cobra striking and the agonising death of the victim, obviously taken from life. . . .

After each item he rose from the floor, grinned, louped towards my *charpoy*, opened his mouth to breathe on me and let me smell the sort of grub he ate. I sweated with apprehension in case he touched me. . . .

All this time I was too ill to move, and not quite certain whether what I saw could be real. Indescribably thirsty I was about to make an effort to get some water, when a visitor walked into the room.

He had a huge, close-cropped square head, two double chins at the back of his neck, and eyebrows like those on a Chinese executioner. He belonged to a German mission opposite the bungalow and said he had only just been told a Sahib was lying ill, so he came to see about it. . . .

Padre Stern, once he considered he had earned his pay by preaching woe, devastation and hell's torments to a sick youth, turned out to be quite decent. He detailed a man to look after me and sent little delicacies from the Mission, always prayed when he called but having paid that toll became a normal human being.

The story of my alarm at what I thought was a night-mare greatly tickled him. He told me something about the freak's history.

Some villagers had brought him to the Mission with a story that he had been found in a cave. At that time he was about ten years' old. He was suspicious, tried to bite those who held him and struggled to escape. Years of care in the Mission had improved him without taking away all traces of his jungly ways but there was still much of the savage in his nature.

After the padre left, the wolf-child sneaked in again and I examined him more closely. His knees were large and flat, showing traces of years of crawling; to the best of my recollection he had no tongue but once I knew all about him he did not seem so uncanny, although it was uncomfortable to see such a morbid affliction slouching about like a refugee from Madame Tussaud's. . . .

Three years later I was again in Gorakhpore but the old bungalow with its bats and civet cats had been pulled down and a comfortable building stood in its place.

A genial crowd of fellows happened to be staying there over the week end. A Police Superintendent, a tailor's traveller, an optician, and a railway man. After a cheery dinner we sat late and played nap for pice and of course my experiences with the wolf-child were brought up.

Just after breakfast the next morning we were wondering how to pass the time when someone spotted him in the compound. Of course he was welcomed, and given a drink and biscuits. It was Sunday so he had on a clean shirt and dhoti. After two more drinks he took on with a Trichy cheroot while the policeman prepared a cocktail in a half-gallon bathroom dipper which he was sure would take quite a bit of beating. The foundation was some beer left over from the previous night fortified with two pegs of whisky, a dash of brandy, some Perry Davis's Pain Killer, a liberal helping of Lea & Perrin's Worcester sauce, a lump of Day & Martin's blacking to give it body and a hearty shake of the pepper pot to put a top on. The wolf-child put it out of sight with evident enjoyment . . . Just as the drink was getting a good hold, scores of Indian Christian girls, beautiful pocket Venuses, marched two deep out of the Mission compound on their way to Church.

. . . Immediately the wolf-child saw the converts . . . we saw he was half inclined to join them. Someone gave him a push-off and he took post at the head of the column, waving his cigar like an alderman applauding an after-dinner speech. With half a hundred girls giggling behind, he staggered along the road to Church.

Of course it was little less than an outrage but that is what happened. Nearly a hundred people thoroughly enjoyed themselves and perhaps he afterwards looked back on that Sunday morning as the greatest time in his life when so many Sahibs took a friendly interest in his welfare.

MAJOR H. HOBBS
Indian Dust Devils (1937)

The Prisoner

At the time of this tale of the North West Frontier, George Younghusband was a Captain with the King's Royal Rifles and had just taken part in the relief of the British force cut off in Chitral. (His brother was the famous traveller and explorer, Francis Younghusband.) (1895)

After the Relief of Chitral in 1895, it was decided to send the opposing General, Sirdar Sher Afzul, whom we had captured, to India, as a prisoner of war. He was placed in my charge, and I was given a company of British Infantry and a small Cavalry escort to guard him through two hundred miles of mountainous country that lay between us and the Indian railway. The party was to move down slowly, march by march, and at each halting-place would find a camp pitched, and a relief escort ready.

The prisoner was most amenable, and gave no trouble. His only complaint was that he found it "difficult and embarrassing to dress and undress, and to say his prayers, with a Highlander's bayonet within eighteen inches of his back." This legitimate grievance being removed, the march continued pleasantly, day by day, till the cavalcade reached a place called Khar in the Swat Valley. Here, whilst taking a short rest under some trees during the heat of the day, a mixed deputation approached.

This consisted of the Adjutant, some other Officers, the Sergeant-Major, and some Sergeants of one of the oldest of His Majesty's regiments, which chanced to be encamped close by. They had a complaint to make. It was that the prisoner of war, Sher Afzul, was wearing their regimental buttons, and they wished to flay him alive, or otherwise horribly dispose of him, for so doing. Sher Afzul's costume, when we took him in the cold heights near Chitral, was an Astrakhan fur cap, a double-breasted Russian greatcoat of the warmest description, thick breeches, and long Russian boots. We had certainly mildly wondered why he retained this exceedingly inappropriate costume in the extreme June heat nearing the borders of the plains of

118

India. But, beyond noticing that he had brass buttons on his greatcoat, no one had appreciated that they were British, and belonged to the old and gallant Bedfordshire regiment.

This fact, however, being verified, the enraged soldiery were pacified with soothing words, and it was promised to retrieve the buttons in a possibly less sanguinary manner. As we rode on, therefore, I ranged up alongside Sher Afzul, and explained to him that the English were a quaint and curious nation, with some quite unexplainable habits and customs, and that one of these was to adorn certain regiments with buttons of divers metals and devices. Further, that they bitterly and hotly resented any one who did not belong to that particular regiment wearing the peculiar buttons it affected.

Sher Afzul looked sideways in a somewhat furtive and fearful manner, as if he suspected that this parable concealed some deep and horrible design. Then getting very pale, and dropping great beads of sweat, partly doubtless attributable to the heavy Russian coat, he replied with caution:

"Without doubt, the English are a nation of princes!" which, however polite, did not seem very relevant.

"Yes, quite so; but to get to the matter in hand. On that greatcoat of yours you have the buttons of the regiment we have just passed through, and they are somewhat displeased, and would be obliged if you would return them to the regiment."

A look of immense relief came over the General's face, and he beamed on me; a smile which implied, "Is that all?" Yet with Oriental gravity, he merely said:

"Your Honour has only to give the order, and they shall be yours to do as you will."

"Thank you; you shall have another set to replace them. May it be asked where you got them? They probably have a curious history, for you come from Central Asia, far from where that British regiment has ever been quartered."

"I bought them in Kabul, and know nothing more about them," he replied, with a slight return of anxiety. . . .

At the next halting-place, before five minutes had elapsed, the buttons came over in a curiously prompt manner, and were in due course returned to the regiment that owned them.

Next day the General appeared in the same greatcoat, though the weather was now excessively hot; its glory perhaps somewhat dimmed by the hasty substitution of tin trouser buttons of the most impoverished description, in place of their gorgeous predecessors.

"Surely you are rather hot in that coat?" I ventured to remark. "Can I lend you, or buy you, some cooler garment?" Again the General looked at the British Officer furtively and with great suspicion, and answering somewhat shortly:

"No, I prefer this."

Everyone to his own tastes. If he liked to be turned into an Irish stew, inside a double-breasted Russian greatcoat, by a June sun, that was his affair.

The following day the prisoner and his escort arrived at their journey's end, where it had been arranged to hand General Sher Afzul over to the Civil authorities. Under their arrangements he would be conducted to his future place of residence, a salubrious station in the Himalayas. On taking over a State prisoner it is apparently the custom of the Civil authorities to fill in an identification paper, giving his height, appearance, and any particular marks or crosses he may have; a swivel eye, or what not. Also an exact list is taken of the clothes he has on, or off, and of his other possessions. This seemed an ordinary, and not too obnoxious a procedure, but the querulous objection raised to it by the General was quite pathetic. He implored and beseeched that he might be saved this indignity; he even went down on his knees and wept bitterly, and implored the military to intervene, adding that they were his father and also his mother. . . .

Being a guileless soldier, not very deeply versed in Oriental subterfuges, I put in a good word for him to the head of the Police. But that official was adamant. He knew the Oriental, and he knew his business. He added in English:

"Very sorry, but I must obey orders. After all this fuss I shall be exceedingly surprised if there is not something very important concealed about his person."

As I could do no more, I took my leave, first handing over to my late charge a new and gorgeous and unexceptionable set of buttons, procured by telegram; at the same time bidding him be of good cheer, and wishing him better fortune in the future.

That evening the Police Officer came to me, grinning broadly.

"I told you so. I knew all that fuss meant something. We found nearly £20,000 worth on him, in money and stones, besides some most important papers!". . .

After the trip to India with Sher Afzul I returned to headquarters, and there found my tent standing, and everything as I had left it. My Indian servant came forth beaming to meet me.

"Hullo! Luckoo, how goes it?"

"Very well, Sahib; all is well. Save only your Honour's money, which I have had the misfortune to lose."

"Lost my money, you scoundrel; what do you mean? I left ninety rupees with you."

"Without doubt, Sahib, you did; but, owing to misfortune, I have lost it all in gambling. This is a very shameful fact, and I place dust on my head in obeisance. Nevertheless let not the Lord be angry, he shall cut it from my pay to the last coin.

"Tea is now ready," and he waived the matter aside.

On the camp table, possibly as a peace-offering, reposed an important-looking cake. This, with much guile and some bribery, he had induced a friendly cook to make, asking that suitable words might be inscribed on it in pink sugar. The cook was a Christian, and scratched his head a good deal over a suitable inscription. Finally, after consulting his Bible and taking into consideration the general situation, it occurred to him that he could not do better than

"Prepare to meet thy God."

MAJOR-GENERAL SIR GEORGE YOUNGHUSBAND
A Soldier's Memories in Peace and War (1917)

MAGIC AND MYSTERY

ON ONE occasion when Commissioner of Chattisgarh I was travelling through certain very jungly districts, preparing the minds of the people for the coming of the new railway. . . . I ran down to the end of the line to meet the Chiefs, whom I had often met before in the course of my tours. I had a talk with them on the evening on which I arrived; and we then retired to rest.

I was awakened in the night by the weird sound of jungle music. I knew that the tribes were at worship. Next morning I asked the local Chief where the shrine was at which they had been worshipping. After some hesitation he told me that there was no shrine, but that his people had been offering a goat to my engine. He apologised for having disturbed me, and hoped that I would not mind this liberty having been taken with the engine by these simple people. I found the engine sprinkled with blood, and beside it the signs of the sacrificial feast which had been held. These superstitious people had wished to conciliate the unknown Power; and I was thankful that their ignorance prompted that desire, and not the smashing of the engine to pieces and vengeance on all connected with it, as it might have done. (c. 1890)

SIR ANDREW H.L. FRASER
Among Indian Rajahs and Ryots (1911)

The Marked Bullet

Eastern magic was usually the preserve of local people; but Thomas Lewin – then Deputy Commissioner and Political Agent of the Hill Tracts of Chittagong – knew how to beat them at their own game. As the aggressive Lushai people were continually raiding the Hill Tracts for plunder, Lewin went to confront their chief, Rutton Poia, determined to make a forceful impression. (1866)

A little after sunrise the "karbari," with two or three other Lushais, came to say that Rutton Poia would receive me; accordingly, accompanying them, I entered the low, dark door of the chief's house. Inside, I found myself in a long, low room, where, although the hour was so early, numbers of men were assembled, sitting along the wall with their backs against the mat, smoking, while down the centre of the room was the inevitable line of huge earthern pots full of hill beer, and at each pot two drinkers sucking up the liquor through reeds.

Making our way through this crowd, who did not incommode themselves by moving out of the way too much, we passed on to the further end of the room, where, in a small partitioned recess with a window looking out over the hills, sat Rutton Poia, with sundry other chiefs. . . .

At length Rutton Poia grunted. The "karbari" translated this sound by saying that the chief wished to know why I had brought a formidable party of armed men to his village. I replied that my men were armed in order to defend themselves from the dangers of the road; but that, having reached Rutton Poia's village, I had now no need of arms, as my presence showed. I requested that the chief would dispose of the contents of a bale which I had brought with me. The said bale was quickly opened and the contents, consisting of scarlet cloth, cotton sheeting, beads, looking-glasses, &c., were carried off by the chief's retainers; but Rutton Poia and the rest of them still sat like brown images.

"I am glad to hear," said I, "that Rutton Poia disclaims all participation in the outrages which have recently been committed in my country to the south; and I have come here in consequence, to confirm the friendship between us."

No reply. Some brass cups containing a strong spirit were handed round.

"The prevention of such occurrences is my duty," I continued; "or, when not preventible, we can punish our enemies, and Rutton Poia knows that what I say is true."

This was a side shot at the chief personally; for I knew that he had been himself in command of the party which was so effectively routed by my predecessor, Captain M——. On this, Rutton Poia took a big gulp of spirits, and then addressed a remark to the interpreter. I noticed that he stuttered in speaking, but whether this was through nervousness or habit I could not tell. I hoped he was nervous.

"The chief says that Captain M—— was a magician. Is it true that he had a charm against shot and steel?"

"All Sahibs," I rejoined impressively, "are alike gifted with this power by Government on their taking charge of the Hill Tracts. If you have a gun handy I can easily prove this to you."

On a sign from Rutton Poia a gun was brought; the chiefs communed with each other in low tones, the drinkers left their pots, and a crowd of heads peeped over the partition.

"Now," I said, "charge that gun." The "karbari" carefully put in a measure of powder. "Now a bullet." He was putting in the bullet when I stopped him – "Stay! let me see the bullet." It was handed to me. "Lend me a knife." One of the chiefs produced a knife, and I proceeded to cut a cross on the bullet; then, raising it up so that all could see the mark, I said: "You would all recognise that bullet again?" Murmurs of assent. "Then see, I take that bullet and I place it in the gun, thus; then I ram it home in this manner. Now, prime the gun."

It was a heavy flint-lock musket; the "karbari" carefully primed it. Rutton Poia rose and carefully examined the priming.

"Now," said I, "fire at my chest." The "karbari" hesitated.

"Do as the Sahib tells you," said Rutton Poia.

I covered my eyes and face with my arm, and the "karbari," at a distance of about ten yards, took a careful aim and fired. I staggered for a moment, as if receiving a shock, and then, putting my hand to my mouth, from between my teeth I took the marked bullet.

"Is that the ball that was in the gun?" I asked calmly, handing it to Rutton Poia. The excitement was intense. The chiefs were now all standing, and the bullet was rapidly passed from hand to hand amidst exclamations of astonishment. It was indeed the marked ball!

We resumed our seats. Conversation among the Lushais now became vivid; their immobility had disappeared.

At last one big fellow, Vanlula I think his name, got up and began to make a speech. I need not further describe the pow-wow which followed; suffice it to say, that by 4 o'clock that afternoon I was on my way back to the boats, having contracted a solemn alliance, offensive and defensive, with Rutton Poia and his allied chiefs, the compact having been duly ratified by the sacrifice of a guyal, with the proper ceremonies, and sealed by infinite potations.

Skilled magicians, I suppose, are never nervous, or it is, at any rate, part of their profession to appear imperturbable; but I confess that, as I lay in my canoe on my way down stream, it was with a shiver of excitement that I recalled the scene at the Lushai village, and thought of the moment when I changed the pewter bullet of the Lushai and substituted for it a waxen ball carefully blackleaded outside, according to Professor Houdin's receipt, which I had prepared before starting, and which was of course mashed to pieces in the gun when rammed home, while I concealed the marked bullet under the base of my thumb. When the "karbari" was about to fire at me, I covered my face with my arm to keep the powder and pieces of wax out of my eyes, the same movement enabling me to pass the bullet into my mouth, whence I was of course able to produce it after the explosion. I went straight down the river, stopping only one day at Chandraguna, and reached Chittagong on the 24th October 1866, being anxious to report what I had done to the Commissioner.

LIEUT.-COL. THOMAS H. LEWIN
A Fly on the Wheel (1885)

The Feast

*While staying at a military camping ground in northern India
W.S. Burrell was told by his native servant of a curious
happening which occurred every evening in the grounds of a
jungle temple close by. Together with some of his men Burrell
went out to investigate. (c. 1870)*

. . . A flight of broken stone steps led up to the temple, before which
hung suspended on a crossbar a beautiful old bell of silver-bronze.
Two rows of simply-built cells or cubicles occupied part of the longer
sides of the courtyard. Before each cell sat a priest – naked saving the
waistcloth and sacred Brahmin string – and busily engaged in cooking
chuppattees. Not a word was said by any of the priests. The
chuppattees were not ordinary ones, but singularly thick and
coarse. . . .

The setting sun struck horizontally on the gleaming thatch of the
temple. The priests sat, silent and stolid, before their fires and cakes,
as if ignorant of our presence. As the last rays of sunlight died off the
temple and the topmost buds of the mighty hedge round us, a man of
extreme age, clad in white robes, and closely shaven, issued from the
shrine. It was the chief priest. Moving slowly forward, he took up a
bronze hammer and began to strike the bell. . . .

At the sound all the priests arose, as if for vespers, and moved
solemnly, and still in dead silence, round the quadrangle, bearing with
them their huge *chuppattees*, which they broke up as they walked, and
deposited in great pieces on stones and old tree trunks, and on the
steps of the temple.

What could it all mean?

Just then a rustling sound, and a startled exclamation from a soldier
behind me, made me look round. A jackal, big and plump, brushed
past my leg with an upward curl of his lips, and upward look of
surprise and resentment in his red-bronze gleaming eyes!

Simultaneously, from every lane and passage in the darkening thicket, came other jackals, singly and in pairs, and even a whole litter together, and filled the space before the temple.

Soon the feast was spread. The high-priest ceased to toll the bell, and, at a shout and a wave of the hand, every jackal trotted, without rivalry, and without snarling or confusion, to what was evidently his accustomed place and feast, seized the cake in his jaws, turned, and disappeared through the thicket.

There was no fondling of the animals, no sign of any worship of them, no ceremonial, nothing but this silent, business-like almonry.

The rite was over, the priestly office performed, and one by one the soldiers went back to camp. In vain did I fee the priests to learn the meaning of this strange bounty. "It had always been so," was the answer – the best argument, the most ample *raison d'être* of anything in the East.

W.S. BURRELL and EDITH E. CUTHELL
Indian Memories (1893)

Something to Think About

Mr A.M. Jacob (more correctly Ali Muhamad Yaaquob), a well-known resident of Simla, was a successful art dealer and jeweller who probably came originally from the Levant. But it was Mr Jacob's reputation for occult powers rather than jewels that interested "Tautriadelta", a magician from Yorkshire, who sought his acquaintance on a visit to the Hills. (c. 1895)

My next reminiscence is an experience at Simla. I had made the acquaintance of many fakirs, and had examined their feats and probed their mysteries; but I heard of one man to whom common report attributed all the powers of Moses – and more. This was a native jeweller and diamond merchant at Simla, a man of immense wealth, highly educated and polished. I determined to go to Simla, in the hills, and interview him.

I knew a man who had been sent up there to recover after an attack of enteric fever, a captain of Bengal Lancers, and I prepared to visit him. In brief I did so, and arrived at the bungalow, jointly occupied by my friend and a Scotch surgeon-major of Ghoorkhas, just before sunset. During the evening, over our cheroots and brandy-pawnee, I asked if they knew Mr. Jacob. "Rather! who didn't, at Simla?"

I expressed my intention of making his acquaintance, but my friend said that he did not think I should manage it in the few days I had at disposal. . . .

The next morning I went to Mr. Jacob's bungalow, higher up, about three-quarters of a mile from where I was staying. His bearer informed me that he was away, and was not expected home for three days, when he had invited three gentlemen to tiffin. I left my card and promised to call again, as I was obliged to leave Simla the day after his expected return; and I left word that I had come hundreds of miles to see him.

To strengthen my chances, I marked in pencil a hieroglyphic on the card . . .

The result exceeded my wildest expectations. Three days after-

Simla, the Bazaar

wards, I returned from an early morning ride to find that Mr. Jacob
had himself called at our bungalow, and left his card for me, with the
hope that I would join his party at tiffin that day. My Scotch friend
looked very glum, and was sure some harm would come of it.

However, at the appointed time, I gaily mounted the captain's tat,
and set forth. When I arrived, the other three guests were there – one
of them, a general officer whose name is a household word in England
and India. I was received with great empressement by Mr. Jacob
(thanks to the hieroglyph), and we proceeded to enjoy the repast.

Afterwards, when the Trickinopolis were lighted and desultory
conversation set in, our host was asked by the General to show us
some, what *he* called "tricks." I could see that Jacob didn't like the
word; but he simply said, "Yes, I will show you a trick." Then he told
a servant to bring in all the sahibs' walking-sticks. Selecting one, a
thick grape-vine stick with a silver band, he said, "Whose is this?" It
was claimed by the General, and a glass bowl of water, similar to
those in which gold-fish are kept, was placed on the table. Mr. Jacob
then simply stood the stick on its knob in the water and held it upright
for a few moments. Then we saw scores of shoots like rootlets issuing
from the knob till they filled the bowl and held the stick upright; Jacob

standing over it muttering all the time. In a few moments more a continuous crackling sound was heard, and shoots, young twigs, began rapidly putting forth from the upper part of the stick. These grew and grew; they became clothed with leaves, and flowered before our eyes. The flowers became changed to small bunches of grapes; and, in ten minutes from the commencement, a fine, healthy standard vine loaded with bunches of ripe black Hamburgs stood before us. A servant carried it round, and we all helped ourselves to the fruit.

It struck me at the time that this might only be some (to me new) form of hypnotic delusion. So, while eating my bunch, I carefully transferred half of it to my pocket, to see if the grapes would be there the next day.

When the tree was replaced on the table Jacob ordered it to be covered with a sheet; and, in a few minutes, there was nothing there but the General's stick, apparently none the worse for its vicissitudes.

I then described the performances of different fakirs whom I had seen, especially the only one which puzzled me – the transfixion of the body with a tulwar. Mr. Jacob smiled and said, "Oh, that's nothing. Stand up." I did so, and he, taking down a superbly mounted and damascened yataghan from Persia, which formed part of a trophy of arms on the wall, drew it from its scabbard and held the point to my breast, saying only "Shall I?" I had absolute confidence in him, so simply said "Certainly." He dropped the point to about two inches below the sternum (breast-bone) and pushed slowly but forcibly. I distinctly felt the passage of the blade, but it was entirely painless, though I experienced a curious icy feeling, as though I had drunk some very cold water. The point came out of my back and penetrated into the wood panelling behind, which, if I remember rightly, was of cedar wood. He left go of the weapon and laughingly remarked that I looked like a butterfly pinned on a cork. Several jokes at my expense were made by the others; and, after a minute or two, he released me. I looked rather ruefully at the slit the broad blade had made in my clothes, but Jacob said, "Never mind them; they'll be all right by-and-bye." He began to show us another wonder, and I forgot all about it. But about an hour afterward there was no trace whatever of any damage to the clothes. . . .

Presently he asked us if we would like to look at his gardens (a most unusual proposition there). We consented out of politeness, and went outside. We found there an artificial lake or large pond, of which we took no particular notice, and lounged about in the shade chatting and smoking. Presently, the officer to whom Jacob was talking at some little distance from the rest, called out: "Mr. Jacob is going to walk on the water." Jacob said "Why not?" and immediately stepped not into but *on* the water, and deliberately walked right across the pond. The water being very translucent, we could see the astonished fish darting away in all directions from under his feet. When he got to the other side he turned round and came back again. As he stepped on the ground I requested to look at his shoes, to see if they were wetted at all. The soles appeared just as if he had walked over a wet pavement, and that was all. He said: "That is nothing; anyone who can float in air" (*Anglice* levitate) "can walk on water; but I will show you something that really requires power."

It was a baking hot day in the hot season, and although considerably cooler up there in the hills than in the plains, it was still as ardent as a hot summer's day in England.

Bringing out the baguette [wand] again, he waved it slowly round his head. Presently the air was full of butterflies. They came by thousands, by millions, till they were as thick in the air as a heavy snowstorm. They settled on everything, on us, on our hats, our shoulders, anywhere, like bees swarming, till we presented a ridiculous spectacle. The scene was so ludicrous that we burst into roars of laughter. This seemed to offend Jacob, who was rather touchy on some points, so he said: "Ah! you laugh; we will have no more of it." The butterflies rose from where they had lit, rapidly went up into the air, higher and higher, till they formed a dark cloud passing the sun, and then drifted off out of sight altogether.

We went into the bungalow again, but there was a decided coolness perceptible in our host's manner, and I, for one, was not sorry to prepare to leave.

Before we broke up, however, Mr. Jacob requested a few words privately with me. I followed him out to the verandah, and we spoke on occult subjects for a few minutes, and then he said to me. "I will give *you* a special experience, which will give you something to think about." Just what I wanted!

He said, "Shut your eyes and imagine that you are in your bedroom in your bungalow." I did so. He said, "Now open your eyes." I opened them to find that I *was* in my bedroom – three-quarters of a mile in two seconds! He said, "Now shut them again, and we will rejoin our friends." But I wouldn't have that at any price; because the idea of hypnotic delusion was still present to my mind; and, if it were so, I wanted to see how he would get over the dilemma.

He did not try to persuade me, but only laughed, saying, "Well! if you will not, then good-bye," and he was gone. I instantly looked at my watch, as I had done in his verandah at the commencement of the experiment, and *two minutes* had barely elapsed.

I walked straight out of my bedroom to the dining-room where both my friends were sitting. They stared and wanted to know "How the deuce I got there?" So I sat down and told them all that occurred. The doctor said, "Let us see the grapes." I felt in my pocket and they were there all right, and passed them to him. He turned them over very suspiciously, smelt of them, and finally tasted one. "They're the real thing, my boy; genuine English black Hamburgs," he said, and proceeded to devour the lot. Then the captain said, "But where's the tat?" I replied that I had forgotten all about it; I supposed that he had better send for it. Calling a servant, he told him to go to the stables and send a syce up to Sahib Jacob's bungalow for the tat. In a few minutes the bearer returned with the syce, who said that the tat was at that moment safe in his own stable. We stared at one another, and then went to see for ourselves. Sure enough he was there.

"TAUTRIADELTA"
Stories from the Life of a Magician
Borderland Vol.III. No. 2. April,1896

Haunted

Was it artistic temperament which made E.M. Merrick more susceptible to . . . what? She was in India for the winter to paint portraits, having decided that there must be scope for a lady artist to paint wives in purdah. At Bhaunagar – where she hoped to paint "the Maharajah's favourite wife" – she was staying at the house of the chief engineer when she had "experiences" (c. 1899)

I had a curious experience at Bhownugger, which I must relate, although I do not in the least believe in the supernatural. The house where I was staying, which was of two storeys, was built round a Hindoo temple, and the rooms had formerly been occupied by priests. The servants objected to sleep in any of the passages, as is usual for Indian servants, because they said they were haunted by an old woman, who sat on their chests. My room, which was at the end of a long passage, was occupied before my arrival by my host's son, who then used a tent in the garden. I continually heard curious noises, but persuaded myself they were caused by wild cats and squirrels on the roof. A slow and measured tread up and down the courtyard, in the dead of night, I made myself believe was a stray cow. But I did not mention any of these noises, until one night, about half-past three, I was suddenly startled out of my sleep by my bedroom door being violently shaken; at first I thought by a tremendous gust of wind, but all again was silent, except the measured footstep up and down the courtyard. The following night this happened again, and as I could not see anyone in the courtyard, or in any way account for the noise, I asked the former occupier of my room if he had had a similar experience, and he acknowledged that he had, it generally occurring about half-past three, and he could not understand it. The next night I had my heaviest trunk leant against the door, a *chick* or curtain made of fibre hung on the outside, and asked if a native servant might sleep on the mat. My ayah was sleeping on the floor at the foot of my bed, and at half-past three we were both suddenly awakened, not by the

135

shaking of the door this time, but as if hands were pattering hard upon it; the native sleeping outside said he heard nothing at all. I began to dislike these experiences, especially as, in the morning, the lady housekeeper entered my room, with a very white face, to tell me that she had had a wretched night. She slept upstairs, and between three and four o'clock she heard something, apparently very heavy, being dragged along the verandah outside her room, and then round and round her bed, the furniture being knocked as it passed. She hurriedly lit her candle, but could see nothing, and as soon as it was put out the noise commenced again. I related what had occurred in my room; and to our astonishment, when we sat down to breakfast, a very stolid old gentleman, who was only up from Bombay for a few days, announced that he had had what he called a ghost in his bathroom, and that it was the cleanest ghost he had ever heard of, as it had had a bath between three and four in the morning. Bath-rooms are attached to every bedroom in India, and he said he heard some one splashing and making such a noise in his that he lit his candle and took in his dog, who was all excitement, to see who it was, and to his surprise found the room empty, and not a spot of water disturbed; there was nowhere for anyone to make their escape, except a small window near the ceiling with iron bars across. After returning to bed he heard a second bath being taken, but did not trouble to get up again. A few days after I left, so did not hear if the mystery was solved.

E.M. MERRICK
With a Palette in Eastern Palaces (1899)

AFFAIRS OF STATE

. . . IT IS a fact, and not one to regret in the least, that both tradition and personal experience make an Englishman a born chief among Asiatics, and any disregard of the colour of his skin is high treason.

And, reader, never forget this if you find yourself among dark-skinned races, that *dominion is your birthright*. Let trouble overtake you, one Englishman with a thousand Orientals, and they will all turn to you for protection as certainly as flowers turn to the sunlight. (1879)

PHIL ROBINSON
Chasing a Fortune (1884)

Private Revenge

The Andaman islands in the Bay of Bengal had been used as a penal settlement for almost fifteen years, and Lord Mayo – the Viceroy – now had plans to establish on Mount Harriet a sanatorium for Bengal. After a visit of inspection with Major Burne, his secretary, and General Stewart, the Superintendent of the Settlement, the Viceroy lingered on admiring the view. Major Burne tells what happened next. (1872)

We were all, indeed, in good spirits, and almost off our guard, seeing that we had spent the day in various parts of the Settlement without mishap; and we started off on our return journey as soon as we could, although Lord Mayo was unwilling to leave the spot. Nothing unusual occurred on our return to the pier until we arrived within a few yards of our naval escort and steam launch. It had, however, become suddenly dark (there being no twilight in the Andamans), when Stewart, addressing the Viceroy, asked to go back for a few moments to speak to an overseer as to the arrangements for the next day. In doing this he had to pass through the guard in rear of us, when in a moment a tall, muscular Afridee rushed through the opening, and, fastening on Lord Mayo's back, stabbed him twice between the shoulders before any of us could get hold of him or prevent the occurrence. It was, alas! all over; for the stabs proved fatal, and, while myself and others of our party got hold of the assassin with difficulty, Lord Mayo, half stunned, fell over the pier (where the water was fortunately shallow), exclaiming to me, as I quickly jumped down to his help, "Burne, they have done it."

We did our best to raise him and place him in the boat, and, after binding up his wounds, rowed off to the *Glasgow*, which was anchored about half a mile away. It was a dreadful half-hour, during which our dear Chief almost imperceptibly breathed his last, and our party of joy was turned into a band of mourning! With unspeakable grief I had to break the awful news to poor Lady Mayo, while the sailors carried the body to the quarter-deck, where they soon erected a partition of flags,

139

and constructed a rough coffin, over which we breathed a prayer of farewell for one of the most lovable of men and best of Viceroys. . . .

It was only on the following day that some light seemed to be thrown upon the event by the court of inquiry then convened. It appeared, in fact, that this man, Shere Ali, who was about twenty-five years of age, was a Pathan whose home was near the Khyber Pass, that he had been in the police, and was found guilty in 1867 of a blood-feud murder in the streets of Peshawar, a crime which he himself denied, but for which he was sentenced to transportation for life to the Andamans. He was by repute a well-conducted man, and behaved so quietly in the Settlement that he had been allowed to act as barber, and in this capacity had for years past had a free run of the Hopetown ground . . .

The conclusion arrived at by the Government was that the deed was one of private revenge for what the man considered to be unmerited transportation . . .

Shere Ali was eventually hanged for the crime without making any confession of his reason and objects, for he was a proud obstinate Pathan. Shortly after the crime, Lady Mayo's children telegraphed from England a message to the murderer of their father, "May God forgive you." In a letter from General Stewart (10th March, 1872) he said: "I gave the message from Lady Mayo's children last night to Shere Ali. It was not easy to make him comprehend the meaning of it, but when he did grasp it he insolently told me to go away, as he was very angry. He said if they had sent a message ordering him to be cut into pieces he would have been glad, but a prayer for God's forgiveness he could not take from them."

MAJOR-GENERAL SIR OWEN TUDOR BURNE
Memories (1907)

Our Portuguese Hosts

*Lady Curzon, the daughter of a Chicago millionaire, was the
only American-born woman to become Vicereine of India.
Here, in a letter to her family, she re-lives an official visit with
the Viceroy to the Portuguese territory of Goa, south of
Bombay.*

14 November 1900

. . . After lunch I went on board the Portuguese gunboat and met
George, and we sailed across the harbour to Panjim, which is only five
miles away, but we were 3 hours getting there in the gunboat, which is
a silly old tub which can't start under forty minutes and only goes 2
knots an hour. The bulwarks were 7 feet high and we could see
nothing, and we sat in a crowd of Portuguese who smoked vile cigars
and drank vermouth, and could speak no language we could
understand. We were at our last gasp when we reached Panjim, where
we drove round and round a small public square in a carriage, while
the crowd threw fire crackers and squibs under our horses' feet,
howling "Viva". It was diabolical. The palace was only twenty yards
away, but we kept driving past in order to make the drive seem long!
In the palace, which consisted of acres of barnlike emptiness, the
Portuguese ladies met us. They were vast and brown, and I never
made out who any of them were, as the introductions were in
Portuguese: but a kind official pointed at first to one lady and then the
other and said "Dat's de oldest" – "Dat's de youngest" – and these
thus designated were the Governor's daughters I believe. After a sort
of levee and George meeting all the officials in the Throne Room
while I sat in a row with the ladies, we drove to our residence, which
was five miles away. It was *pitch* dark, and there was no escort – only
two wild creatures acting as outriders, who yelled and whooped and
ran down every carriage we met. The Natives there lighted fireworks,
which exploded like bombs under our carriage, and when I remons-

trated with the Portuguese who was with us he only said "Dey mean it for ze best." The horses were too miserable to run away, so we drove over bursting squibs and bombs and resigned ourselves to the inevitable. The house we are to stay in is called Cabo, and used to be a nunnery when Goa was a flourishing place in the sixteenth century. The comforts have remained mediaeval, and the night and day we spent in inside rooms swarming with red ants, and no sanitary arrangements of any sort, made the most ghastly experience we have had in India. We stayed in this place until Tuesday afternoon, and as my bedroom was over the poultry yard I got no sleep. George said most of the party started for old Goa at 2, but as they went by the awful gunboat I elected to go by road instead, and Major Baring went with me, and we drove 11 miles and got to old Goa just as the gunboat did, although we left two hours after it! . . .

After seeing the churches we drove back to Panjim and again ran the gauntlet of fireworks hurled under the carriage. Our clothes had been brought to the Governor's house, Panjim, and here we dressed for the State banquet. No bath of course, and no blinds to the windows and thousands looking in, so Garland pursued me round the room with a bath towel, which she held in front of me. Nine of the Staff dressed in one small hole with one wash basin, and their clothes laid out on the floor, and an enthusiastic audience gazing in upon nine furious Englishmen trying to dress for a State banquet in this black hole! About 9, after waiting and nearly fainting for an hour of intolerable heat and delay, we sat down at the banquet of 65. We were all placed according to precedence strictly, and as no one spoke any language his neighbour could understand the dinner passed off in silence, save for two bands, one in the next room and one outside in the street, which played different tunes simultaneously! The Governor made us a speech in Portuguese and George replied in English, and at 11, dead with fatigue, we said Goodbye to our Portuguese hosts and walked to the gunboat through a disorderly crowd. The local police were drunk and one charged the Governor, on whose arm I was hanging (as he insisted on arming me everywhere) and nearly knocked him over. We boarded the gunboat, and no sooner did we start than we ran aground and were stuck for an hour and in absolute despair of ever getting out to the *Clive*, which was lying two miles out to sea. After frantic efforts we got off, and only got to the *Clive*, to which we were rowed in a small boat as the gunboat could not get alongside, at 1.45 a.m.

The whole Goanese visit was too much for me, and I was ill all night, and next day George – who is dead beat too – went to Gersoppa Falls without me . . .

LADY CURZON
Lady Curzon's India
Letters of a Vicereine (1985)
ed. John Bradley

Anti-British Feeling

Security arrangements for the Prince and Princess of Wales were, of course, planned very carefully during their tour of India. Sir Walter Lawrence, a friend of Lord Curzon, the Viceroy, was appointed to accompany their Royal Highnesses, and here he reveals the lengths to which the secret service had gone to protect the future King George V. (1905/1906)

Among other places visited by the Prince and Princess was Peshawar and the Khyber Pass and well-meaning persons both in England and in India sent me messages of warning and protest, urging that it was wicked to risk these precious lives. There was a risk all through the Tour, and no one knew this more clearly than the Royal visitors. But they trusted the people, and the people responded. They were safe in that dare-devil city of Peshawar, and safe among the Afridis of the Pass. But when we returned to Peshawar after the visit to the Afghan end of the Pass, I received a budget of letters from Calcutta urging that Calcutta should be omitted from the Tour, as the anti-British feeling ran high and there might be trouble. Always contrasts, always the paradox in India! It was safe to pass through the wild and undisciplined country of the Pathán̄s: it was dangerous to visit the Capital of India, the second largest city in the Empire. The visit to Calcutta was, of course, made, and not a single item of the programme was altered, though to the last moment there were anxious suggestions that certain functions should be omitted. . . .

After some months of travel, the Prince and Princess were staying at the Nadesri House at Benares, a bungalow belonging to the Maharája of Benares. On one side of the bungalow was an old-fashioned Indian rose garden; on the other side, by the front door, was the shrine of the goddess Nadesri, and a park in which were the tents of the Prince's suite. The Prince and Princess had gone out early to give rewards to some Gurkha soldiers who had done good service in saving life in a recent earthquake. I stayed at home to finish some work. As I was waiting for their return I walked up and down the long

144

Hindu Beggar.

Fakir ("Hindu beggar")

rose garden, and suddenly noticed a naked faqir hidden in the rose bushes. I beckoned to him to come out of the bushes, but he shook his head. I saw the British sentry pacing up and down the veranda of the Nadesri house, and said to the faqir: "If you don't come out I shall call the sentry, and there may be trouble!" On which the faqir took out from his beggar's bowl his card and photograph of identification. He was one of the Mahrattas, whom I knew well, but smeared over with ashes, with his long matted locks, I did not recognise him. I had always been warned to look out for the faqirs and their begging bowls, for the bowl often held a murderous knife. "You can see everything from this garden?" "Yes," he said. "No one can enter the bungalow from this side without my knowing."

At breakfast the Prince asked me the proper name of the house. I said it was Nadesri. "Well," he said, "I met a Sanskrit scholar this morning, and he told me that the proper name was Nandesri." Some years before this, when Lord Curzon was about to visit Benares, I had ascertained from the Maharája of Benares that the shrine after which the house was named was sacred to a local goddess, Nadesri, so I urged her claims against those of the perhaps better known Nandesri. But after breakfast, to make sure, I went to the shrine, and found there, at his devotions, a venerable Hindu dressed in a spotless white tunic. I said: "Rám, Rám," and he, looking beyond me with viewless eyes, replied: "Rám, Rám." "What is the correct name of this shrine?" He answered, to my satisfaction: "Nadesri." "Good," I said; "and how many years have you been guardian of this shrine?" "I came yesterday," he replied. "Then what can you know about the correct name of the shrine?" I asked. On this, without a smile or change of devout countenance, he drew from his tunic his pass and photograph. "Where is the real guardian of the shrine?" I asked. "We have sent him away on holiday," was the reply.

SIR WALTER ROPER LAWRENCE, BART.
The India We Served (1928)

The Amir

William Montagu, 9th Duke of Manchester, was travelling with the Duchess in a round-the-world yacht party at the invitation of an American millionaire. The chief event of the winter season, when they called at Calcutta, was the State Visit paid to the Viceroy by the Amir of Afghanistan. Amir Habibullah Khan was pro-British, cosmopolitan, and something of a card. (1907)

. . . The day after our arrival Lady Minto's bazaar and fête opened. I forget what charity it was in aid of, but it certainly was a wonderful *tamasha*, with all the doubtful joys of a bazaar and a full-blown Coney Island attachment, the whole affair culminating in a military display in the evening and a sham fight about midnight. Here we again met the Amir of Afghanistan. He appeared delighted to see us, and on leaving the bazaar insisted on walking hand in hand with my wife and me. Just inside the entrance the Viceroy's car and that of the Amir were drawn up: amid general bowings and "Good nights" the Viceregal car drove off, and the Amir then asked me where our conveyance was. We confessed that we were about to take a hack, whereupon he insisted on driving us home in his own car.

Arrived at our hotel, we thanked him profusely and bade him good night, but he looked at us in blank amazement.

"What," he said, "you not give me supper?"

I replied: "Of course, Sir, if we can get any." And not without considerable misgivings we took the Amir upstairs to our rooms. It was by this time not far short of one o'clock, and the whole hotel staff was asleep, but after arousing our native servants we managed to dig out a quantity of stodgy cake, a half-empty tin of Huntley and Palmer's biscuits, and two dozen bottles of stone ginger-beer. Then began what threatened to be an all-night orgy. There was a piano in the sitting-room, and when thoroughly primed with stone ginger the Amir decided to sing Persian songs, accompanying himself on the piano with wholly irrelevant notes thumped out with the forefinger of

147

his right hand. He ran lightly through the whole of the poems of Hafiz, and then, in order to prove that Hafiz was superior to Omar Khayyam, he also recited the complete works of Omar Khayyam, just for comparison – at least that was what I gathered from the length of the performance, although, my Persian not carrying me to the extent of understanding every word he spoke, I could not check it all. . . . In the full tide of his enthusiasm the Amir would probably have introduced us also to all the Persian minor poets, but at a quarter to five in the morning we managed by broad hints to convey to him that it was time to go.

It seemed that we had scarcely crept between the sheets when I was aroused – at eight-thirty – by a loud and insistent knocking on the door of my bedroom; going on to the verandah, I found it crowded with a mob of bowing Afghans. There were twenty-five or thirty of them: first and foremost, three very important-looking gentlemen whom I had frequently seen in the Amir's suite; then six men carrying three huge parcels covered with *kingkhab* (gold brocade); two or three interpreters; and, finally, a crowd of miscellaneous camp-followers. The interpreters took a deep breath apiece, and proceeded to explain to me simultaneously and antiphonally that these were presents from the Amir – that, at least, was as much of the trio's florid address as I could gather. Then the gold brocade was unwrapped and the gifts were disclosed. The centre parcel contained a clothes-basket full of the most delicious fruits just arrived from Kabul; this basket was flanked on each side by scarcely smaller packs, one consisting of rolls of beautiful camel's hair cloth, and the other of a pile of Persian lambskins, topped off with two wonderful skins of golden lamb; the Amir subsequently told me that they exported two hundred thousand skins a year from Afghanistan and scarcely ever were there more than two of the golden lamb. My anger at being awakened after so little sleep speedily subsided, and I accepted the gifts in a speech so flowery that I am glad to think that it was wholly unintelligible even to the interpreters, apart from the remainder of the crowd.

This early-morning offering was the cause of a great deal of subsequent trouble. My wife, when she finally woke up, had only just time to get dressed for luncheon, and in the rush of the afternoon's amusement completely forgot to write a note, as she had intended, to thank the Amir. That night we dined together, and I noticed that all through the dinner the Amir's countenance seemed overcast; at last he broke his brooding silence:

"Did you get the offering I sent you?" he enquired.

My wife hastened to assure him that she had, and, according to the usages of society, carried the war into the enemy's camp by asking: "Did Your Majesty get my letter thanking you?"

The Amir's face immediately brightened, as he replied, "No; I thought you had not answered." And we all quickly chipped in, praising the wonderful gifts.

When the sham fight at that evening's military display was over we retired to bed at once, trying to make up for our loss of sleep the night before. But about two in the morning I was roused to receive a note from the English official in charge of the Amir, imploring me to write and say that there was a mistake about the letter from the Duchess having been delivered, as the Amir was beating all his servants in turn to find out who had failed to hand it to him. So I sat down and wrote a hurried note, saying that the whole affair was the fault of the Duchess's *kitmutgar*, who had said that he had delivered the note but had not done so. This necessitated immediately paying off the man and telling him to make tracks for Poona, his native city, in order to escape the wrath of the Afghan monarch.

THE DUKE OF MANCHESTER
My Candid Recollections (1932)

Their Majesties

Some six months after his coronation in London, George V visited India – the first British Emperor ever to do so. Major-General Nigel Woodyatt found himself responsible for many of the arrangements in connection with the Coronation Durbar and other ceremonies. (1911)

One incident in the Durbar proves how short a step it is from the sublime to the ridiculous. In India there is a saying that it is impossible to eliminate the sweeper and his broom from any function or gathering. Still, one would think it impossible for him to figure in a royal durbar. Nevertheless, he did in 1911, and photos snapped of the amphitheatre when all had taken their seats, and we were awaiting the arrival of Their Majesties, depict this menial with his attendant broom emerging round a corner of the dais! He was soon hunted off by a terribly shocked political.

Two other never-to-be-forgotten functions are stamped on my brain, the homage ceremony at a bastion of the Delhi Fort, and the fire at the Investiture.

As regards the homage ceremony it must be stated that over a million inhabitants of the surrounding district had been collected and assembled by the civil authorities in the *bela* of the River Jumna, close under the walls of the fort. This multitude was to march by and do homage to the King and Queen seated, fully robed, in a bastion jutting out from the fort wall.

My wife and I had got seats in an enclosure a few feet to the right of Their Majesties. In common with the majority, we had looked upon this particular performance as a vast piece of humbug – a sort of "by order" function got up to please the King and Queen. But Lord Hardinge and Sir John Hewett had known better, and this we realised when we saw this huge mass of people of all ages surging forward in excited batches, through the well-arranged barriers, to do homage to their King-Emperor.

It amazed us to behold with our astonished eyes the spontaneous,

150

genuine and impulsive feelings by which they were undoubtedly actuated. To hear their cheers, shouts and excited cries of "Badshah! Badshah!" (Emperor! Emperor!) as they passed the Presence. Finally to note, with big lumps in our own throats, that below the eyes which blazed with so much enthusiasm, tears were running down the cheeks. . . .

The fire at the Investiture was a very near thing. The function was held in a huge canvas hall draped in light blue muslin, the colour of the "Star of India" order. This was festooned in wave after wave along the ceiling, and right down to the floor all round. It can easily be imagined how this would have blazed to nothingness in a few seconds had flames once touched it.

What happened was, a telegraph messenger, bringing a wire to the tent next but one to this hall, and windward of it, leant his bicycle with its lighted lamp against the ropes of the tent while he tried to find someone to whom to deliver his message. The breeze blowing over the bicycle, the lamp set fire to the tent, and in less than two minutes there was nothing left but charred canvas and bits of burnt furniture. Fortunately the tent in between, belonging to Lord Crewe, was cut down immediately, and that really saved the situation.

Inside the hall we could plainly hear the roar of the flames, which sounded only a few feet away, and every second we expected to see them. There was a sudden movement amongst the large audience of ladies, British officials, non-officials, Indian nobles and native gentlemen. Many rose up, turning towards the one entrance, but all with their eyes on the royal dais.

Seated in the third row and actuated by a sudden impulse, I remember standing on my chair, and shouting in a loud voice, which sounded quite strange to me: "Sit down, oh! *do* sit down."

Near by this had a good effect, but it appeared to me that the spectacle of the King calmly persevering with the investments, as if nothing had happened, did more than anything else to stay the excitement.

It was not as if he did not know. For one thing, he could not fail to hear the roar of the flames, and besides this the Duke of Teck had slipped out at the back at once, and returning had whispered the news to His Majesty. Adding, I fancy, that Crewe's tent had been cut down, because King George appeared much amused.

Early in the evening an entertaining thing happened. The heralds having proclaimed by fanfare the arrival of the King and Queen, and Their Majesties, after the processional entry, having taken their seats on the dais, the Queen suddenly got up and, with a small escort, walked out again.

An excited Rajah, exactly in front, turned round to me to say she must be ill. Shaking my head, he insisted on repeating his remark, enquiring what else could it be? Not satisfied with my further negative motion, he jumped about on his seat, and informed his right- and left-hand neighbours that the Queen must be sick, very sick. Being just as ignorant as he was of the cause, we felt puzzled, but it seemed extremely unlikely to be sickness with a private way out behind the dais, if required. When just about to ask the Rajah if he was *obliged* to be so fidgety, a flourish of trumpets was again heard, and in marched the Queen, through the audience, in the sky-blue robes of the Star of India. Making an obeisance to the King, she was invested with the order of Grand Commander, after which His Majesty, assisting her to rise, kissed her full on the lips in front of us all. I very nearly cheered!

MAJOR-GENERAL NIGEL WOODYATT
Under Ten Viceroys (1922)

Memorable March

While stationed at Bangalore, Frank Johnson realised that only some seventy or eighty miles down the road was the scene of a famous British victory – the Fort at Seringapatam, where in 1799 Tipu Sultan was killed and his army defeated.

Thinking that a visit to this historic spot would improve the morale of his troops, Johnson managed to obtain official permission even though the Fort was in an independent native state ruled by the Maharajah of Mysore. It was just possible that the present day ruler would also remember the events of 1799. (1916)

My Brigade handed me written orders to proceed to Seringpatam at the rate of fifteen miles per day and without fail to return to Bangalore by a certain date. On the other hand, my friend, the Resident, was obviously a little worried when he knew that I had been living among South African natives for years.

"Now, for Heaven's sake, Johnson," he begged, "forget you have ever been in South Africa. Remember that these are not your naked savages, but an educated, sensitive people who would resent the least slight or disregard of their customs. I look forward to your visit doing much good, but on no account let any regrettable incident take place, and, whatever you do, avoid hurting their feelings."

With these instructions ringing in my ears, we approached Seringpatam, having been given a sort of official reception, with garlands, at Closepet and other towns *en route*. Nearing Seringpatam I was met by a charming Indian A.D.C. on the staff of the Maharajah, who had come in a Rolls Royce car, bearing a letter from His Highness in which he expressed his pleasure at hearing that British troops were in his State, and inviting the Battalion to visit his capital city of Mysore as his guests.

I was in a fix. How, on the one hand, was I to carry out definite military orders and yet, on the other hand risk hurting Indian feelings in defiance of the civil authority? Risking the result, I decided to accept gratefully the Maharajah's invitation. So, after a day and night at the Fortress, we covered the sixteen miles to Mysore in a day. The City was *en fête* and the streets lined with flags and decorations. The old Government House had been turned into an Officers' Mess and elaborate *shamianahs* (marquees) were pitched for the men on either side of the drive. It was a truly lavish reception that will remain engraved in the minds of the men of the 2/6th the Royal Sussex as long as they live, for it was their first experience of truly oriental luxury.

His Highness inspected the Battalion, the first British troops seen in Mysore since the Duke of Wellington's days. Incidentally the Regimental Band had a hectic time practising and mastering the Mysore national anthem, with which the Maharajah was greeted on parade.

For two days elephants and camels – riding and draught – were placed at the disposal of the men. Masses of fruit, vegetables, etc., were issued regardless of "rations" and, had I not intervened, His Highness was about to supply each man with a bottle of whisky *a day*, such was his exaggeration both of the calls of hospitality and the British soldier's capacity!

Our programme was to end by the Battalion forming into mass in the square facing the palace after dark. Then, at a given signal, thousands of electric lights were to be switched on to illuminate the splendid Palace. We arrived and formed up in mass according to plan, the lights came on, and I then saw that one side of the square was occupied by the Mysore Lancers (dismounted) with an unarmed infantry battalion on the other side of the square, facing them. Then, to my intense surprise, out came a majordomo bearing a message from His Highness that he wished *all* the British soldiers to see over his Palace, but that they would, of course, enter unarmed, leaving his Lancers to take charge of their rifles! Here was a nice dilemma. In a flash I remembered that the commencement of the Mutiny, nearly seventy years previously, had its genesis in the seizure of arms whilst the British battalions were attending Church Parade unarmed. Every instinct, therefore, within me rose against this idea of surrendering our arms in the dark, but again the words of the Resident came ringing in my ears: "For goodness sake, don't hurt their feelings." What was I to do? It was, indeed, a hard case to solve. But, a minute later, the Battalion had been called to attention and had piled their arms in front of each platoon. The Mysore Lancers then posted sentries and the Battalion marched off in half-sections into and through the magnificent principal rooms of the Palace.

At last it was over, our arms recovered, official and other farewells said, the Mysore followed by the British National Anthem played, and then, after hearty cheers for the Maharajah and Mysore, the Battalion swung from the Palace to the tune of "Sussex by the Sea." It was then I noticed that we were being surrounded by the native infantry battalion, armed only with lighted torches, this being in accordance with an old Mysorean custom which considered that guests were supposed to have been so well "done" that an escort on the homeward journey was essential! These torch-bearers accompanied us well beyond the city boundaries. Thus ended the memorable march to Mysore City, considered by the civil authorities to be such a political success that my disregard of the official time-table was overlooked by my military superiors.

LIEUT.-COLONEL FRANK JOHNSON
Great Days (1940)

DANGERS AND DISASTERS

AND THEN there was the other interesting experience! The three of us were sitting with several friends at a bachelors' tea-party on the roof of the highest house in Calcutta one Saturday afternoon when we had the biggest fright of our lives . . .

The sponge cake was just being passed round for the second time when someone said, "Hallo!" For an instant we looked at one another, and began to feel pale. It seemed as if the house was suffering from a bad attack of delirium tremens or St. Vitus' dance, or both. It was in a violent tremble. . . .

"Stand not upon the order of your going, but go at once," was the command, and helter-skelter, with affrighted haste, the walls cracking as we fled, and lumps of plaster hitting us to spur us on, we jumped and tumbled down those four flights of stairs and made a dash from the door just as the front of the adjoining building fell in with a fearful crash.

Horses were scampering away, crowds of people were rushing out upon the Meidan, women were fainting, the earth was heaving in waves, there was the roar of riven walls, and it was tolerably clear that the last trump was about to be sounded. . . . In truth, had the earthquake of June 12th, 1897, continued one minute longer, the whole of Calcutta would have been ruins.

JOHN FOSTER FRASER
Round the World on a Wheel (1899)

Famine Camp

Over five million people died between 1876 and 1878 when famine spread across the southern parts of the sub-continent – just at the time Queen Victoria assumed the title Empress of India.
Valentine Prinsep was commissioned to paint the "Delhi Durbar" celebrations as a present from the Government of India to their new Empress. After the Durbar, Prinsep spent a full year travelling in India and observed contrasting scenes to those of Imperial splendour. (1877)

At Bangalore I renewed my inquiries about the famine.

"Was it bad?"

"Bad? This was one of the worst places! – the dead bodies used to lie all about the cantonment. I have seen as many as thirty collected in one night out of holes and corners by the road, into which the poor creatures had crawled to die."

"It is all over now, I suppose?"

"Oh, yes, it's all over now; the crops are splendid."

"I should have liked," said I . . . "to see some famine camp;" and so I was sent to a kitchen. A large quadrangle, surrounded by a high wall, and with one large guarded door, and inside, round the wall, sheds with pens made of bamboo; and down the middle were two rows of sheds, and under the sheds and in the pens, little huddled heaps mostly asleep. "Are these animals or human beings?" I think, and then a thing comes towards me – a skeleton! It is easy to *say* a skeleton, – to realize it with all its ghastliness is impossible. The limbs with no flesh, and the joints with nothing to conceal their articulation, are horrible enough; but far more dreadful the head, – mostly shaved here, – showing not only bone but suture; and, worst, the poor ribs back and front, with the shoulder-blades sticking on as if they had been an afterthought; and the poor stomach, now full, but with skin stretched on so tight that one can fancy one can trace the organs within.

Now, this is not exaggerated in the least. I have described one; they are all the same. Add to this horrible skin diseases that would make even a Scotchman scratch himself; and imagine 490 of these beings in one relief kitchen! yet the famine is over, and many of these are convalescent and making sheds for the rest.

The superintendent, who showed me as much of this misery as I could stand, told me that these were only bad cases – men and women who had wandered from the relief works, from a desire to escape working, and been picked up by the police.

"These," said he, pointing to the pens, "are those brought in last night. We give 'em lots to eat, but, Lord, sir! There's no satisfying 'em. They lie and steal to get more, and that's what makes them ill with fever and dysentery and diarrhoea. They're sure to get it if they eat too much.

"Do many of them die?"

"About ten a night on an average, – sometimes as many as eighteen."

I pointed to one woman with swelled feet, and asked whether that was dropsy. "Yes, sir, that's dropsy. That's what they get last. When they have had that bad, there's no saving them. These are the orphans; they're well looked after," said he, with a smile; and I saw a Sister of Charity wandering about them, who was anxious to save their bodies that she might have a turn at their souls. Then we came to the women. I was much struck by the patient silence of all those I had seen, but the women were not silent. Many of them had petitions to make. One old creature was most clamorous. "She wants to be let out, and prefers begging about in the bazaar to being here," said the superintendent. "It's useless feeding up the old people. Give 'em as much as you like, you cannot fatten them."

"Do parents care much for their children?" I asked.

"Not much, sir. I've known 'em steal their children's food, saying they were certain to die, and the food could do them no possible good. It's astonishing what they'll eat. Now, this little chap," said the superintendent, tapping a little boy on the head, "he'll eat enough for two grown-up men, and it don't seem to do him any good either."

The superintendent is a tall stout Eurasian, who was evidently a credit to his feeding, and the contrast between him and the mite was terrible. The boy was scarcely human, squatting on the ground, and progressing in that squatting position, like a monkey. He crawled thus up to us and laid his upturned palms on the ground, and cried. He was covered with filth, and perfectly naked: a truly horrible spectacle.

"It's no use clothing him; he won't keep on anything. He's mad, sir, and this is not the right place for him."

The poor boy cried on, making creases in his thin face like a hideous caricature.

"Poor boy!" said I.

"We have great trouble with him sometimes. He can be most abusive, I assure you. Would you like to see the infirmary, sir?"

But I had had enough of horrors. Infirmary! were these not infirm enough? So I left, with an impression I shall never forget. The whole thing, hideous as it was, was rendered almost grotesque by the inhuman aspect of these poor creatures. If they had been white, I could not have stood the sight a moment; as it was, I could hardly realize that I was of the same genus as these ape-like beings. And the famine is over! There were double the number here formerly, and ten times the number in other camps! Only a fourth of the famine-stricken here were men.

My host, a high official, told me that the famine had been coming on for a year, that up to August there had been no showers, and that then the bravest-hearted despaired, for all hope of rain was past. Happily in August it poured hard – a most unusual thing – and the country was saved. I saw the food being given out to these poor people. Their rice and meat to me did not look appetizing, but I was told that it was better than what they usually had. God help them! I wonder how many of them will live? They seemed all treated with kindness, though of course a small amount of discipline has to be exerted. Famine seems to deprive the poor creatures of all sense of respect or decency.

VAL C. PRINSEP
Imperial India (1879)

Indian Life

In the summer heat of the plains the Collector's wife, Mrs Robert King, waits for the monsoon to break and chronicles her day-to-day experiences in Meerut. (1878)

June 26. – We have just had another practical sermon on the words "In the midst of life we are in death." It would be strange if we did not remember them. At the band-stand last night, where every one was assembled, the Riding Master of the Artillery was seized with heat apoplexy. He was taken away by two doctors, and we hear he never spoke again. This afternoon a notice has come round to say his funeral takes place this evening. Riding to the band one night – carried to the cemetery the next. Such is Indian life.

June 28. – Yesterday evening a cloud of locusts suddenly made its appearance, coming from the north, and darkening the air as it came. It is a wonderful sight anywhere, but not nearly as striking on the plains as when seen in the hills, as then you can form a better idea of the vastness of the flight. You see valleys 2,000 feet below you filled with the fluttering wings, you yourself are nearly blinded by the whirling mass of insects round you, and you look up and see mountain-tops 3,000 feet above you encircled by reddish clouds, still of locusts.

Here you lose much of this effect. You can only see that the whole sky above you is darkened by the fluttering host, and that as far as the eye can reach the air is thick with them, looking like snowflakes where the sunlight falls on them, and like dark red spots where they come between the sun and you.

A tremendous hullabaloo was set up by all the people about the place to prevent them from settling here, and where they did alight they were screamed at and stoned till they rose again and fluttered further. They *must* settle somewhere for the night, and woe betide the hapless spot where they alight. They have jaws like horses, and appetites like ogres. We shall, no doubt, trace their course through

162

the newspapers, which never fail to chronicle such "fashionable arrivals."

June 29. – No rain, nor sign of it, but an abominable dust-storm in the evening,which caught us when out driving. We noticed a very lurid ominous light on a heavy bank of clouds, but thought we should have time to get home. Five minutes later we saw the vultures and kites swooping about in great disorder, evidently beating up against a wind that had not yet reached us, and then we knew the storm was on us. In another moment the first gust of cold wind had struck us, and we were in the midst of a dense pall of dust, and darkness so great that we had to pull up and stand still until the worst of the storm was past. The coachman and syces were sorely exercised about their hats, which are much the shape and size of bread-platters, and offer a good surface to the wind. . . .

July 9. – Joy at last! The rains seem really to have set in, and four inches have fallen in the last two days. The frogs are having a perfect jubilee; there are two sets of them apparently, and they sing antiphonal chants all the evening, each set letting the other have its turn in the fairest manner. What they have done with themselves all through the hot weather I do not know, no one sees or hears them, but the moment the rains begin they swarm. The sweeper goes round the house and collects a water-can full of juveniles every evening, and deports them to a distance. Another rain creature that appears with the toad tribe is a lovely red velvet insect about the size of a huge lady-bird. He is exactly like a button of softest crimson velvet. The natives believe he is rained from the sky. . . .

Aug 20. – A most singular phenomenon occurred to-day. Heavy rain had been falling, and a perfect stream was rushing out from our compound by an outlet near the stables. Suddenly a large shoal of little fish was noticed in the shallow water, and the servants turned out with sticks and baskets and killed and caught four pounds' weight of them. The kitmatgár caught one which he declares he *saw* fall from the air, and brought it to Robert, who weighed it and found it to weigh one ounce. Another man says he was standing under a tree when he saw a fish fall from the branches, and tried to catch it, but lost it in the grass. Now, our compound has no water in it, nor any hollow where water can lie, nor is there any inlet for water; the whole compound being enclosed by a bank and low wall, with only the carriage gate at the upper end, and an outlet for flood water at the *lower* end, towards which the fish were being swept by the stream from the garden. Therefore the question arises, Where did these fish come from if not from above? . . . . I merely record the facts, an account of which we have sent to the newspaper. I am by no means prepared to defend the theory of the fish having fallen from the clouds, but at the same time I have no other conceivable theory to suggest. Fish are not likely to have jumped over the wall in any numbers, even if any chance had brought them to the other side of it.

The heat continues frightful. Ten days ago an officer left here invalided for England; sleep was of the utmost importance to him in his weak state, but it appears that the guards all along the line had received orders to wake any passengers who appeared to be asleep, for fear they should in reality be dead or dying from heat apoplexy, so fearfully numerous have the deaths been. So the poor fellow was constantly roused from sleep during the weary journey of three days and three nights to Bombay.

So many people are away at the hills that Meerut seems perfectly deserted. I think there are only nine ladies now here, no garden parties or entertainments, and one expects to see the Mall grass-grown.

The only rendezvous now is on Thursdays, when there are public sports and races, tent-pegging, riding at the ring, and so on. One of the "events" one week was the following:-

"Z O O L O G I C A L S T A K E S

A HANDICAP FOR ALL ANIMALS EXCEPT HORSES, MULES, PONIES,

OR DONKEYS. ANIMALS NOT SUITED FOR RIDING MAY BE

ACCOMPANIED BY THEIR OWNERS ON FOOT."

Among the entries were a bullock, a mongoose, a camel, a partridge, and some deer! The partridge came in first . . . .

MRS. ROBERT MOSS KING
The Diary of a Civilian's Wife in India 1877-1882 (1884)

Wild Endeavour

Politically, Sikhim was a "native state" under British guidance. But, as Major Waddell of the Indian Army Medical Corps found when he took his large party of servants and coolies exploring in the little-known hills north of Darjeeling, Nature was still very largely in command of the country. (1889)

Early in the morning, we descended the gloomy gorge of the roaring river, amid rank decaying vegetation which suggested deadly malaria. As we reached the bridge, our men sent up a loud shout, calling on the malignant water-spirit to let us cross in safety. And, certainly, it looked as if special prayers for our safety were really required, for the bridge, dangerous at all times, was a mere ragged skeleton of itself, and slippery with green slime. . . .

I had already crossed several of these primitive bridges in Sikkim . . . but none were ever so alarmingly rickety-looking as this. On climbing up on to it, it proved on examination to be not only frail but *rotten!* And we now found that the men who had been sent two days before to repair it, had declined the hazardous task and had decamped without touching it. These bridges last only about two seasons, and this one was already several years old and had not been repaired at all. But we must cross this river anyhow, as a night's detention in this gorge meant fever in a fatal form.

I sent one of my Lepchas, who was accustomed to these bridges, to examine it, and he managed to go over it, and returned to say that he thought it was crossable. Sending him across again, I prepared to follow, having first taken off my boots, as the bamboos on which I had to walk were so slippery. But I had not gone many yards ere I found that there was only a single line of bamboos for foothold, and that these single bamboos were neither lashed end to end nor tied to the V-slings, and that many of these V-slings were untied or wanting altogether. I therefore retraced my steps, and sent the Lepcha to tie it up a bit.

I then mounted the bridge again, and I almost shudder, even now, to think of that awful passage. Had I known what was in store for me I should never have attempted it. The instant that you step on to these bridges they recoil from you, and swing and shake in an alarming way, rolling from side to side and pitching with every step you take, like a ship in a storm. . . . So, seizing the two suspension cables, one in either hand, for a railing, you have to work your way across this jerky swinging, shaking, writhing thing. I got along a short way without much difficulty, so long as I could look to see the bamboo rod on which I had to walk, although the open sides heightened the sense of insecurity. But on clearing the bank, the instant you look down to see where to place your feet, the rush of leaping water in the deeply sunk torrent underneath you, gives you the giddy sensation that both you and the bridge are running swiftly upstream. . . . But it was now too late to turn back, as I could not swing round; so, I went forward with long strides . . . At last, after what seemed an age, the other bank was reached and the danger, so far as I personally was concerned, was past. . . .

View from Darjeeling

Glad were we to get away from this fluvial horror, and emerge from the stifling gorge up on to a cool flat, where we encamped . . . And here a refreshing cup of tea and the hot lunch that Achoom had awaiting us made us forget our troubles and fatigues of the day.

Next morning we were off early along the bold and cliffy upper valley of the Teesta . . . But oh, the hateful leeches and the climb.

The damp forest through which we passed swarmed with legions of voracious land-leeches. No thicker than a knitting-needle when they are fasting, they stood alert on every twig of the brushwood that overhung our track, and on every dead leaf on the path. And as we approached they lashed themselves vigorously to and fro, in the wild endeavour to scize hold of us. The instant they touch their victim, they fix themselves firmly and then mount nimbly up by a series of rapid somersaults till they reach a vulnerable point; and then they lose not an instant in commencing their surgical operations. Our poor servants and coolies who walked bare-footed were of course badly bitten. From their ankles and legs little streams of blood trickled all day, and at every few steps they had to stop and pick off these horrid little pests, and it was often difficult to dislodge them. We had dusted our stockings with tobacco-snuff, and had not felt the usual sharp nip; and our legs were well encased in *putties* or thick woollen bandages, which are wound round the leg from the ankle to the knee, over the boots and stockings, and give grateful support to the leg and more freedom to the calf muscles than leggings. We had each picked off thousands of leeches during the day, from outside our boots and *putties*, and were congratulating ourselves on having escaped, but on taking off these articles to cross the small substantial cane-bridge over the Dik-chu river, after having walked about sixteen miles through forest, we found that a large number of leeches had sucked their fill of us. They had insinuated themselves through the eyelets of our boots, and between the folds of our *putties*, and thence through the meshes of our stockings. And, after gorging themselves to repletion with our blood, some had withdrawn themselves and were lying under the *putties*, their thread-like bodies swollen with our blood, to the size of small chestnuts; while others had crept down into our boots, and had there got squashed, bathing our feet in gore; and all this had happened quite unconsciously to us. Washing our wounds only made them bleed the more profusely. B. was less bitten than I was, probably owing to his blood being so saturated with nicotine, as he smokes all day long. . . .

The leeches and the pelting rain, all day long, had so delayed us and disorganized our men, that, although it was now about 3 p.m., we had not yet had breakfast, only the morning tea and toast. We were now ravenous; but there was little chance of our getting anything till we reached the Rajah's residence on the hill, about 3,000 feet above us; for we found that Achoom and the lunch-basket had gone on ahead. So after climbing over some boulders on the river bank to wash again our bleeding leech-bites, we began the steep climb up the short cut to Toomlong.

MAJOR L.A. WADDELL
Among the Himalayas (1899)

The Old Diamond Mines

Mervyn Smith, a mining engineer representing a London syndicate, had come out from Britain to find the mines of Buwapatam. When he arrived in the area, however, the local Chentsu people warned him that the old workings would be too dangerous to visit because of cobras. In fact he found there was more to it than that. (c. 1892)

I told Permal I was determined to go, even if he would not go with me, as I had come to see the old pits, and the old pits I must see. After much cogitation with his fellows he said if *Davaru* (Lord) insisted on going, then he would devise a means to outdo even the *Raj-Nag* (King Cobra). His grandfather had done so years and years ago, when a mad gentleman who broke stones (a geologist!) had visited these parts. Permal promised to come again next day. With this the Chentsus took their departure, and we saw nothing of them till next afternoon, when my servant called out "Sar! Sar! the village-mans bring the cock-coop." On going out to see what was up, I perceived Permal and another Chentsu with two enormous wicker baskets of the kind known throughout South India as cock-baskets or hen-coops. The baskets were a little larger and rather more strongly made than those ordinarily sold for penning fowls. Permal said these baskets were to be put over our heads when we got near the haunts of the king-cobra, and that we should then be perfectly safe. The meshes of the basket, he explained, were too small for the serpent's head to pass through, so that it could not bite us, and when it attacked all we had to do was to squat down with the basket over us (like a candle extinguisher) and fire at the brute through the meshes. I laughed at the idea of being cooped up in a cock-basket; but as there was no other method of inducing the Chentsus to show me the old mines, I agreed to this plan, and arranged to go next morning. Nothing would induce any of my camp-followers to accompany me, cock-coop or no cock-coop.

Starting off early next morning, we had a good ten miles to go before we got to the low hills, some two hundred feet above the broad valley of the Nullamullays, where the old pits were said to be. The jungle was very dense – giant bamboos and large forest trees, with much tall grass and under-growth of thorns. The Chentsus stalked on in front, with the baskets on their heads. As we neared the site of the old pits, I noticed that the large trees had disappeared, but the undergrowth was more dense, showing that at one time this had been a forest clearing. Permal now advanced with great caution, and asked me to put one of the baskets over my head, he and his fellow getting under the other. After some demur I did so, and we had gone less than half-a-mile in this fashion, when suddenly a peculiar whistling noise was heard on our right. The Chentsus immediately squatted down and seized the cord hanging from the centre of the basket, so as to hold it firmly down without exposing the hands. Permal made signs to me to do the same, and said there were two king-cobras about; and that the whistle was that of the female calling to her mate, and that we should be attacked almost immediately. Down we all three squatted therefore, with the baskets over us, and firmly held on to the centre cord, so as to fix them hard on to the ground. We waited perhaps five minutes in this position, but no snakes were visible. I could see the Chentsus gesticulating to one another, but could not make out what it was all about.

It was only now that I began to realise the danger of our position, and the value of the wicker baskets as a protection from a sudden attack of these fearful brutes. The undergrowth was so dense that it was impossible to see more than a yard or two around. It would not, therefore, be difficult for the snakes to attack us unperceived, nor would it be possible to use a gun before they were on us. The Chentsus still continued to gesticulate and point in my direction. Keeping a firm grasp of the rope, I turned round, and, there, above me and within eighteen inches of the top of the basket, I saw the expanded hood and gleaming eyes of the dreaded *Ophiophagus*. How it got there without my knowing it I cannot say, but there it was, looking down at me, and apparently bothered by the novel structure between it and its prey. Immediately I turned the creature set up a hissing that made my blood run cold. It resembled nothing so much as the hissing noise made by steam escaping from an engine. The hood appeared to be fully nine inches wide, and over a foot in length, and the forked tongue, which shot in and out, was quite three inches long. I began to feel quite sick and my eyes to swim, whether through the fascinating power said to be exerted by the eye of the serpent, or from the strong musky odour emitted by the snake at each hiss, or from sheer funk, I cannot say. Why I did not use my gun when I might easily have blown the head off the horrid monster, I do not know. I now saw the utility of the cord hanging from the apex of the basket. As I felt my head spinning, I threw my weight on the cord and kept the basket firmly planted on the ground. It was well I did so, for suddenly I heard a dull thud, and then a succession of blows on the sides of the basket, and saw the great cobra wriggling on the ground endeavouring to extract with its mouth an arrow deeply imbedded in its body about three feet from the head. A second and a third arrow were now planted in its body by the Chentsus, who shot from under their basket, raising it for the purpose. I now felt a violent tug at the top of the coop, and looking up saw a second king-cobra biting the knot of the cord outside the basket, and by which I held it down, and shaking it just as a dog does a rat. The terror of that moment I cannot express. What if it should overturn the basket! The strength of thirteen feet of muscle must be enormous, and if used in the right direction would soon overcome my pull at the cord. What would then happen? Certain death for me I felt sure. Again the whiz of an arrow, and I saw a gaping wound along the neck of the fierce brute as it quitted its hold to look for this new foe. Fixing my knee on the cord, I now placed the muzzle of my gun just through one of the square openings of the baskets, and, aiming at the hood, fired both barrels in rapid succession, and had the satisfaction of seeing the horrid brute fling up the leaves and dust in its death throes. I looked round for the first assailant, and found it lying in the path with several more arrows planted in it, but still biting fiercely at the arrow that had first entered its body. A shot in the head soon settled this brute also.

Permal said we might now leave the shelter of the baskets, as there could be no more full-grown king-cobras in the place. . . .

The snakes were at once skinned by the Chentsus, who used the sharp iron heads of their arrows for this purpose. The poison fangs and glands, the palate, and the gall were carefully preserved by them for medicine. Diluted with gingelly oil, the poison is drunk in small portions, and is said to be a wonderful preservative against snake bites.

I measured the skins when we got home late that evening. The larger one was fourteen feet eight inches, and the other thirteen feet. Leaving the younger of the Chentsus to finish the skinning, I went on with Permal to visit the old diamond mines . . .

Permal led the way to the old pits which were situated on some rising ground a little way to the east. He said there were several hundreds of these pits extending over some miles of ground . . . Selecting one of the largest and best preserved of the pits for examination, the Chentsu's axe quickly cleared away the brushwood. A strong light rope, which I always carried on these expeditions, was fastened to a stump, and I prepared to descend the old mine, but, before doing so, I threw in a wisp of lighted grass to test the condition of the air – a very needful precaution – and to get some idea of the depth I would have to descend. The grass kept alight at the bottom of the pit, showing the air was fit to breathe, and the depth appearing to be not more than thirty feet, I began the descent, first sticking a lighted candle to a piece of damp clay attached – miner fashion – to my cap. On arriving at the bottom, I found myself on the top of a mound of *debris* fallen in from the mouth of the pit. The ground sloped away on all sides, to a very considerable distance, making a very large chamber, the full extent of which I could not see, owing to the darkness, thc glimmering light of my candle not extending very far. After waiting a little time, to accustom my eyes to the darkness, I proceeded to examine the sides, in order to discover the nature of the "working", and whether it was for diamonds . . .

. . . Great Heavens! What was that? A distinct hiss as of a cat, and then in the distance a gigantic cat itself. As I looked it appeared to grow in size . . . I hurried back to the mound in the centre of the shaft, and shouted to Permal to join me and bring my gun with him. . . . There was no mistaking the hiss and growl, which again emanated from a far corner of the mine on our throwing a stone in that direction. Permal at once declared he could smell tiger. He kept sniffing about, and said, "*Ullee, davaru* (tiger, my lord)." . . . Cutting up several candles into pieces, we soon had a brilliant light about us, and this enabled me to see that the underground chamber was very irregular in shape, about thirty feet wide from east to west, and somewhat longer towards the north. It was from the latter direction that the hissing and growling seemed to come, and Permal declared he could see a large tiger crouching down behind a piece of rock in the far corner. But if it was a tiger, why did not it attack us, as it could not be more than twenty paces away from us? I was inclined to believe it was a hyena, and therefore plucked up heart to have a shot at it, as I would not have ventured to attack a tiger at such close quarters, and on foot. Cocking both barrels, I directed Permal to throw stones at the creature to induce it to break cover; but no, the brute would not move, but continued spitting and growling. I was now convinced it was a hyena, and advanced more boldly until I could just see a dark object behind a rock. I could see the gleaming eyes distinctly, so, taking careful aim, I fired, and then retreated hastily to the mound. We waited some time, but could hear no sound, and the smoke made it more difficult to see. We threw several large stones in the direction, but there was no movement. The hissing too had ceased. Re-loading the empty barrel, we again advanced cautiously, and then I made out the body, in the same position apparently. Again aiming carefully, I tried a second shot. There was no missing so large an object within a few paces, so I felt quite sure the creature was hit, but not so sure that it was dead. We retreated once more to the mound, and after some time advanced again to the attack, but not a movement had taken place in the object. Feeling quite sure it was dead, we now got close up and examined it, and found it to be a tiger of the largest size, in a most emaciated condition – nothing but skin and bone. Probably its last effort was to rise on its legs on my first intrusion. It had not strength for any further effort and must have died in a day or two from sheer starvation. The Chentsu surmised that it had fallen into this natural trap while in pursuit of wild pig, and I could well understand the tiger's inability to get out again, as the widening out of the chamber began about fifteen feet above our heads, so that it would require a leap of that height in order to fasten its claws into the narrow neck of the shaft . . .

After the tiger was flayed we tied the skin to the rope. I then made my way up, hand over hand, and the Chentsu followed, and together we drew up the skin. On examination it proved to be in splendid condition, the fur being beautifully soft and long. It measured ten feet one inch from snout to tip of tail, and from ridge of shoulder to fore-claws three feet ten inches; so that it must have stood a greater height than most tigers. Thus, two king-cobras and a large tiger were the spoils of one of the most exciting day's adventures I have ever experienced in all my journeyings in the wild places of India.

A. MERVYN SMITH
Sport and Adventure in the Indian Jungle (1904)

Bullets Everywhere

*Young Winston Churchill, approaching his twenty-third birth-
day, was in India as a Lieutenant in the 4th Hussars. At that
time, however, he found that the only way he could manage to
see some action was to get himself attached as a war
correspondent – for the* Pioneer *newspaper – to the Malakand
Field Force operating against rebel tribes on the North West
Frontier. Here, in the Mahmund Valley, he not only saw action
in a skirmish with tribesmen, but Britain's future war leader
came very close to an early death. (1897)*

At last we reached the few mud houses of the village. Like all the
others, it was deserted. It stood at the head of the spur, and was
linked to the mass of the mountains by a broad neck. I lay down with
an officer and eight Sikhs on the side of the village towards the
mountain, while the remainder of the company rummaged about the
mud houses or sat down and rested behind them. A quarter of an hour
passed and nothing happened. Then the Captain of the company
arrived.

"We are going to withdraw," he said to the Subaltern. "You stay
here and cover our retirement till we take up a fresh position on that
knoll below the village." He added, "The Buffs don't seem to be
coming up, and the Colonel thinks we are rather in the air here."

It struck me this was a sound observation. We waited another ten
minutes. Meanwhile I presumed, for I could not see them, the main
body of the company was retiring from the village towards the lower
knoll. Suddenly the mountain-side sprang to life. Swords flashed from
behind rocks, bright flags waved here and there. A dozen widely-
scattered white smoke-puffs broke from the rugged face in front of us.
Loud explosions resounded close at hand. From high up on the crag,
one thousand, two thousand, three thousand feet above us, white or
blue figures appeared, dropping down the mountain-side from ledge
to ledge like monkeys down the branches of a tall tree. A shrill crying
arose from many points. Yi! Yi! Yi! Bang! Bang! Bang! Bang! The

whole hillside began to be spotted with smoke, and tiny figures descended every moment nearer towards us. Our eight Sikhs opened an independent fire, which soon became more and more rapid. The hostile figures continued to flow down the mountain-side, and scores began to gather in rocks about a hundred yards away from us. The targets were too tempting to be resisted. I borrowed the Martini of the Sikh by whom I lay. He was quite content to hand me cartridges. I began to shoot carefully at the men gathering in the rocks. A lot of bullets whistled about us. But we lay very flat, and no harm was done. This lasted perhaps five minutes in continuous crescendo. We had certainly found the adventure for which we had been looking. Then an English voice close behind. It was the Battalion Adjutant.

"Come on back now. There is no time to lose. We can cover you from the knoll."

The Sikh whose rifle I had borrowed had put eight or ten cartridges on the ground beside me. It was a standing rule to let no ammunition fall into the hands of the tribesmen. The Sikh seemed rather excited, so I handed him the cartridges one after the other to put in his pouch. This was a lucky inspiration. The rest of our party got up and turned to retreat. There was a ragged volley from the rocks; shouts, exclamations, and a scream. I thought for the moment that five or six of our men had lain down again. So they had: two killed and three wounded. One man was shot through the breast and pouring with blood; another lay on his back kicking and twisting. The British officer was spinning round just behind me, his face a mass of blood, his right eye cut out. Yes, it was certainly an adventure.

It is a point of honour on the Indian frontier not to leave wounded men behind. Death by inches and hideous mutilation are the invariable measure meted out to all who fall in battle into the hands of the Pathan tribesmen. Back came the Adjutant, with another British officer of subaltern rank, a Sikh sergeant-major, and two or three soldiers. We all laid hands on the wounded and began to carry and drag them away down the hill. We got through the few houses, ten or twelve men carrying four, and emerged upon a bare strip of ground. Here stood the Captain commanding the company with half-a-dozen men. Beyond and below, one hundred and fifty yards away, was the knoll on which a supporting party should have been posted. No sign of them! Perhaps it was the knoll lower down. We hustled the wounded along, regardless of their protests. We had no rearguard of any kind. All were carrying the wounded. I was therefore sure that worse was close at our heels. We were not half-way across the open space when twenty or thirty furious figures appeared among the houses, firing frantically or waving their swords.

I could only follow by fragments what happened after that. One of the two Sikhs helping to carry my wounded man was shot through the calf. . . . I looked round to my left. The Adjutant had been shot. Four of his soldiers were carrying him. He was a heavy man, and they all clutched at him. Out from the edge of the houses rushed half-a-dozen Pathan swordsmen. The bearers of the poor Adjutant let him fall and fled at their approach. The leading tribesman rushed upon the prostrate figure and slashed it three or four times with his sword. I forgot everything else at this moment except a desire to kill this man. I wore my long cavalry sword well sharpened. After all, I had won the Public Schools fencing medal. I resolved on personal combat *à l'arme blanche*. The savage saw me coming. I was not more than twenty yards away. He picked up a big stone and hurled it at me with his left hand, and then awaited me, brandishing his sword. There were others waiting not far behind him. I changed my mind about the cold steel. I pulled out my revolver, took, as I thought, most careful aim, and fired. No result. I fired again. No result. I fired again. Whether I hit him or not I cannot tell. At any rate he ran back two or three yards and ·plumped down behind a rock. The fusillade was continuous. I looked around. I was all alone with the enemy. Not a friend was to be seen. I ran as fast as I could. There were bullets everywhere. I got to the first knoll. Hurrah, there were the Sikhs holding the lower one! They made vehement gestures, and in a few moments I was among them.

There was still about three-quarters of a mile of the spur to traverse before the plain was reached, and on each side of us other spurs ran downwards. Along these rushed our pursuers, striving to cut us off and firing into both our flanks. I don't know how long we took to get to the bottom. But it was all done quite slowly and steadfastly. We carried two wounded officers and about six wounded Sikhs with us. That took about twenty men. We left one officer and a dozen men dead and wounded to be cut to pieces on the spur.

During this business I armed myself with the Martini and ammunition of a dead man, and fired as carefully as possible thirty or forty shots at tribesmen on the left-hand ridge at distances from eighty to a hundred and twenty yards. The difficulty about these occasions is that one is so out of breath and quivering with exertion, if not with excitement. However, I am sure I never fired without taking aim.

We fetched up at the bottom of the spur little better than a mob, but still with our wounded. There was the company reserve and the Lieutenant-Colonel commanding the battalion and a few orderlies. The wounded were set down, and all the survivors of the whole company were drawn up two deep, shoulder to shoulder, while the tribesmen, who must have now numbered two or three hundred, gathered in a wide and spreading half-moon around our flanks. I saw that the white officers were doing everything in their power to keep the Sikhs in close order. Although this formation presented a tremendous target, anything was better than being scattered. The tribesmen were all bunched together in clumps, and they too seemed frenzied with excitement.

The Colonel said to me, "The Buffs are not more than half a mile away. Go and tell them to hurry or we shall all be wiped out." . . .

But meanwhile the Captain had made his commands heard above the din and confusion. He had forced the company to cease their wild and ragged fusillade. I heard an order: "Volley firing. Ready. Present." Crash! At least a dozen tribesmen fell. Another volley, and they wavered. A third, and they began to withdraw up the hillside. The bugler began to sound the "Charge," Everyone shouted. The crisis was over, and here, Praise be to God, were the leading files of the Buffs.

Then we rejoiced and ate our lunch. But as it turned out, we had a long way to go before night.

THE RT. HON. WINSTON S. CHURCHILL
My Early Life (1930)

An Eater of Men

"Czarist Russia was fading out of the picture on India's Frontier, but the Russian Bear, in a coat of rapidly deepening red, was creeping in."

This was how Patrick Alexander of Political Intelligence summed up the situation shortly after the Russian Revolution. Now the Russian Bear, in the person of agent Gregory Kruylov, was spreading revolutionary propaganda among the wild hill tribes. Disguising himself as a hillman, Alexander set off with two local colleagues on a man-hunt towards the border fort at Landi Kotal. (1920)

. . . early the next morning, riding hired horses, we were in the shadow of the Fort. Dismounting, we strolled past mud-walled houses and fierce-visaged vendors of sherbet and other commodities, into the walled enclosure which housed passing caravans. There I immediately recognised Dawid Shah, a sub-inspector of the D.C.I.'s staff [Director of Criminal Intelligence], and was about to forget my role and speak to him, when I saw two men watching him, and two more, one of whom I thought was Gregory Kruylov, hurrying toward a sweet-meat stall.

Thrilled with excitement, I wandered after them. They were heading for a mud hovel behind the stall, and I looked round for my companions, but they had disappeared. All was well, however, and I chuckled over the fact that a native police officer in ordinary dress was being watched while I went by unnoticed, to capture single-handed the noted agitator. Alas for my dreams! Squatting around me was a group of Turkis arguing loudly with a half-dozen Afridis over the merits of two mares, one black and one grey. Like horse traders anywhere, the Turkis had been indulging heavily in the cup that cheers. One of them looked up as I passed and, seeking an arbitrator, appealed to me. I made the sign of the Prophet and stalked on, but not far, for two of the drunks seized my shirt tail while another said, "By the Beard of the Prophet, tell us, Haji, which is the better horse."

Wali Shah's voice from behind answered, "He has sworn, my

178

Arab horse dealers

brothers, to kill his brother's slayer before allowing words to pass his mouth. Let him go in peace, and I will judge your mares."

The Afridis sat and glowered, honouring my quest, but the Turkis dragged out their goat-skin of kumiss and slapped my shoulders swearing that I and no other should judge their mares. I was willing enough to try the kumiss, which was a new drink for me, but Wali Shah shook his head, so I slapped the grey, indicating that she was my choice. She was the better mare, but it was a wrong play because she belonged to the Turkis, who let off a loud shout, and one, in his glee, threw his arms around my neck with such abandon that we both crashed to the ground. Everyone roared with laughter as I threw him off, except the man, who had been slightly hurt. In a drunken rage, and angered still more by the ridicule of the crowd, he flew at me like a catch-as-catch-can wrestler. Perhaps all would still have been well had I pulled my knife and threatened to slit his throat; but instead I hit him a beautiful uppercut. He was down, but up again in a flash with a knife in his hand. The rest of the crowd had also drawn knives, the Afridis ready to back me, one of themselves, against the foreign Turkis. I hit my man again as he attacked; and Wali Shah yelled something about my being a lion and an eater of men; but someone cried that I was "a dog of a Feringhi." Instantly, as with all mobs, the sympathies of the crowd changed like lightning, and became murderously hostile. I had a revolver strapped under my shirt, but didn't pull it; instead, as an old Mullah struck with a lathi, I snatched the stick from his hands and laid it about like a flail.

For a moment the ugly crowd hesitated, some still shouting that I was one of them and to help me against the Turkis, but again a voice in the rear proclaimed that I was Christian offal. They only required a leader and I felt that my seconds on earth were numbered. It was useless to try and rush through, for the brawl, like a fracas at a county fair, had drawn a hundred people around us; but for a moment their very numbers were to our advantage, for when they did rush they were in each other's way. Moinda Ali saved us. Just as we were about to be cut down, his voice yelled "Ashkar Haiga, Ashkar Haiga!" (Soldiers come! Soldiers come!), and he came charging in, lashing his horse and leading ours. The cursing crowd scattered like chaff, and Wali Shah and I dived for the saddles of the led horses. As it was, someone grasped my baggy trousers and snatched them off, exposing my bare pink buttocks for all to see. For a moment I hung like a sack of flour across the saddle of the kicking, plunging horse; and then, with the crowd roaring its rage, galloped as though pursued by the hounds of hell for the Fort. We made it, with my shirt tail flying behind like a chariot-driver's cloak, one jump ahead of the frustrated mob. A sentry challenged, and as he flung himself out of our way, yelled, "Look aout, maik wy, 'ere come Mister Godiva hisself!"

We did not find Gregory Kruylov; but heard that the tribesmen were so incensed at all Christians that his friends had difficulty in smuggling him away. . . . The D.C.I. was satisfied to have chased him off; and over a dinner in his bungalow, after I had bathed and shaved for the first time in over three weeks, he expressed the opinion that I was better suited to his department, the Criminal Intelligence, than to the Political.

PATRICK ALEXANDER
Born to Trouble (1942)

A City of Death

The Quetta earthquake of 31st May 1935, was one of the most disastrous ever recorded. Gordon Sinclair, a foreign correspondent for the Canadian newspaper the Toronto Star, *was already in India for his paper, so when the quake struck he was quickly at the scene.*

When I got there smell pervaded everything. I wondered if I could possibly stand that appalling odour. No words can describe the smell of decaying human flesh; yet no man who has suffered it can ever obliterate it from his mind. I was soon violently ill and sat in a pot-hole to rest. There was a dead girl in the hole. A man came along and fell into the hole. His eyes were wide and staring; he turned the dead girl over and then came and tried to roll me over too. I guess he thought I was dead. He went along from pit to pit, turning the dead over to see who they were. Soldiers kept shouting at him to stop but he paid no attention. Another man came and sat beside me with two little girls. His arm was broken. He said that when the crash hit he was buried, but close by was an alarm clock which was going. He kept winding and ringing the alarm for an hour, then another hour. It finally attracted a soldier who dug him out, but three of his five children were dead. . . .

I pushed on to the race-track, where survivors were lying in tents. Two men were stolidly playing chess, others nonchalantly smoking long hookah pipes. A well-dressed Indian girl went among the refugees, giving them money. She gave me money, but I gave it back; then she got me a bottle of beer and I took the beer. Beside the club, terribly injured Baluchi women were fighting off male doctors. Even with the last breath of life, these devout followers of Mohammed would not allow a male hand to touch them or even to view their hurts. Some kicked, some pulled the cover over their faces, some screamed in horror if a man came near. . . .

Down by the bazaar, where usually Afghan and Persian caravans came tinkling in with Oriental treasures, everything was quiet and deserted. A dog worried the body of another dog; a vulture was perched on the bloated remains of a man and tugged at his eyeballs. The man held a goatskin bag of money in his hand; no one touched the money. In a corner a woman and three babies lay dead beside a camel. The camel's legs were broken but it still lived and kept grunting terribly. I told a soldier about the camel but he did not shoot it. . . .

Farther along, a woman was humming a lullaby to a baby. I felt sorry for her, because I thought the baby was dead. It was a funny colour, like the colour of an elephant. She saw what I felt and shrieked in English that the baby was not dead; then she undid her shirt and put the baby to her breast to nurse. It was dead, all right, and she knew it.

Pinned to a notice board near the hospital were thousands of telegrams asking about people. They fluttered like dry leaves in the desert wind. Nobody claimed the telegrams because the people they were for were all dead. I passed on toward the hospital.

If ever a man feels like moralizing on the blast that wiped Baluchistan's capital off the map of middle Asia, he has a natural springboard to start from in that hospital and its female patients. . . .

. . . there were 49 mothers, an all-time high, with new and roly-poly babies in Lady Dufferin Hospital at Quetta when the town turned a somersault. Every last one of these was saved. Not a mother and not a baby perished.

Down the road were the prostitutes of "Chip Street." (A chip is a rupee, or forty cents, the usual charge for such a woman.) . . . They were mostly young but well-upholstered tribal harlots from Kashmir or the Baluchi backlands. Of the 600, so far as had been learned, not one solitary woman escaped. All were buried alive in their houses of easy virtue. . . .

Then there were the zenana women. In India they hate to call a place where a rich man keeps his assorted wives, a harem. That's Turkish . . .

Well anyhow, harem or zenana, with or without eunuchs, a startling proportion of Quetta's zenana women went stark mad in the earthquake. I saw a few of them shrieking and screaming about what had once been streets. The only way doctors could calm them was to give them a hypo shot in the arm big enough to quiet a mule; and even then they twitched like a bass on a hook.

Never having made a decision or faced a problem of their own in all their lives, these irresolute wives were now thrown into a city of death entirely on their own puny resources; and they found themselves unable to meet conditions. They developed neurasthenic jitters while their more stolid peasant sisters from the bazaar jogged about the business of saving themselves and their children with the bovine acceptance of these things generally shown by a harnessed bullock.

Finally, there were the white women; and they were magnificent. I've often said or written and oftener felt that the white woman in India, particularly in a big military station like Quetta, was a pampered and spoiled nitwit. Not only was she physically incapable of the most elementary usefulness, but her conversation lacked intelligence, let alone brilliance. What on earth they did with their time all day, I often wondered.

But here they stood. These very spoiled la-de-da-loungers. Having lost homes and husbands, clothes and careers, friends and loved ones, they had also lost that lazy affectation. They were working – bandaging the wounded, soothing the dying, giving food here, a dose of anti-lockjaw toxin there. They were fighting the insane and the terrified. There were no hysterics, and no threats of nervous breakdowns among the white girls; yet they suffered and lost in equal proportion with the rest. . . .

Getting this colour stuff and the more factual information required for a spot news story in the midst of disaster was easy; all a man had to do was keep his eyes open and his stomach under control. But getting the news away was hopeless. The hastily repaired telegraph service was going full blast night and day on much more urgent matters than news stories. Still, I had to keep pestering the army – which had taken control of everything – to dash off just a few fragments to my paper. They refused curtly and absolutely, and I dare say the army was right.

By the third day they had burned or buried 10,000 dead; but the toll had steadily risen to more than 40,000 and corpses lay everywhere blackening in the sun. The army going its daily round among the dead was sweating in gas masks, and there was idle and unconfirmed talk of dynamiting what was left of the one-time garden city of the frontier. Survivors fought furiously against this because there were money and jewels and valuable family possessions in the ruins of what had once been mud homes.

I had a boiled rice breakfast and carried on my ghoulish investigations . . .

GORDON SINCLAIR
Khyber Caravan (1936)

INDIAN SKETCHES

I FORGOT to tell . . . a pleasing story I heard from one of the South Mahratta country clergy. He introduced cricket into his school to foster a manly spirit, and the boys got quite keen on it. Gradually he evolved a team and arranged a match with a neighbouring school. He told his team that they must work their hardest to win, and to encourage them he gave them fifteen rupees to spend on new bats or whatever would be most useful. When the day came, the team turned out for the match full of quiet confidence, but with all their old accoutrements. "Why," asked the *padre*, "what have you done with those fifteen rupees I gave you?" "Well, sir," replied the captain, "we thought it best to spend it *all* on the umpire."

They won.

From a letter of
The Hon. Robert Palmer
quoted in his
A Little Tour of India (1913)

Pot-Luck

*Earle Welby was born in India and spent much of his adult life
working there as a journalist. Not surprisingly he had many a
tale to tell when he came to look back over his Indian years.
(c. 1906)*

I was then at A————, where the frogs were nothing like as bad as I
have known them in some other parts of India, but were bad enough.
I took the usual precaution in a country of open doors of having a
board eighteen inches high put up in every doorway, but always there
would be from ten to twenty frogs hopping about my rooms. Day after
day I had my head servant catch these creatures, and take them out in
a waste-paper basket to the gate, and there deposit them. In time, I
wondered whether all the frogs in A———— visited my house in turn or
the same frogs revisited me after their ejection. And on a Sunday
morning I told that same servant to tie round the middle of each frog
he deported a piece of red tape, that they might be identified on the
morrow if they stubbornly returned. And then I forgot all about this;
and going out, picked up a young man of my acquaintance to come
back with me to pot-luck. When the meal was over, and we were
stretched in those admirable Indian chairs which rest the legs and fix
the gaze heavenward, so that one does not observe the events on the
floor, my guest squirmed and squirmed while I contemplated the
ceiling of the veranda and discoursed at large. Till at last he cried out,
after long speculation whether his was sober vision, "I say, old chap,
do you keep frogs as pets?" I heaved in my long chair, looked down,
and there on the veranda were many frogs belted with red tape and
indeed apparently rather disposed to think that with this livery they
had received the freedom of the house.

One of the points of this anecdote is the calm and absolutely
unsmiling acquiescence of that servant of mine in my request that tape
should be put round the frogs. Only a servant's obedience? But listen
to this story out of another part of India, where all the local notables
of, I admit, a rather remote district gathered in perfect seriousness

187

when, at a time of drought, a certain white official, mentally affected by overwork and hell's heat, summoned them to see him bring down rain by dispatching into the clouds a vulture with a home-made bomb appended to it. The local notables attended and observed with unmoved faces the efforts of the accursed and heavily-burdened fowl to flap upwards. Even when with a fuse burning, it perched on the apex of the official's thatched roof, and he became concerned for things other than rain, they kept their places and their countenances: this too, doubtless, was part of the performance. It was only when an explosion removed all of the vulture and some of the official's roof without precipitating rain that they felt something had gone wrong with the programme. . . .

. . . My main journeys were inevitably done by rail . . . Once there came into my carriage an old Hindu gentleman almost over-refined of feature. Only the nobility of the broad brow and the firm set of the lips saved that beautiful face from a charge of being over-daintily modelled. . . .

I asked him how far he was travelling, a matter of concern in that country where a journey may be one of anything from eighteen to forty-eight hours. He replied, "To Benares," and I was obtuse enough not to catch the significance of what he told me. He saw my failure, and after a little while added gently that he was going to Benares because he had now entered on the last stage of the true Brahminical life, the renunciation of all things worldly and of all family ties to undertake meditation in a sacred place. "I have taught long enough, I now go to learn," he said smilingly, and I think not a little pleased with the neatness of his summarising phrase. At intervals during the many hours that we travelled together I thought of that distinguished and dainty old gentleman sitting half naked among the saints and charlatans of the sacred and filthy city, making his fine mind a blank that there might enter into it – what? . . .

Who would not feel privileged to have such a travelling companion as that Brahmin gentleman? And many a time in Northern and Southern India did I readily share a railway compartment with some Indian who had completely adopted English modes in certain matters. But it would be hypocrisy to pretend that I or any other Englishman going by train was not made somewhat anxious by the prospect of an Indian fellow traveller. It was no question of colour prejudice or racial arrogance, as it was so often made out to be by the worst sort of tourist or stay-at-home friend of India. If you were going to be together for twenty-four hours or so you were both going to use the sanitary convenience attached to your compartment, and, to put things very mildly, a proportion of Indian travellers used it otherwise than we of the West. Then there were those, in their own place no doubt excellent citizens, who chewed betel-nut and squirted the red juice on the floor of the carriage. Again, there were those who made themselves almost entirely nude, and offered to unenthusiastic Western eyes the spectacle of perspiration coursing over their bodies. And, for a few specially luckless white travellers, there could be a companion of that sect which holds it wrong to destroy any animal life whatsoever, and at night on a journey gathers parasites off the body into a little box and in the morning returns them to the body, thus insuring the continuance of food supply for God's most objectionable creatures. . . .

At M—— some twenty of us used to take, what sounds very English and suburban, an office train from the residential to the business part of the city, and a very large first-class carriage was attached to the morning train for our accommodation. One day two highly self-conscious young Indians, obviously students, entered our carriage with a brave strut, but then were abashed because as we all knew each other well there was a great deal of talk and chaff going on, while the representatives of India had no one with whom to converse. At last one of the students plucked up courage to say to his friend at the top of his voice, "I fear poor Ramaswami has committed an unfortunate matrimony." To which his friend, seeking for support from some English proverb which ought to have existed, replied, "But so he has buttered his bed, so he must lie on it." Our laughter was very loud, but the two young Indians realised that it was not in the least ill-natured, and all was well.

T. EARLE WELBY
One Man's India (1933)

A Journey of Salvation

*Every July the Ashadi Fair at Pandharpur – one hundred miles
south east of Poona – attracted many thousands of pilgrims to
visit the celebrated shrine of Vithoba. Unfortunately, Pandharpur was equally famous as a dangerous centre of cholera
infection.*

*Winifred Heston, an American medical missionary, had
come out to India immediately after qualifying and then spent
four years in the country. Here she writes to a friend at home
about the suffering pilgrims. (c. 1908)*

Karad, July 4, 19--

And this is the glorious Fourth! I suppose you are lying low within
doors while all the small boys make the hours hideous with their
explosions and so-called patriotism. . . .

We have attempted to celebrate the day. At the station dinner this
evening we were as stylish and witty as possible, and told all our stale
jokes, laughing uproariously thereat.

But there is no use trying to be gay in this letter. We seek to put on
a smile, and forget for a brief space our gruesome surroundings, but it
is a thing that cannot be done. This country and these people have
become a part of our lives, and everything that affects them affects us.
Just now the vulture's wings are darkening the heavens, and they are
even worse than a brassy sky. This morning twenty-three corpses were
found on the road in front of the compound, having died there during
the night. And the reason is this: a great pilgrimage has been in
process – the annual fair at Pandrapur, a very holy city some little
distance from here, situated upon a very holy river. The papers have it
that between three and four hundred thousand people attended this
year, some going by rail in the cars fitted up like cattle-pens, in which
the rate is less than third-class fare, some in bullock-carts and some on
foot. Hundreds who travelled in carts and on foot passed our
bungalow, bearing banners, tomtoming on their drums, with constant
shouts of victory. To them it was a journey of salvation, and they were

190

filled with a great hope and faith in the benefits to be derived from it. Arrived at Pandrapur, they would crowd in between the temple walls and struggle to reach the inner precincts, where they could fall at the feet of a stone god and kiss the impression in the stone floor made by the priests, pay their money, and, if they could escape the throngs without being crushed to death, go to the holy river, have a bath, wash their clothes, and take a good drink. Of course there are no sanitary regulations there, and it is a perfect breeding-place for cholera and kindred diseases.

For the last few days they have been returning, but oh, to what a different tune! The vultures and crows provide the dirge, and form the advance and rear guard of the endless funeral march. Sometimes there will be a cart whose driver sits up to his task, guiding his bullocks with his stick and hurrying them by a twist of the tail, while behind him are lying one or two corpses, and one or two sick and dying. Now and then a cart passes whose driver has succumbed, and the bullocks follow along the road according to their own sweet will.

This evening Miss Pentup and I went for our usual walk towards the river. By the roadside we came upon a woman, seemingly in the last stages of cholera. We approached, hoping to be of assistance in some way, but she still had life enough to motion us away – she would not be defiled in her last moments by any contact with such as we. She was dying in a holy cause, and gloried in it! We were helpless before her caste and religion, and turned away, sick at heart. She was completely covered with ants, which had already begun the awful work to be finished a little later by the vultures.

We walked on to the river, and found a cremation in progress, the victim having been a Brahmin, and hence worthy of some attention. He was nicely packed in the middle of a square pile of wood, kerosene had been poured on, and the whole lighted, while two Brahmins marched around the pyre, reciting mystic formulae in Sanskrit. They continued until the skull burst, then took a ceremonial bath in a neighbouring well and went home. Held by the weird fascination of it all, and unmindful of the gathering darkness and the approaching dinner hour, we watched the blazing heap until it died down into a mass of glowing coals.

Some of the pilgrims have applied at the hospital for entrance, but we cannot take them in and expose our patients and the whole plant to this dread disease. We can only advise them to go to the government segregation hospital, which they will scarcely ever consent to do. To such as have gone, we send milk and medicine by the good Christian boy who scrubs the operating-room, and he goes gladly, with never a thought of his own danger. . . .

Does it not make you sick at heart? And to feel so helpless against it all, yet with a terrible conviction that there must be no giving up, that we must fight on to the bitter end!

WINIFRED HESTON
A Bluestocking in India (1910)

The Hindu Mother

The Grand Trunk Road was the great strategic highway built across northern India linking the capital, Calcutta, to Peshawar on the North West Frontier. Gordon Enders, son of an American Presbyterian missionary, grew up in north India, and as a young boy would sometimes accompany Jowar Singh, their number-one servant, to watch Life on the Road. (c. 1908)

I stood beside Jowar Singh in comparative shade and watched.

The Grand Trunk Road, down which Kim so familiarly vagabonded, was thronged with the vivid life of India, drawn there by the lodestone of the winter cattle fair. Jugglers and tumblers, Punch-and-Judy shows, beggars and holy men, blind men and mad men, widows, prostitutes, and baby brides, moved together in a sweating, holiday crowd. . . .

The two adults, with the baby still astride its mother's hip, turned into the grove. Not far from where we stood, the father unwound his turban and spread it upon the ground. It had once been white and was almost the shape and size of a big bed sheet. He took the baby from its mother and motioned the woman to sit down.

She had a yellow chuddar, like a cotton shawl, thrown over head and shoulders and pulled down over her face, so that I could not guess her age or see what manner of woman she was. But when she relinquished the baby it was obvious why she had stopped: she was far gone in pregnancy.

Patiently she squatted on her heels, peeking out from behind her chuddar at the women who drew water and washed at the well. She clutched her hands around her throat, and I could see the dozens of glass and silver bracelets on her wrists and the blue tattoo marks on the back of her hands. Her fingers were covered with cheap rings, and along the tops of her bare feet ran lines of silver chains which joined her tinkling, peanut-shaped toe rings. She had gathered her full red skirt beneath her and from time to time moved convulsively. But she made no sound.

Hindu woman

Matters presently became urgent, and the father put the fat baby down to play with the ants which scuttled over the ground. He asked a question of his wife, and I heard the bangles on her wrists tinkle when she pointed toward the well. He hurried across the grove, filled his lota full of water, and stopped to question the women – their faces were covered – who washed and chatted near by. Because of the caste system of India, he might not ask a woman of higher caste to help his wife, nor would he accept the services of a woman of lesser caste. Eventually he found a suitable helper and brought her over to his wife.

Surrounded by people, within earshot of the chaos on the Grand Trunk Road, the Hindu mother turned to a total stranger for the most private and mysterious function of the human race. She had the corner of a soiled turban, less than a quart of cold water, a stolid husband, and an unknown woman to assist her in bringing a new baby into the world.

While the dust-laden sunlight filtered through the mango trees, the mother struggled. Her body arched crazily at times, and her bangles sounded like sudden bells. The father got to his feet and walked about, then squatted down to join the strange woman in encouraging his wife.

Slowly, ever so slowly, before my fascinated eyes, the baby came. The strange woman held, and turned, and helped it. The mother made no sound except to gasp: "Yes! Yes! Yes!" at breathless intervals.

Even before the birth was fully accomplished, the assisting woman, her face now showing through her dishevelled chuddar, proudly announced a son; a man-child to grow up to drive his father's cattle, to marry and have sons of his own. The mother nodded her head, caught her breath, and nodded again.

Then the little fellow was born – all pink and gold and black. I watched him become a separate entity. With quick movements, a large knot was made at his navel, and it became clear to me why little bumps of flesh protruded from the middles of so many naked Indian children. The mother was quit, now, of her child, but not of her pains. Nor did the baby breathe yet.

For a moment the midwife abandoned the mother. Grasping the new child by his heels, she stood up and shook him as a terrier would a rat, banging him over the shoulder blades. She called to the women at the well, and the baby gasped his first breath before an appreciative audience.

The baby's cries had been too much for me, and I joined the group openly. Several women hurriedly investigated the little fireplaces, and one came back with a double handful of the white ashes of cow dung to give the baby his first bath. They doused him with water, and he made full-throated protest. Then they smeared him with the white ashes and began to rub him down as sailors holystone a deck. He objected lustily, which made the women laugh and rub the harder. And saying that he would be a great warrior, the father of hosts of sons, and the head of his village, they scrubbed him until he was nearly frantic with rebellion. At last they dried him and laved him with sweet cooking oil, and between whimpers his little mouth began to water.

The women wrapped him in dry cloths and passed him around for admiration. Catching sight of me, they asked whether I had looked like that, and I retorted that white babies did not look like that when they were born. They laughed and fell to examining the baby's face again, saying it must be like that of his grandfather, or his uncle, or perhaps his little dead brother. For to them a new life was not new, it was merely a disguise for an old life, for the world return of a familiar spirit.

Standing with my hand in Jowar Singh's, with the sounds of the Grand Trunk Road in my ears, I was half convinced, so real and commonplace was their talk.

I looked closely at the little child and saw something which still challenges my imagination.

Babies, in the Orient, are born old.

GORDON ENDERS
Foreign Devil (1945)

The Proper Price

During his years in the Indian Education Service, Nelson Fraser would often take leave away from Bombay to see something of the rest of the country and its people – as here in Kashmir. (c. 1908)

. . . I must relate the episode of the "foccus"-skin. Azad Bat, my headsman, gave me a word of warning when we reached Srinagar. "Be on your guard," said he; "what you hear in the village is half-true and half-false; what you hear in Srinagar is wholly false; and especially do not trust these merchants, and if you want to buy any skins, ask me the proper price." I did not want to buy any skins, and I thought myself secure from danger in that quarter. However, one evening, when Azad Bat was out, there came to my tent a skin merchant, who offered to show me skins. I explained the whole situation to him; I was not interested in skins, but only in old brass; moreover, I did not know the price of skins and had promised Azad Bat not to buy any. He replied that my attitude was very sensible, that he would not even attempt to sell me any, but he saw no harm in my looking at some. He had the pleasantest face and the most insinuating voice in the world; and his recommendations spoke with bated breath of his extraordinary honesty. His skins, too, were perfectly beautiful, and at last my eye dwelt for a moment on that of a Yarkandi fox. He detected at once the wavering of the balance, and mentioned quite casually the price – seven rupees eight annas. Woe is me! I succumbed to it; I counted out the shekels, and he departed. The skin I put away in my trunk, thinking to conceal my guilt. Half an hour afterwards Azad Bat reappeared, and in firm tones addressed me and said, "I hear the Presence has bought a "foccus"-skin; where is it?" I drew it forth from my trunk, and displayed it, and he asked what I had given for it. "Seven rupees eight annas," said I; "but observe what a magnificent ——." "The proper price of this skin," said he, disregarding my plea, "is three rupees; you have brought this on yourself." I looked a doubt I did not venture to express; but every day afterwards, as long as I

197

stayed in Srinagar, Azad Bat introduced a different skin merchant, who offered to sell me a "foccus"-skin for three rupees. . . .

Medical knowledge, though much needed, hardly exists. Accidents of all kinds are common; so are cancer, skin diseases, and sore eyes. There is a firm popular belief in the medical skill of white men, which often embarrasses the tourist. He has the physician's robes thrust upon him. If he pleads ignorance, the plea is not accepted. I did not wholly decline the office myself, trusting chiefly to castor oil, quinine, and boracic acid, and if I may believe all I heard, these remedies are more potent than we generally suppose. I was called in once to a baby; she was gravely indisposed, they said, and had long declined all food. I found her swollen into a perfect globe, with hardly a trace of features or limbs. I do not know what complaint produces these symptoms, and I said so, but I prescribed castor oil and faith in Providence. Fortunately, on passing that village a week later, I learned, at least I was informed, that she had made a good recovery, and gone for a change of air. This was satisfactory; but the most satisfactory of all my medical experiences was different in its character. One day by the roadside I saw a little boy with his face damaged, and plastered over apparently with cow-dung. It appears he had been herding goats the night before, and tumbled off a rock. Now I do not much believe in cow-dung, whatever its mystic virtues may be, and I had my zinc ointment handy, so I halted the expedition and prepared to treat the case (not having been asked to do so). Within a few minutes a concourse of people had gathered, including the father of the boy, and I thought it a good opportunity to inculcate in their rude minds the virtues of scientific cleanliness. So I had some water boiled, and a nice strip of lint prepared, and when everything was ready I sat down to wash off the cow-dung. But behold! it was not cow-dung at all, but chewed grass of a kind esteemed for this purpose. And I found it made an excellent plaster, adhering very firmly, positively curative, and certainly calling for no interference. So I left it alone; and I doubt if the assembly appreciated the higher wisdom of this course.

J. NELSON FRASER
In Foreign Lands (n.d.)

Dreadful Disease

Arley Munson came to India directly she had qualified as a medical doctor in New York. Working at a Wesleyan Mission Hospital in north west India proved to be a challenge as much to her courage as to her skills. (c. 1910)

I had heard much in the West of the oriental lepers who kept a distance between themselves and the rest of the world by their cry, "Unclean! Unclean!" but in India, though a man be positively falling to pieces with leprosy and yet have money enough, many a girl is glad to marry him. Almost every day I treated lepers at our hospital, and I never noticed the slightest shrinking on the part of their friends who had come with them.

A leper woman, the wife of the richest man in Ramyanpett, came to our hospital; her attendance was of the best, her palanquin of the most luxurious, and her silks and jewels of the choicest, all this in sad contrast to her face eaten away with the dreadful disease, the blurred eyes, the ulcerating hands and feet, the awful stench of leprosy uncleansed. Even as these thoughts came to me, she stepped forward; and, *salaaming*, embraced me heartily. I succeeded in my effort not to shrink from her, but, like *Lady Macbeth*, I felt that not even the "perfumes of Araby" could ever make me quite clean again.

As I heard her story of distress and discouragement, my eyes filled with tears and my throat ached with a longing to weep with her; nevertheless, I could but marvel at her companions, as they sat beside her, one with her arms about the leprous woman's neck and the other resting against her knee, fanning her vigorously, neither seeming to mind in the least the close contact with the unfortunate creature.

The prevalence of hydrophobia among the pariah dogs gives rise to many cases of this terrible disease in the village people; but, with their usual fatalism and lack of imagination in regard to the future, the wound caused by the bite of a dog suffering from rabies is carelessly treated, if it be not altogether neglected.

One of our coolies, a lad of thirteen, when bitten by a mad dog, cauterized the wound with a burning torch and told nobody about it. A month later, his mother brought him to us in the last stages of hydrophobia. She was a widow and he her only son. In the West that would mean much, but in India it is all; the son provides for his parents in their old age, and is the one being who can pray their souls into paradise after death. I told the mother as gently as I could that her boy would live but a few hours longer. She gazed at me a moment before she comprehended. Then, with a look of the wildest anguish and before any of us could prevent her, she rushed to the side of the struggling, panting victim of rabies, and placed her arm over his frothing mouth. Again and again he savagely bit the limb. The poor mother shrieked with hysterical laughter at the sight of the dripping blood; and so, laughing and sobbing, beating her breast and tearing handfuls of hair from her head, she was led away by the village friends who had come with her. I had begged them to let me treat her wounds, but they refused, saying: "Why should she live? Will there be aught in life for her when her only son is dead?" While my professional spirit urged me to save her life, my woman's heart told me they had spoken well.

ARLEY MUNSON
Jungle Days (1913)

Taboos

Edward Charles was Principal of a large Hindu-Moslem University College in central India. Among his administrative duties was the regular inspection of the College's kitchens – an experience which could on occasion make him feel more than usually dyspeptic. (1927)

When I got to College I had to deal with the Hindu kitchens. The inspection of a Hindu cook-house is a very tricky business, and it behoves me to record exactly my procedure.

At a quarter to eleven I got hold of the Vice-Principal, whose caste I have never discovered but who is, I fancy, a lax Hindu, and together we walked across the grounds and into the courtyard of the kitchen. In each of the divisions upon either side the Hindu servants of the appropriate caste were squatting indolently, it being apparently too early to begin preparing the midday meal.

The central courtyard runs east and west, and it being before noon and I having entered the courtyard from the west, I was walking into the morning sun, and my shadow, short enough anyway, was tidily behind me, not straying about into the eating compartments, where it would have sullied the soil and vitiated any food which might have been lying about.

It's all bunkum anyway. Does not Gandhi himself eat with Europeans? Not European food, of course, but *with* Europeans? The fantastic rigour of these "collegiate" taboos is simply a method of obstructing administration.

It is extremely difficult for me to inspect the place and satisfy myself that it is comparatively clean from the central courtyard.

I made the servants move the saucepans about and bring them forward for me to examine. I put up, in this way, two scorpions at the back of a quite high-caste partition (the second on the left from the west). I told D—— to order the mess secretary of that mess to reprimand their cook.

Just as I was leaving I turned back unexpectedly and walked quickly east and came into view of the last partition on the right in time to see the cook squatting down and relieving himself on to a piece of paper spread on the floor.

I did not wait for D——.

I stepped quickly in, past another cook who was eating. I didn't give a damn for my shadow. I'm Principal of this College and I'll go where I like and have the place clean, if I empty it of every Hindu student.

When I got to the back of the cubicle the boy had risen and was standing shyly looking down. I took him gently by the hand and led him out up to the astonished D——, who came running up.

D—— told the boy to wait while I took D—— in to see the evidence, what the French call in their criminal trials, "*les pièces à conviction.*"

On the way back again I noticed the other boy still sitting huddled sulkily over his bowl of rice. My shadow had not touched him. But he was anxious, guarding his rice against the pollution of my next passage.

I asked D—— to make the boy stand up. I objected to the attitude he was adopting. I wanted, too, to see behind him.

Hindu cooking

"Ah, Mr. Principal . . . Ah, I'm sorry, that I cannot do . . . he is eating. When a Hindu eats he worships his food as a God."

"It's bad luck," I said, "for him and for his bowl of God; but I must have this place empty and examine it thoroughly. Tell him that he can get up, throw his food away and cook more later, when I have gone; or that he can finish his meal now and leave the College grounds for ever."

Mr. D—— smiled wanly. "Mr. Principal," he said, "I cannot speak to him while he is eating . . . he is not of my caste."

"The responsibility is yours then, Mr. D——. The boy must leave this College and is hereby dismissed. See to it, Mr. D——, that his mess secretary pay him his wages and that he quit the compound this morning. Tie a string across the partition. The group who eat here must eat elsewhere to-day. Their cubicle is 'out of bounds.' If any question of students' money is involved in the loss of that food stacked behind there, the College must and shall refund any deficit. It will be a matter of only a very few rupees. I will draw the cheque myself on the 'repairs and maintenance' account. This place is out of bounds and both these boys are dismissed. Do you understand?

"The first boy is dismissed for reasons which need no explanation, the second boy's dismissal is on your shoulders, Mr. D——."

"Whatever the Principal wishes shall be done. If you have finished your inspection, Mr. Principal, we can leave by this gate."

"Yes . . . I can see the gate, Mr. D——."

"Such a thing has never occurred before, Mr. Principal. I deeply regret it."

"Regret what?" I asked. "The boy's filthy habits or . . . or . . . his dismissal?"

"Ah, Mr. Principal, how you delight to tease! You have a stern humour, Mr. Charles . . . Come, come . . . We will let it be: it does not matter much."

"Very well," I said, "it does not matter, much."

I do not think that I have often been so near to tears as I was when I got back to my cool office with the punka drifting its sigh over my head. That punka, stirring the dirty air . . . What else do any of us do?

What right had I to keep the College clean, forsooth? This College is for Indians. Half its income is government money, half is from public subscription, endowment, fees, Indian money. But all of it Indian money. We have founded an institution for Indians, which Indians frequent and support. They want to learn English literature. *I* don't know why . . . *They* don't know why . . . Nobody knows why.

They want to call themselves B.A., or, failing that, *B.A.*, *Plucked*, which seems almost as good. (Where did they get the word "plucked"?) They want to become *vakhils*. Talk, talk, talk.

They don't want to learn the elements of hygiene, as we understand those elements. They don't want to learn about honesty, as we understand honesty, about cleanliness as we understand it. We talk in terms of germs: they talk in terms of the sacredness of life. We talk of drains: they talk of the cycle of decay.

EDWARD & MARY CHARLES
Indian Patchwork (1933)

Talks with Gandhi

*Mary Barr got to know Gandhi and his family in the early '30s.
Originally in India to work at a Mission School, she was soon
drawn instead towards working with Gandhi. While visiting
the Wardha Ashram near Nagpur, Mary became seriously ill,
and Gandhi (Bapu, or Father) closely supervised her care and
recovery. (1933)*

Soon my temperature went up to over 104 degrees and stayed there,
so next day three doctors came to see me. My diary account of this,
written the following day, takes up the story thus:– "Bapu brought
three doctors to see me yesterday morning, and the usual little crowd
of hangers-on came into the room with them. Bapu sat on a chair
behind the doctors while they were prodding my tummy and testing
my chest, so that he could not see what they were doing. But another
man, whom I did not know, was standing at the head of my bed
watching all that was going on. Seeing this, Bapu immediately got up,
spoke to this man, and took him away into another place." Sometimes
there are disadvantages as well as advantages in the extreme publicity
of Indian India, but on this occasion Gandhi's kindly tact saved me
from undue annoyance. That afternoon I was taken to the Government Hospital, as typhoid was suspected, and Nila, another Ashram
member, came to be with me, for, as in many Indian hospitals, there
was only one nurse to three doctors, and the many patients were
nursed very largely by their own friends and relations. In the evening,
having heard that I was suffering from Malaria and not Typhoid, and
knowing that I might be inclined to refuse injections on account of his
ideas which are all in favour of "Nature Cures," Gandhi sent me a
little note:-

"Chi. Mary,
I think it is better for you to take the orthodox medical
treatment and get well. Injections are the order of the day
now-a-days. You had better take them. And take what
food they permit. If you don't need Nila's help, let her

come away. I know that the introduction of strangers
disturbs doctors in a well-managed hospital. May God be
with you.

Love,   28-9-'33
Bapu."

The advice in this letter is interesting in face of the general impression
one gets from his writings as to his ideas on the subject of "Western"
medicine. The fact of the matter is that he always deals with
individuals as such, and not according to any rule of thumb. . . .

After a few days in the hospital, I was removed to a tiny
one-roomed cottage in a sort of park belonging to the All India
Spinners' Association, so it was more than a fortnight before I saw
Gandhi again, though I had a few cheery little notes from him. When I
felt strong enough to go to the Ashram again, I sent him a message
and he arranged for a friend to take me there in a car. His letter about
this was the first one I had from him written with his *left* hand, which
he sometimes uses when his right hand is suffering from writers'
cramp.

"Chi. Mary,
I am glad you have been free from fever. If it is not
inconvenient, you should come at 4 p.m. and I will see
you in your car – you won't come up.

Love,   13-10-33
Bapu."

Gandhi came downstairs from his room on the roof that afternoon
to talk to me in the car, and as usual two or three friends came too. At
first I used to object to having others present during talks about my
affairs, but I have learned to appreciate their presence instead of
resenting it, even when they are unknown to me. The later pages of
my diary do not constantly refer to other people being there during
talks with Gandhi.

After a few enquiries about my health he said, "Well, fire away."

I fired away, reminding him that the Missionary authorities had
asked me to return to the work in Hyderabad, and he himself had
suggested that I should serve a year's probation, and the year was
nearly up. My illness made me wonder if it was presumptuous to try to
"go Indian" though for my part I was wishful to see it through and
much preferred to continue working under him. He replied:-

"No, it is not presumptuous if you feel mentally and spiritually
fitted for it. Certainly you cannot continue in this life if you do not

take a few ordinary precautions such as all Europeans need to take in India. Do not eat and drink everything that is offered to you as you go about."

"But," I argued, "it would hurt people's feelings if I refused food. *You* can do so, because you are a Mahatma."

"Well, I used to do so before I was a Mahatma," he naively remarked. "It is better for you to fast a day rather than take all sorts of unwholesome food that you are not accustomed to. But the solution to the problem is always to carry some dried fruit and dog-biscuits about with you on your travels."

I burst into laughter at the mention of 'dog-biscuits'.

"Yes," he continued, "I can give you a good recipe for making a hard, wheat biscuit, which I have christened 'dog-biscuit.'

"They are very crisp and will keep good for a long time under the most unpromising conditions. Be sure you get Ba to show you how to make them before you go back to your village. Then always carry boiled water with you for drinking, and you should be alright. I have no objection to your 'becoming Indian' but I must warn you that you may sometimes meet opposition from others. But if you do, you must just regard it, as Father Elwin does, as penance for the sins that English people have done to India. I feel similarly that any sufferings which we have to bear at the hands of the British must be regarded as penance for our sins to the Harijans."

After giving me news about other Ashram members, in whom he knew I was interested, he went upstairs again, and I returned to my wee cottage in the park. A day or two later, when I had been allowed to walk up the steps to his room, he suddenly looked up from his correspondence and said:-

"Mary, Ba must show you how to make 'dog-biscuits' tomorrow."

I suggested that I should go and fix up a time with her at once, but he stopped me saying, "No, I'll get round her. She is worried and not very well to-day. She was allowed out of prison to look after me when I was very weak and to-day she has written to tell the jail officials that I am now better and that she is ready to complete her sentence."

When I heard this I tried to back out of the engagement altogether, but he preferred to keep it, saying that it would be good for her mind to be occupied.

Next morning, I found her in the kitchen where a Harijan servant was also working, and I realised afresh how sincere are their own efforts to do away with untouchability. A non-Hindu can hardly imagine what a sacrifice it is for a woman like Mrs. Gandhi to have an outcaste preparing food in her kitchen. The "dog-biscuits" turned out to be a thin, hard, wheat biscuit, an excellent substitute for "Vita-Wheat" tinned goods. I found I could make a pound for about twopence.

F. MARY BARR
Bapu (1949)

TRAVELLERS AND TOURISTS

UP THERE [in Darjeeling] we found a fairly comfortable hotel, the property of an indiscriminate and incoherent landlord, who looks after nothing, but leaves everything to his army of Indian servants. No, he does look after the bill – to be just to him – and the tourist cannot do better than follow his example. I was told by a resident that the summit of Kinchinjunga is often hidden in the clouds, and that sometimes a tourist has waited twenty-two days and then been obliged to go away without a sight of it. And yet went not disappointed; for when he got his hotel bill he recognised that he was now seeing the highest thing in the Himalayas. But this is probably a lie. (1896)

MARK TWAIN
Following the Equator (1897)

The Best Hotels of India

*Being a journalist George Steevens was used to foreign travel
and knew a good hotel when he saw one. But, as he soon
discovered, this was not one of the sights of India. (1899)*

Within the hour of your landing India begins playing its jokes upon
you. You drive through piles of palace and masses of palm to a hotel
whose name is known throughout the world. A Goanese porter
receives you, and requests you to inhabit a sort of scullery on the roof.
I do not exaggerate a jot. I have seen the European cell in a remote
district jail, and it was very appreciably larger, lighter, cleaner,
cooler, and more eligibly situated than the first room I was offered in
an Indian hotel.

As the first, so was the second, and the third, and all of them. By
the time I left the country I had been in almost all the best hotels of
India. Four, throughout the 1,800,000 square miles, might indulgently
be called second-class; all the rest were unredeemedly vile. When they
were new they may have had the same pretension to elegance and
comfort as a London public wash-house has; but by now they are all
very old, and suggest anything rather than washing. There can hardly
have been a depreciated rupee spent upon the herd of them. The walls
are dirty, the carpets shabby, the furniture rickety, the food
uneatable, the management non-existent. The only things barely
tolerable in an Indian hotel are the personal service and the bedding,
both of which you bring with you of your own. . . .

And after all, what do you expect? Why should there be good hotels
in India? In Bombay, it is true, a really good hotel is wanted, and
would pay: they say that one is on the point of arriving. Everybody
that comes to India comes to Bombay, and nearly everybody can
afford to pay to be comfortable, or at least clean. . . .

But for the rest of the country, what can you expect? If a hotel is in
the plains, it will be empty in the hot weather; if in the hills, it will be
empty in the cold. The European population of India is sparse and
scattered, and of measureless hospitality. The white man sees less of

211

hotels than of tents, of dak bungalows on lonely, half-made roads, or rest-houses by lonely, half-empty canals. His work is always hanging on his back, and will not let him travel at large; if he goes for a day or two into a town, it is to a friend or to the club. So the hotel languishes. Presently the European owner sells it cheap to a native, and he puts in first a Eurasian manager and then a babu; and the owner will not spend a pie to renew the furniture or new-stain the walls, and the manager will not spend an hour to see that they are clean. Presently the place comes to look like a haunted house crossed upon a byre, and the Indian hotel is complete.

So that the tourist wallows in discomfort. He and she are, like tourists in most other lands, dazed by the unfamiliar into all-accepting meekness. Most of them did not know where India was till they arrived there. They carry in their pocket-books a piece of paper, whereon Mr Cook pitying the lost sheep, has written down the names of the places they are to go to, with the times of the trains by which they are to arrive and leave. They bring native servants . . . who show them such sights as can be compassed without walking, and then smoke and doze under the back verandah of the hotel, while their wards smoke and doze under the front. As a rule the tourist is too broken-spirited even to dress for dinner; how, then, should he complain of a hotel?

G.W. STEEVENS
In India (1899)

Christian Sadhus

Dr Pennell was an experienced medical missionary stationed for many years on the North West Frontier. Developing an interest in the lives of Indian ascetics he decided, as an experiment, to try living like one. So, dressed in "ochre-coloured garments" and accompanied by a young Afghan as his disciple, he set off on a long journey through northern and central India, taking no money, but travelling by bicycle to save time. The story begins at the River Beas in northern Punjab. (c. 1900)

. . . Reaching the river, we found that the toll-keeper was on the farther side and the river itself unfordable. Asking the boatmen whether we could cross without paying toll, as we had no means of doing so, they said the only way was for one of us to cross over and ask. We thought on our part that it would be better for both of us to cross over and ask, and as the boatmen saw no objection to this, we heaved our machines on board one of the boats and crossed over with a number of camels and bullocks. Safely arrived on the other side, we went to the toll-office and did what most Easterns do when they are in a quandary – sat down and waited to see what would turn up. The official in a leisurely way took the toll of all the passengers, quadruped and biped alike, eyed us narrowly without speaking, and then, in still more leisurely fashion, began to smoke his hookah. As time passed we both became contemplative, he on the wreathing columns of smoke from his pipe, I on the bucolic landscape around me. His patience was the first to waver, and he broke the silence with: "Now, Sadhu-ji, your pice."

"Indeed, I carry no such mundane articles."

"Then what right had you to cross the Sarkar's river in the Sarkar's boat?"

"Indeed, our purpose was to crave a favour of your worthy self."

"What do you desire of me, O Sadhu-ji?"

"Merely that, as we are on a pilgrimage to India and have no money, you would allow us to cross without paying toll; and as you were on this side and we were on that, and nobody would take our message, there was nothing for it but to come in person to ask the favour."

"Very well, Sadhu-ji, your request is granted, and may you remember me."

As an instance of the reception we got in a Hindu village, I may cite the case of one which we reached in the late afternoon in the Sirhind district. Most of the men must have been working out in the fields when we arrived, for we scarcely saw anyone as we wended our way to what seemed the principal house in the village, and, sitting down outside it, my companion began to sing a popular Indian hymn . . . First some children and then some men collected, chief among the latter being a venerable and stately old Sikh, the owner of the house and the religious *guru* or *sodhi* of the place.

The song ended, he enquired who we were, and what were our object and destination; and when he had been satisfied on all these points, he informed us that, though he had never entertained Christian Sadhus before, yet if we were ready to be treated like other Sadhus, he would be very glad to offer us the hospitality of his house. We thankfully accepted his offer, and he prepared a room for us and later on brought us a supper of rice and milk in his own vessels, which to us, after a long and tiring day, seemed quite a royal repast.

It was not often that I was recognised as a European, until I had declared myself, but the following occasion was a notable exception. I was sitting in the little jungle station of Raval, and a party of gentlemen in semi-Indian costume arrived from a hunting expedition. The chief was an elderly thick-set man with an iron-grey beard, dark piercing eyes and gold spectacles. He eyed me narrowly a short time, and then said to one of those with him in the Persian language: "That man is an Englishman." I replied, "I recognize you gentlemen as Afghans." He assented, and I entered into conversation with one of the Afghans with him, who told me that it was His Highness Yakub Khan, ex-Amir of Afghanistan, who had thus recognized me.

On the other hand, at Allahabad I was going on my bicycle along a road which was slippery from a recent shower of rain. In turning a corner the machine skidded and I fell, and as I was picking myself up, an English girl who was passing, called out: "O Sadhu! you must have stolen that bicycle, and that is why you do not know how to ride."

Finally we made our way to Bombay, having been helped the last part of our journey by a friend who bought us our railway-tickets. Here we desired to return homewards by taking the steamer to

Karachi. We then had no money, but I was asked to give a lecture on my travels, and after the lecture several of the audience gave me sums amounting altogether to eleven rupees. When, however, we went down to the docks to take passage, we found that our steerage fare cost ten rupees, and five rupees was demanded for each of the bicycles too! We purchased our tickets and stood on the quay awaiting developments. Among the crowd was a Brahman holy man, who was sprinkling the passengers with holy water and receiving a harvest of coppers in return. He came to sprinkle us, but we declined the honour. He then asked why we were waiting instead of going aboard with the other passengers. I told him that we were waiting because we could not pay the fare of our bicycles. He retorted that unless we invoked his blessing (for a remuneration) we should assuredly never start, but that, having done so, everything would turn out well. When we still declined, he went away prophesying that all sorts of misfortunes would befall us.

The last of the passengers had gone aboard, the appointed time for starting had arrived, but no friend had appeared to help us out of the difficulty. The Brahman came back and taunted us with our position, and what it might have been had we but accepted his offer. All I could say was, "Wait and see." Just as the steamer was about to start a ship's officer called to us and said that the captain was willing to take our bicycles free of charge. With a friendly nod to the Brahman, we crossed the drawbridge and in a minute more were under way.

We had now one rupee left for food, but still we were not left in want, for when that was finished the Goanese cooks came and inquired about us and gave us a share of their own dinner. At Karachi the steamers anchor out in the harbour a considerable distance from the landing wharves, and passengers are taken ashore in native boats, a number of which crowd alongside the moment the ship is moored. But these boatmen naturally require remuneration, and we had none to give, so that it now seemed as though we should have greater difficulty in getting off the steamer than we had in getting on. Just then a launch came alongside for the mails, and a ship's officer came up and asked if we would like to go ashore on it. Of course we accepted the offer with alacrity, had our machines on board in a trice, and were safely on *terra firma* again before the native boats had got away from the steamer.

This pilgrimage gave me many opportunities for philosophizing on the rôle that a man's clothes play in gaining him a reception or a rejection. My missionary brethren took various views on the subject.

Most exhibited incredulity as to the expediency of donning native garb, while showing some sympathetic interest; few were antagonistic on principle, though one missionary brother, indeed, weighed the matter a long time before admitting us into his house. He thought that the gulf between East and West was *a priori* unbridgeable; therefore no attempt should be made to bridge it, and that the relation between a missionary and his native associates should be sympathetic (patronizing?), but not familiar. To go about with an Indian brother, sharing the same plate and same lodging, seemed to him the height of unwisdom, even to shake hands being to go beyond the bounds of propriety; while as for an Englishman donning native clothes, he was dimming the glamour of the British name in India, which in his eyes was next door to undermining the British rule itself.

T.L. PENNELL
Among the Wild Tribes of the Afghan Frontier (1909)

Inspector of Inspectors

After graduation and a year of teaching, Harry Franck decided to leave the USA and devote the next twelve or fifteen months to world travel. Wanting to observe ordinary people's lives, he worked at lowly jobs along the way to keep himself – although in Madras he glimpsed occupational depths he feared to plumb. (1905)

It was my good fortune to find employment the next morning. The job was suggestive of the spy and the tattle-tale, but the most indolent of vagabonds could not have dreamed of a more ideal means of amassing a fortune. I had merely to sit still and do nothing – and draw three rupees a day for doing it. Almost the only condition imposed upon me was that the sitting must be done on a street car.

Let me explain. The electric tramways of the city of Madras are numerous and well-patronized. The company does not dare to entrust the position on the front platform to aborigines; for in case of emergency the Hindu has a remarkable faculty of being anywhere but at his post, and of doing anything but the right thing. But as conductor, a native or Eurasian of some slight education does as well as a real man. He has only to poke the pice and annas into the cash register he wears about his neck and punch and deliver a ticket. Yet it is surprising, nay, sad, to find how many accidents befall him while engaged in this simple task. He will forget, for instance, to give the passenger the ticket that is his receipt for fare paid; coppers will cling tenaciously to his fingers in spite of his best efforts to dislodge them; he has even been known, in his absent-mindedness, to overlook his friends on his tour of collection through the car. Don't, for a moment, fancy that he is dishonest. It is merely because he is a Hindu and was born that way.

To correct these unimportant little faults, the corporation has a force of inspectors, occasionally sahibs, commonly Eurasians, clad in khaki uniforms and armed with report pads, who spring out unexpectedly from obscure side streets to offer expert assistance to passing conductors.

But, of course, mathematical experts do not dodge in and out of the sun-baked alleyways of Madras for the good of their health. The spirit of India is sure to attack them sooner or later, even if it has not been with them since birth. Cases of friendship between inspectors and conductors are not unknown, and it is not the way of the Oriental to attempt to reduce his friend's income. In short, the auditors must be audited, and, all unknown to them or its other servants, the corporation employs a small select band of men who do *not* wear uniforms, and who do *not* line up before the wicket on pay day.

It was by merest chance that I learned of this state of affairs and found my way to a small office that no one would have suspected of being in any way connected with the transportation system of Madras. An Englishman who was ostensibly a private broker deemed my answers to his cross-examination satisfactory, and I was initiated at once into the mysterious masonry of inspector of inspectors. The broker warned me not to build hopes of an extended engagement, rather to anticipate an early dismissal; for the uniformed employees were famed for lynx-eyed vigilance, and my usefulness to the Company, obviously, could not endure beyond the few days that might elapse before I was "spotted." He did not add that a longer period might give me opportunity to form too intimate acquaintances, but he wore the air of a man who had not exhausted his subject.

My duties began forthwith. The Englishman supplied me with a handful of coppers that were to return to the corporation through its cash registers. I was to board a tramway, find place of observation in a back seat, and pay my fare as an ordinary passenger. The distance I should travel on each car, the routes I should follow, my changes from one line to another, were left to my own discretion. Upon alighting, I was to stroll far enough away from the line to allay suspicion and return to hail another car. The company required only that I make out each evening, in the private office, a report of my observations, with the numbers of the cars, and sign a statement to the effect that I had devoted the eight hours to the interests of the corporation. What could have been more entirely mon affaire? If there was a nook or corner of Madras that I did not visit during the few days that followed, it was not within strolling distance of any street-car line. . . .

My devotion to corporate interests brought me the surprise supreme of my Oriental wanderings. At the corner of the Maidan, where the tramway swings round towards the harbor, a gang of coolies was repairing the roadway. That, in itself, was no cause for wonder. But among the workmen, dressed like the others in a ragged loin-cloth, swinging his rammer as stolidly, gazing as abjectly at the ground as his companions, was a white man! There could be no doubt of it. Under the tan of an Indian sun his skin was as fair as a Norseman's, his shock of unkempt hair was a fiery red, and his eyes were blue! But a white man ramming macadam! A sahib so unmindful of his high origin as to join the ranks of the most miserable, the most debased, the most abhorred of human creatures! To become a sudra and ram macadam in the public streets, dressed in a clout! Here was the final, lasciate ogni speranza end. A terror came upon me, a longing to flee while yet there was time, from the blighted land in which a man of my own flesh and blood could fall to this.

Again and again my rounds of the city brought me back to the corner of the Maidan. The renegade toiled stolidly on, bending dejectedly over his task, never raising his head to glance at the passing throng. Twice I was moved to alight and speak, to learn his dreadful story, but the car had rumbled on before I gathered courage. Leaving the broker's office as twilight fell, I passed that way again. A babu loitering on the curb drew me into conversation and I put a question to him.

"What! That?" he said, following the direction of my finger. "Why, that's a Hindu albino.". . .

Two days later, the broker confided to me the sad news that I had been "spotted."

HARRY A. FRANCK
A Vagabond Journey around the World (1910)

The Sanctity of Life

After attending George V's Coronation Durbar at Delhi, The
Hon. Robert Palmer took the opportunity of seeing something
more of India. Here, in one of his letters home, he tells of a
visit to the Jains' Holy Mountain near Palitana, in Kathiawar.
(1911)

The guide-book said there was a dak bungalow there – *i.e.*, a little
rest-house provided by Government where there are no hotels; so I
telegraphed for breakfast to be ready there, and travelled by night
from Ahmedabad.

Railway travelling is a vile business here. The trains are very slow
(well under twenty miles an hour), dirty, and roundabout (*e.g.*, to get
from Udaipur to Abu last week, fifty-five miles as the crow flies, I had
to travel three hundred and seventy-five miles by train, as the map will
show you). You invariably start, arrive, or change at about 3 a.m. But
what is far worse is the native crowd. A native who wishes to travel
always comes to the station twelve or fifteen hours before the train is
due. Innumerable others who don't wish to travel come to gossip with
the passengers and guard. Consequently every station is choc-a-bloc
with a very dirty and malodorous horde of men and women, all
chattering as loud as they can bawl, pausing only to spit every tenth or
eleventh second (they chew betel-nut, which produces pints of
crimson spittle, too disgusting for words), jostling each other and
blocking the whole platform with their bundles of bedding, while at
intervals the hawkers of glutinous foodstuffs utter intolerable droning
calls from the midst of a seething, pestilential swarm of flies.

This is a true picture of every station; and every train (except mails)
stops at every station a quarter of an hour for purposes of gossip, and
at all large stations half an hour or an hour . . . Consequently we took
twelve and a half hours to cover a hundred and seventy miles.

However, I got to Palitana at last at 9 a.m. and was met on the
platform – to my natural surprise – by the Prime Minister of the State!
There was no dak bungalow, and so my telegram had been taken to

the Administrator, the only white man in the place, and he, having a proper sense of what is due to *sahib-log*, had told the Prime Minister to meet me and see that I was cared for in the Maharajah's guest-house. So I was put into a *tonga* and told that I should find breakfast at the guest-house. The servant here, however, in spite of my telegram, was of opinion that I should prefer to climb the mountain on an empty stomach, and had only provided tea and biscuits. I could get nothing else but *chapathi* (an alias for dough rolled out flat): as for bread, there was no such thing in the city. Fortunately, I had brought some provisions, and managed to make a sort of meal. But before starting for the mountain I impressed on the Prime Minister's A.D.C. that I hoped for something more substantial when I came down.

The *tonga* took me to the foot of the Satranjaya Mountain. It stands two thousand feet straight out of the flat plain, and there is a Pilgrims' Way up the side – a steep paved path varied by flights of steps: an average gradient of one in ten and about four miles in length. . . .

I was taken up in a *dholi*, which is a square small mattress slung on two poles and carried by four men. It took an hour and a quarter to get up. The whole top of the mountain is occupied by a city of Jain temples. . . .

The Jains are not a very big sect: they are analogous to the Quakers in Christendom. . . . The best-known characteristic of the Jains is their extreme doctrine of the sanctity of life. The Hindu does not kill wantonly, but except for cows, monkeys, and peacocks, and local sacred beasts, he will kill under provocation. The Buddhist is much stricter, and won't even kill snakes. But with the Jain it amounts to fanaticism. Not only won't he kill even a flea (their holy men carry brushes to sweep insects out of their path, lest they should tread on one), but he makes great efforts to keep things alive at all costs. . . . At Ahmedabad I met a string of about fifty Jain women carrying canvas bags from which water was trickling. On inquiry I found they were carrying all the fish from a pond ten miles away, which had dried up, to another pond where there was water.

Their whole character seems to be of a piece with this. Like their namesake, they are gentle and as good as gold. They are men of peace, devout and simple: and in Palitana at least they were most friendly, showed me everything, though none of them knew a word of English, and made no demands for *backshish*. The very *dholi*-coolies only asked for eight annas each for carrying me up the mountain and down again – I wouldn't walk it for eight rupees. . . . I got back to

Palitana about half-past three, had a bath, and found a solid five-course meal prepared, which I gladly consumed. After that I went to call on the Administrator. He, his wife, and her sister were the only white people in the State. He had been there six years . . . He runs the State autocratically, for the Rajah is only eleven. I saw him, poor little boy! and felt very sorry for him. He has to live with the Administrator, since his life would not be worth a month's purchase in the zenana, among his mother's rivals. He can only visit his mother occasionally and in charge of a trustworthy guardian, and of course mustn't touch any food there. He was one of the Queen's pages at Delhi, and when I saw him he was dressed up in his Durbar clothes and jewels, as he was going to visit his mother and show them to her.

THE HON. R. PALMER
A Little Tour in India (1913)

The Eye of Faith

Travelling round the world, the novelist Aldous Huxley crossed India from Bombay to Calcutta. When he reached the sacred city of Benares, in January 1926, a partial eclipse of the sun occurred – an event of great religious significance to the Hindus. Huxley rowed out on the river to watch the spectacle of their devotions along the ghats.

There were, at the lowest estimate, a million of them on the bathing ghats that morning. A million. All the previous night and day they had been streaming into the town. We had met them on every road, trudging with bare feet through the dust, an endless and silent procession. In bundles balanced on their heads they carried provisions and cooking utensils and dried dung for fuel, with the new clothes which it is incumbent on pious Hindus to put on after their bath in honour of the eclipsed sun. Many had come far. The old men leaned wearily on their bamboo staves. Their children astride of their hips, the burdens on their heads automatically balanced, the women walked in a trance of fatigue. Here and there we would see a little troop that had sat down to rest – casually, as is the way of Indians, in the dust of the road and almost under the wheels of the passing vehicles.

And now the day and the hour had come. The serpent was about to swallow the sun. (It was about to swallow him in Sumatra, at any rate. At Benares it would do no more than nibble imperceptibly at the edge of his disk. The serpent, should one say, was going to try to swallow the sun.) A million of men and women had come together at Benares to assist the Light of Heaven against his enemy.

The ghats go down in furlong-wide flights of steps to the river, which lies like a long arena at the foot of enormous tiers of seats. The tiers were thronged to-day. Floating on the Ganges, we looked up at acres upon sloping acres of humanity.

On the smaller and comparatively unsacred ghats the crowd was a little less densely packed than on the holiest steps. It was at one of

223

these less crowded ghats that we witnessed the embarkation on the sacred river of a princess. Canopied and curtained with glittering cloth of gold, a palanquin came staggering down through the crowd on the shoulders of six red-liveried attendants. A great barge, like a Noah's ark, its windows hung with scarlet curtains, floated at the water's edge. The major-domo shouted and shoved and hit out with his rod of office; a way was somehow cleared. Slowly and with frightful lurchings, the palanquin descended. It was set down, and in the twinkling of an eye a little passage-way of canvas had been erected between the litter and the door of the barge. There was a heaving of the cloth of gold, a flapping of the canvas; the lady – the ladies, for there were several of them in the litter – had entered the barge unobserved of any vulgar eye. Which did not prevent them, a few minutes later when the barge had been pushed out into mid-stream, from lifting the scarlet curtains and peering out with naked faces and unabashed curiosity at the passing boats and our inquisitive camera. Poor princesses! They could not bathe with their plebeian and

The Burning Ghat, Benares

unimprisoned sisters in the open Ganges. Their dip was to be in the barge's bilge-water. The sacred stream is filthy enough under the sky. What must it be like after stagnating in darkness at the bottom of an ancient barge?

We rowed out towards the burning ghats. Stretched out on their neat little oblong pyres, two or three corpses were slowly smoulder-ing. They lay on burning faggots, they were covered by them. Gruesomely and grotesquely, their bare feet projected, like the feet of those who sleep uneasily on a bed too short and under exiguous blankets.

A little further on we saw a row of holy men, sitting like cormorants on a narrow ledge of masonry just above the water. Cross-legged, their hands dropped limply, palm upwards, on the ground beside them, they contemplated the brown and sweating tips of their noses. It was the Lord Krishna himself who, in the *Bhagavad Gita*, prescribed that mystic squint. Lord Krishna, it is evident, knew all that there is to be known about the art of self-hypnotism. His simple method has never been improved on; it puts the mystical ecstasy *à la portée de tous*. The noise of an assembled million filled the air; but no sound could break the meditative sleep of the nose-gazers.

At a given moment the eye of faith must have observed the nibblings of the demoniacal serpent. For suddenly and simultaneously all those on the lowest steps of the ghats threw themselves into the water and began to wash and gargle, to say their prayers and blow their noses, to spit and drink. A numerous band of police abbreviated their devotions and their bath in the interest of the crowds behind. The front of the waiting queue was a thousand yards wide; but a million people were waiting. The bathing must have gone on uninterruptedly the whole day.

Time passed. The serpent went on nibbling imperceptibly at the sun. The Hindus counted their beads and prayed, made ritual gestures, ducked under the sacred slime, drank, and were moved on by the police to make room for another instalment of the patient million. We rowed up and down, taking snapshots. West is West.

In spite of the serpent, the sun was uncommonly hot on our backs. After a couple of hours on the river, we decided that we had had enough, and landed. The narrow lanes that lead from the ghats to the open streets in the centre of the town were lined with beggars, more or less holy. They sat on the ground with their begging bowls before them; the charitable, as they passed, would throw a few grains of rice into each of the bowls. By the end of the day the beggars might, with luck, have accumulated a square meal. We pushed our way slowly through the thronged alleys. From an archway in front of us emerged a sacred bull. The nearest beggar was dozing at his post – those who eat little sleep much. The bull lowered its muzzle to the sleeping man's bowl, made a scouring movement with its black tongue, and a morning's charity had gone. The beggar still dozed. Thoughtfully chewing, the Hindu totem turned back the way it had come and disappeared.

ALDOUS HUXLEY
Jesting Pilate (1926)

An American Tourist

While in India researching a book, the successful French writer and journalist Maurice Dekobra enjoyed a chance meeting with one of his American readers. The enjoyment was all on his side. (1928)

On arriving at Benares, the city of two thousand temples which extends for three miles along the left bank of the Ganges, I noticed, in the station, a lady with lorgnette and a Colonial helmet, dressed in a tailor-made khaki suit and carrying under her left arm a copy of *The Saturday Evening Post*. She seemed lost in the midst of her baggage. She was an American tourist. I asked her very politely if I could be of service. She accepted gratefully and begged me to help her get the coolies together because the hotel representative was occupied elsewhere. Some twenty minutes later, we arrived at our destination.

When I had introduced myself, the traveller thanked me a second time and confided her name: Miss X——— of Boston. Then with that delightful nasal accent which is one of the charms of English as it is spoken in the United States, she suggested:

"If, by any chance, you care to see the curiosities of the city, we could share the same automobile and the same guide – Because, I really know you very well, you know."

"Not possibly?"

"You are the author of a novel which was censured in Boston two years ago. Am I correct?"

"Perfectly, Miss X———. I have shared with your great writer, Sinclair Lewis, and several others, the distinction of being banned by Boston society or, more exactly, by the book-stores of your illustrious city."

Miss X——— scrutinized me through her lorgnette. Then she added:

"Well, it just happens that I belong to the virtuous association which caused the authorities to take action – Odd, isn't it?" . . .

The following day at dawn, Miss X——— and I started for the center of the city where, in an inextricable conglomeration of houses and streets scarcely wide enough to give comfortable passage to a cow, half a dozen important temples are to be found. There is a complex perfume of faded frangipanis, rotting jasmins, burned myrrh, raised dust, dry bovine excrement and fetid water running under the flat stones outside the buildings.

We went down a street which led to the gilded temple consecrated to Siva. Along the wall, forty or more old women were crouched. Clothed in rags, sometimes exhibiting long flopping breasts, they held out their wooden plates for our offering. One of them, her bosom completely bare, approached Miss X——— who turned away, properly shocked.

"Oh! Disgusting! –"

"They are poor widows who are totally dependent on charity," I told her.

When she heard that, Miss X———, who had a kind heart, subdued her outraged modesty and dropped a few annas into the wooden receptacle.

We entered the temple. The guide explained that it was like nearly all the temples dedicated to Siva. He enumerated the emblems exhibited on the altar: the statue of the god and the sacred bull, kneeling before the *lingam*. Miss X———, failing to understand, repeated:

"The *lingam*?"

The guide pointed to the emblem which resembled a candle, three quarters burned, stuck on a plate. Miss X——— looked at it through her lorgnette. Then she asked:

"Is that the god's finger?"

"No, madam, it is not his finger. It is the symbol of reproduction. Because, you know, Siva is the god of creation as well as of destruction."

Miss X——— had quickly turned her back. . . .

She made as if to leave the place. I followed her without saying a word. The impassive guide was on her heels. Then, to change the trend of our ideas, Miss X——— having spied, in a shadowy corner, a sort of chapel with a grilled window but elegant in its construction and with a sculptured pyramid roof, exclaimed:

"What a pretty miniature temple! What's inside?"

Drawing near it, she adjusted her lorgnette. In the middle of the tiny edifice, an enormous phallus, painted a brilliant red, stood up, still wet with the ritual water which the faithful had sprinkled on it.

"What is that strange red thing?"

"That is the *lingam*," the guide replied.

Miss X—— from Boston, thoroughly revolted, recoiled . . .

"Can't you show me a temple where that horror is not offered to the eyes of decent people?"

The ever placid guide replied:

"Certainly, madam, I can take you to the temple of Nepal which is celebrated for its wood sculpture."

Miss X——, evidently much relieved, agreed:

"Well, I'm glad to hear that. Let's go to the temple of Nepal." . . .

The latter is a pagoda in stages, made of black wood, remarkably carved – an excellent specimen of the art of Nepal.

The guide led us around the temple and called our attention to the sculptured bas-reliefs at the bottom of the oblique pieces of wood which support the roof of the temple. The first was a group of three, entirely naked – a man and two women. They presented, with extreme immodesty, Fragonard's "Comparison." The guide showed us the ensuing bas-reliefs. One showed a woman with a radiant smile, standing between two other women and, with the most casual glance, it was easy to determine that this scene represented satisfied desire. The rest of the bas-reliefs went to complete a series of excessive gallantries, conceived by an erotic and facetious sculptor.

Miss X—— contemplated each one of them through her lorgnette, the while maintaining the most severe and condemning expression imaginable. When she had examined all sixteen, she turned indignantly to the guide and exclaimed:

"That's sufficient! – We'll return to the hotel!"

Walking rapidly, she found herself face to face, in a nearby street, with a young Hindu, whose white vest was covered with red stains. She asked the guide:

"The poor boy isn't badly hurt I hope?"

"No, madam, he isn't hurt at all – We have recently had the Hindu holiday known as *Holi*, in the course of which the young people, as they do all over India, amuse themselves without restraint and pour that red liquid all over one another."

"It's a sort of carnival," I told Miss X——. "And the red liquid corresponds more or less to the confetti and the serpentines of the Europeans."

"Oh, I see – I see – But, tell me, guide, why the red liquid?"

The guide explained:

"Because, madam, the *Holi* fête is at once the fête of springtime and of love. The red liquid symbolizes the first wound of nubile virgins."

"Oh!!!"

This was the last straw. Miss X—— precipitated herself toward the stairway which led to the *Ghats*. The guide was worried and he asked me:

"Isn't the lady pleased?"

"No. She didn't expect to find that sort of thing in Benares.". . .

We had to run to catch up to Miss X—— who was fleeing as fast as her legs would let her from these scenes of horror. We finally caught her in an alley about two yards wide which led to the copper bazaar. Suddenly, Miss X——, still leading the procession, was obliged to stop. Completely obstructing the passage, a yellow zebu, an extremely enthusiastic young bull, was doing his utmost to explain to a sacred little cow that her first duty was to become a mother so that one day her calf might honour the Hindu Olympus. It was impossible to get by on account of the narrowness of the street and the spirited conversation of the two bovines. Miss X—— did a right about face with a last desolate "Oh!" We would have liked to retrace our steps but the street behind us was already jammed with Hindus, some serious and some laughing, who were admiring the pantomime of the sacred beasts. We couldn't budge. When Miss X—— saw the crowd she was more disgusted than before and when she turned the other way she was thoroughly disillusioned to discover that little cows are not conceived in the hearts of roses.

MAURICE DEKOBRA
The Perfumed Tigers (1930)
Trans. Neal Wainwright

Separate Tables

In the middle of the Great Depression, Robert Bernays spent five months in India as a special correspondent for the Liberal daily paper, the News Chronicle. *(Soon after his return he was elected as Liberal M.P. for Bristol North.)*

At Bombay he mixed with the young expatriates and questioned the liberality of their attitudes. But, before long, Indian experience forced him to recognise there were limits to his own liberality. (1931)

. . . The young men are the most interesting in Bombay. I fell in with a group of them after a Rotary lunch, and have been having in consequence ever since a most generous supply of free meals at the Gymkhana Club. It is a delightful place, where everybody seems to have been at school with everybody else. Here again the vocal element is overwhelmingly Liberal. They believe that the Raj in the Jubilee sense is at an end, and that responsible government is inevitable.

But I discovered one significant fact. Their Liberalism ends with constitutional reform. They are not prepared to admit the Indian socially into their own circles. This is not merely true of the young men, but of the whole of Bombay. There are three great English clubs in Bombay. The doors of every one of them are tight closed against the Indian. Even the Willingdon, so useful in perorations, where the two races meet in the same club-house, is a failure. They may play on the same golf-course or eat in the same room, but it is in exclusive foursomes and at separate tables.

It is understandable. The Englishmen on the whole are having a hard struggle to keep their businesses afloat in this hurricane, and they can hardly be expected to employ their leisure in political gestures.

Moreover, amongst their own people there is the most ludicrous snobbery in social relationships. I heard more talk in Bombay of men who had "accents", or were not "sahibs", than I have heard since boyhood days in a London suburb. The conditions of admission to some of the clubs are preposterous. At one of them it is necessary to be personally interviewed by members of the committee. Absurd tales are told of wholly eligible young men being turned down because the name of their public school is unknown to the chairman of the committee. There is a fantastic line drawn between commerce and trade. If a man is in commerce he is eligible to be a sahib; if he is in trade he is in outer darkness. A man may sell wine from an office. All is well. That is commerce. He hands it over the counter. That is trade. He is an outcast. Such a system produces extraordinary results. A clerk on the railway may be welcomed with open arms, while a managing director of stores, though he was at Eton, may be shut out.

Side by side with this are, of course, the usual rigid Eurasian prejudices. To say that a man has "a touch of the country" is almost as damning as in England to say that a man is a gaol-bird. The ban is carried to monstrous lengths. It extends often even to domiciled residents, to use the grim census term for those Europeans who are permanently living in India. An unfortunate young man with not a scintilla of colour in his veins may find himself socially doomed if he has been seen in Bombay at fifteen, when his contemporaries were away at an English public school.

I once heard an Indian say at a public dinner, "We know that you English have in your society as many 'untouchables' as we Indians do. We often talk about it amongst ourselves." I am not surprised. It is the most interesting phenomenon in Bombay, and explains to a great extent the yawning gulf between Indians and Europeans. It is, after all, the *a fortiori* argument. If Englishmen take such precautions against the society of their own race, it is not surprising that they show some reluctance to meet the representatives of another.

I began to meet some of these Indians, and was struck, as, I suppose, every traveller is, by their extraordinary courtesy. I was the representative of an alien race with whom they were in violent and embittered conflict, and yet they treated me as an honoured guest.

. . . I have now moved on to Bahawalpur, a native state. It is strange that though to use the word "native" in ordinary conversation is to be regarded as having said something positively indecent, one can still talk unrebuked about native states.

On the way here I tried the experiment of travelling second class. Railway fares in India are crushing burdens on slender finances. It is the distances. One tends to think that to journey from Bombay to Delhi is like running up from London to Manchester. It is as a matter

of fact rather more than the distance between London and Warsaw.
. . . However, I was tempted by the thought that I should be saving
fifty per cent. on every fare and decided to be brave. My bearer, who
looks like the sort of man who in England will be Lord Mayor in
twenty years time, was obviously pained. He pointed out that I should
never get all my luggage into the carriage, and that there might be
"Indian sahibs master would not like." I was adamant and tumbled
into the first second-class carriage I saw, to find it completely empty. I
cursed myself for all the tens of rupees that I had poured out
unnecessarily in buying a solitude that I could have had for half the
price. But at the junction I had to change and then the fun began. For
in my next venture into a second-class carriage, though it was eleven
o'clock in the morning an Indian gentleman was still in bed, and
though the temperature, even on a cold weather morning, is at least
that of a fine day in an English May every window was shut. I opened
one in the hope that the prestige of the white race would suffice to get
it kept open. But at the moment three more Indians appeared from
the lavatory in various stages of *deshabille* and the window is tight
closed again. By the rule of the majority I was beaten. . . . They then
all began to eat oranges and to spit the pips to the four corners of the
carriage. I could stand it no longer and after the next station I tried to
explain through the medium of a supercilious bearer to a suspicious
ticket-collector why I was travelling first class with a second-class
ticket.

The whole incident, trivial though it is, illustrates the difficulty of
contact between English and Indian. To put it bluntly, to the peculiar
nostrils of the Englishman the ordinary Indian smells. I do not mean
that offensively. Probably our bodies are to them equally malodorous.
Nor do I refer to the ordinary Europeanised Indian whom one meets
in England. But in general, owing to different conceptions of hygiene
and social habits, close casual association between the two races is
very often physically unpleasant. It is a difficulty that ought to be
faced and overcome. It would be perfectly easy on a railway to have
carriages labelled "for Indians" and "for Europeans." Neither race
desires the intimate association inevitable to railway travel. Several
times I have seen an Indian enter my carriage and on finding me there
deliberately go away and seek out an Indian as a fellow-traveller.

ROBERT BERNAYS
Naked Fakir (1931)

Social Graces

Author and journalist Beverley Nichols spent over a year in India and travelled widely around the country. Wanting to have the last word – or at least know what it was – when dealing with Indian servants, he sought local advice. (1943)

Riding in my first Indian train, from Gwalior to Delhi, I asked a very red-faced Colonel the Indian for "thank-you". The coolies who had carried the luggage were waiting to be paid; it was very hot and they had worked quickly and well; it seemed ungracious merely to tip them and send them off.

"Thank-you?" ejaculated the Colonel. "Thank-you?"

"Yes," I repeated. "Thank-you." (If you say the word "thank-you" often enough it sounds quite peculiar, like a sort of Chinese fish.)

"But my dear fellah," he spluttered, "you *don't.*"

"Don't say thank-you?"

"Certainly not. Nevah. It isn't done." He shook his head violently, and began to climb the steps into the carriage. Then he turned his head: "S'matter of fact, doubt if there *is* such a word. Been in India thirty years. Know Hindi. Know Urdu. Never heard anybody say it. Thank-you!" And he retired into the railway carriage, making old-fashioned noises.

I gave the coolies an extra tip to make up for the lack of a "thank-you" and there is no need for the cynic to tell me that they greatly preferred this *bakshish* to any social graces by which it might have been accompanied. Their wages are so miserable that they would let the sahibs spit in their faces for an extra anna. Sometimes the sahibs come very near to doing it. . . .

I went through India asking this question, feeling stranger and stranger, wondering if I was the victim of some odd personal complex. Nobody else – British or Indian – ever seemed to feel the lack of this word. Servants staggered into hotel bedrooms with monstrous tin trunks on their heads. Nobody said "thank-you". Waiters yawned at midnight tables while the sahibs guffawed over their brandy. Nobody

234

said "thank-you". People picked up things that had been dropped, made way in buses, gave directions in strange, winding streets. Never a "thank-you". It made me feel more and more dumb and churlish. I found myself inventing a "thank-you" of my own – an odd sort of hiss accompanied by a smile and a nervous twitch. It appeared to alarm those who were its recipients, but it salved my conscience.

It was the Princess of Berar who first told me the word for "thank-you". Of all the women in India she was the one who really needed it least, for she was so beautiful that she had only to smile to make a man feel that he was being paid the most eloquent compliment. However, she was not an Indian at all; she was the daughter of the ex-Caliph, and she had royal manners as well as royal blood. She had experienced the same feeling of discomfort over the lack of a "thank-you", and she made me a present of two words. You will not find them in any of the elementary textbooks for Europeans. Presumably, they are so rarely used, that nobody thought it worth while to mention them. The first word is "mihrbani", though that may not be the correct spelling. It means something like "graciousness". The second word is "shuggrea", and that means, apparently, "sweetness", or something like it. I used to say both words in loud ringing tones to the dirtiest and most degraded beggars in the vicinity, to the horror of the sahibs and the high-caste Hindus, but to the evident delight of the degraded ones, who had never heard such words cast in their direction before.

BEVERLEY NICHOLS
Verdict on India (1944)

EASTERN ENIGMA

I WATCHED a scene in south India, not far from Coimbatore, where rival magicians pitted their powers against each other. . . .

. . . A very large circle had been outlined on the ground with chalk, and in its centre the challenger placed his sandal, defying his opponent to move it.

As the opponent advanced into the circle to pick up the sandal, he appeared to strain every muscle and to move only with great physical exertion. The challenger was a little less agitated, but his muscles stood out like the muscles of a wrestler and his half-naked body glistened with perspiration. Advance and strain, retire and relax, seemed to be the sequence of the opponents' movements for more than an hour, when suddenly with a terrific effort and blood spurting from his nose, the challenged party managed to pick up the sandal. . . .

A European who was also present, related to me how he had seen a similar contest, which had a different result. When the challenger had worn his opponent to a shred, the sandal, with no other volition than its owner's power, got up from the ground and so soundly whacked the opponent that he had to flee from the ground. I hinted to my informer that native toddy was quite strong in some districts, but Indians present confirmed the story. (c. 1933)

ARTHUR MILES
The Land of the Lingam (1933)

Rope-Trick

Very few people (if any) had actually witnessed the Indian rope-trick, so Lord Frederic Hamilton, diplomat, traveller and writer, was delighted to hear from one who had. He faithfully recorded the Colonel's strange experience – something the Colonel's camera failed to do. (c. 1910)

Colonel Barnard, at one time Chief of Police in Calcutta, told me a most curious story. We have all heard of the Indian "rope-trick," but none of us have met a person who actually saw it with his own eyes: the story never reaches us at first-hand, but always at second- or third-hand . . .

In the same way Colonel Barnard had never met an eye-witness of the rope-trick, but his policemen had received orders to report to him the arrival in Calcutta of any juggler professing to do it. At length one of the police informed him that a man able to perform the trick had reached Calcutta. He would show it on one condition: that Colonel Barnard should be accompanied by one friend only. The Colonel took with him one of his English subordinates; he also took with him his Kodak, into which he had inserted a new roll of films. They arrived at a poor house in the native quarter, where they were ushered into a small courtyard thick with the dense smoke arising from two braziers burning mysterious compounds. The juggler, naked except for his loin-cloth, appeared and commenced salaaming profoundly, continuing his exaggerated salaams for some little while. Eventually he produced a long coil of rope. To Colonel Barnard's inexpressible surprise, the rope began paying away, as sailors would say, out of the juggler's hand of its own accord, and went straight up into the air. Colonel Barnard kodaked it. It went up and up, till their eyes could no longer follow it. Colonel Barnard kodaked it again. Then a small boy, standing by the juggler, commenced climbing up this rope, suspended to nothing, supported by nothing. He was kodaked. The boy went up and up, till he disappeared from view. The smoke from the herbs smouldering in the braziers seemed almost to blot out the courtyard

239

from view. The juggler, professing himself angry with the boy for his dilatoriness, started in pursuit of him up this rope, hanging on nothing. He was kodaked too. Finally the man descended the rope, and wiped a blood-stained knife, explaining that he had killed the boy for disobeying his orders. He then pulled the rope down and coiled it up, and suddenly the boy reappeared, and together with his master, began salaaming profoundly. The trick was over.

The two Europeans returned home absolutely mystified. With their own eyes they had seen the impossible, the incredible. Then Colonel Barnard went into his dark room and developed his negatives, with an astounding result. *Neither the juggler, nor the boy, nor the rope had moved at all.* The photographs of the ascending rope, of the boy climbing it, and of the man following him, were simply blanks, showing the details of the courtyard and nothing else. Nothing whatever had happened, but how, in the name of all that is wonderful had the impression been conveyed to two hard-headed, matter-of-fact Englishmen? Possibly the braziers contained cunning preparations of

Clive Street, Calcutta

hemp or opium, unknown to European science, or may have been burning some more subtle brain-stealer; possibly the deep salaams of the juggler masked hypnotic passes, but somehow he had forced two Europeans to see what he wished them to see.

LORD FREDERIC HAMILTON
Here, There, and Everywhere (1921)

The Abominable Snowman

*H.L. Davies was a young officer with the Garhwal Rifles
based at the military hill station of Lansdowne in the
Himalayas. In later life, when he came to pen his auto-
biography, he felt able to describe the Abominable Snowman
as a "mythical beast"; but at the time, the experience must have
raised a question mark or two in the younger man's mind.
(c. 1921)*

Much has been written about the Abominable Snowman, the "yeti" of
the higher Himalayas. In upper Garhwal, round the bleak out-skirts
of Trisul and Nanda Devi, the legend of this creature also persists.

On one occasion, while hunting the blue Himalayan sheep in these
parts, I came across these mysterious footprints. They stretched
across the snowclad hillside straight as an arrow as far as one could
see. I knew nothing about the yeti in those days and it was my shikari
who pointed them out and who evinced extreme unease as we
surveyed the gigantic tracks. He wanted to give up the stalk forthwith
and return to the friendly cover of the forests some thousands of feet
below. But we were well placed for our stalk; I could see the herd we
were following with the big ram whose head I coveted, not half a mile
away and I reckoned we would certainly get our shot if we continued.

After an argument the shikari reluctantly agreed to continue, but he
was ill at ease and unhappy. Maybe it was this that caused the accident
which occurred when we were negotiating a steep ice slide which ran
down the hillside. We could have avoided it, I suppose, by climbing a
few hundred feet but time was precious and we decided to cut steps in
the ice and avoid the detour. The slide was not very wide, three or
four yards at the most and though steep it was by no means a
dangerous incline, provided one did not slip.

My shikari led across, punching footholds in the ice with his khud
stick. He got over and I made to follow him. I reached the last
foothold and was stretching out my right leg to reach the solid rock,
when the ice crumbled below my foot. The shikari grabbed me as I fell

but failed to hold me and himself overbalanced. Together we slid down the icy slope, gathering momentum with fearful rapidity. Sometimes on our backs, sometimes on our faces, tearing out our finger nails in a useless attempt to stop our progress. Somewhere below the slide disappeared over a fearful drop, hundreds of feet down to the rocks beneath.

But we were lucky. On the verge of the drop we crashed against some rocky outcrops in the ice and came to a standstill. Gingerly, we climbed off the slide with aching limbs and bloodied finger tips. My rifle had gone over the edge; we recovered it later with the foresight missing and the bolt jammed. The stalk was over and the shoot was ruined for I had no other rifle.

My shikari was very hurt about the whole thing. "You would not take warning, Sahib" he said. "The yeti brings bad luck; we should have turned back when we saw his footprints."

I'm afraid this little experience does not qualify me to express any views as to the reality or otherwise of the Abominable Snowman. . . . But the local inhabitants have no doubts as to the existence of this mythical beast.

H.L. DAVIES
Small Green Men (manuscript)

Damned Nonsense

When he was put in command of the Mule Corps and posted to Nowshera on the North West Frontier, Mark Channing took over his predecessor's bungalow and arranged for a brother officer to share it. Work was soon underway to convert the untidy compound into a proper garden – but the saint's tomb had to be left strictly alone. (c. 1936)

It was curious, having a saint's grave in the middle of one's garden.

The grave of a saint, if it is not a built-up tomb, is generally covered by a longish mound of earth and stones. At the head of it is a low, mud-brick erection shaped somewhat like a Gothic window. In this there are sometimes one or more niches in which little lamps are set on Mohammedan feast days, or on Fridays, the Mohammedan sabbath. This particular grave had such an arrangement, but in a sad state of disrepair.

Now, from out of the opposite end of the mound grew a tree. Whether it originally had any significance I cannot say – there are sects who believe that the souls of the good inhabit fruit-trees, and Hindus sometimes worship Mohammedan shrines – but it is necessary to mention it. It is also necessary to mention two other things: that *dhoob* grass will not grow in the shade, but must have sun; and that one branch of this tree, larger than the rest, cast a shadow under the almost vertical sun.

The *dhoob* grass would not "take" on the shadowed area, and there was an unsightly bare patch. I told my Afridi gardener, Syed Mohammed, to saw off the offending branch.

The order was met by a flat refusal. Whoever sawed off that branch would be haunted by the *bhoot*, or "spirit", of the Holy One, he assured me – "in spite of what has been done in his service!" He was referring to the fact that, disliking the untidy look of the grave, I had had it tidied up and had told him he could spend two annas a week on oil to burn in an earthenware lamp on appropriate occasions. But I felt that he was right, and the branch was pulled up by a rope passed

244

over a higher fork and there knotted. He said he was as pleased as if I had given him five rupees; which I doubt. However, I received through my Indian officer an unofficial message of thanks from the men of the Mule Corps, and a very official visit from the Corps' *protégé*, whom they called "the Säin fakir," a delightful, toothless ancient who went about draped in a red hospital blanket with a rose stuck behind his ear. I used sometimes to think that at his age – he was over eighty – he ought to have known better.

"What would have happened if I *had* sawn off the branch?" I asked.

"The *bhoot* would have come to you in the form of a snake, sahib! Or you might have gone blind, or been killed. This night I shall light for the first time the lamp your Honour has presented to the *pir*-sahib. He will be very contented." It happened to be a Friday.

Knowing my co-tenant's contempt for all phases of the occult . . . I avoided any mention of the incident of the branch.

July on the Frontier is a wicked month, and our veranda thermometer was registering 110° at midnight. That night after mess my tenant cycled to the bungalow ahead of me, I following on foot. It was pitch dark, and his broad shoulders and white mess kit soon dissolved into the surrounding blackness.

Coming up the drive, I saw with a curious sense of content the yellow glimmer of the tiny lamp. Overhead were the glorious stars which the heat haze seemed to magnify to a more than usual brilliancy. Was the old *pir* somewhere up among them and able to see the honour that Syed Mohammed had rendered to his last resting-place? I wondered. From the stars to the grave seemed so very, very far. . . .

My wondering ended abruptly. With a heavy thump a stone hit the lamp and shattered it.

Now, the assassination of British officers on the Northwest Frontier by religious maniacs called *ghazis* not being unknown, I thought for a moment that this missile was a signal for an attack by a band of rascals of some sort, and regretted that my white uniform made me a good target. Also, I was unarmed.

Peering ahead in the direction from which the stone seemed to have been thrown, I discerned a misty-looking figure on the veranda. Our trusty watchman was, of course, nowhere to be seen. It seems to be a point of honour with those men never to be at hand when they are wanted.

"Kaun hai oodher?" ("Who is there?") I called.

My tenant's voice answered.

"Did you throw that stone?" I was half-incredulous.

"Yes!"

"Why?"

"Because I loathe and detest anything that smacks of superstition! Why on earth do they want to stick up a lamp on that grave? It's just damned nonsense and shouldn't be encouraged!"

We separated rather grumpily, and turned in.

At 2 A.M. I was awakened by a furious barking of dogs, mixed up with weird moaning and praying. The sounds were coming from my tenant's bedroom. Every now and then I heard him cry out, "The snake! The snake!" (*The* snake, notice; not *a* snake.)

Padding out into the dividing passage with a cocked 7-inch Webley, I peered round the door-jamb of his room. There was my stone-thrower, leaning against the wall with his pyjama jacket torn to the waist. The hurricane lamp burning in the bathroom revealed that two of the legs of his camp bed were broken. Now, any shaken man is an unpleasant sight; but when he happens to be a soldier surrounded by his own weapons it makes matters worse – especially in that temperature. Nothing I could do or say would soothe him. I managed to get him to sit on a chair, but he was shaking as if he had the ague. Every now and then he would suddenly exclaim, "*The snake! God, the snake!*" I wanted to find out whether he had actually been bitten by a snake, but each time I tried to examine him he beat my hands away.

At this stage the trusty *chowkidar*, complete with naked sword and looking extremely sleepy, put in an appearance.

Him I sent running for a doctor.

By now, of course, all our servants were awake and my bearer suggested imperturbably that we should have tea; and we did.

Five of us with lanterns examined the dust round the bungalow that night for traces of a snake; but there was not even the imprint of a *chowkidar's* foot. Another curious thing is that his dog did not start to bark until the victim of the nightmare started to shout; if there had been a snake he would have lifted the roof off. His master was asleep, lying on his back and was awakened by feeling something thrusting itself under his ankles, so that he shifted his feet a little.

"Immediately the snake – or whatever it was – began to slide more quickly; and, still slithering under my ankles, came across my thighs and slid up under the small of my back. The thing was wrapping itself tightly round me. I struggled with it, but I could see nothing. . . ."

A little Scotch padre who came to live in those rooms – their late occupant having flatly refused to sleep in the house again – suggested that it was all a nightmare. The punkah-wallah, he explained, had fallen asleep, and the punkah-thong had consequently sagged on to the sleeper and given him the impression that it was a snake. But I can swear that was not the case; the thong was hanging in a low loop some four feet above the bed.

The same padre told me later that for the first few nights after he came to the bungalow at about 2 A.M. he heard the sound of footsteps on the grass-matting in the bedroom; but, though there was a light in the room, he could see nobody.

"One of these 'nightmares,' Padre?"

"Do you know, I don't think that boy *had* a nightmare!"

MARK CHANNING
Indian Mosaic (1936)

Rupees Well Spent

Methodist Ministers do not usually have much to do with fortune-telling but George Bassett was soon impressed when he was approached by a Sikh with just this in mind. At the time Bassett was Chaplain to the 17th British General Hospital based in northern India at Dehra Dun. (c. 1942)

Only ten minutes ago an Indian fortune-teller has left me. I don't pretend to believe in fortune-telling but the experience has been so interesting that I am writing this immediately so that I have it in black and white for the purpose of putting it to the test, for this Indian who came to me has told me some things that he could not possibly have guessed. It happened like this. Dinner was over, and stretching before me was the long evening. I had had a busy day and it was time for rest, and as I was sitting on the veranda, along came an Indian of the Sikh caste. He was very well dressed and spoke fairly good English. He asked if he might tell my fortune; I turned him away saying "No" but when he began to speak of Norwich, which, by the way, was my last Circuit before joining the Army, I pricked up my ears and thought that, at any rate, it would be an interesting evening. After a little discussion we bargained that, for ten rupees, he would tell me my fortune; well, here it is just as he told me. As expected, I was first of all to be very lucky. I was to have a long life and would die suddenly at the age of 87. He then told me that I had a lady who cries and misses me a great deal; this I knew, but when he told me that the initial of her pet name that I used was "P" I was very interested. My wife's name is Margaret, I call her Peg. I will only be married once and I have one little child, and again he told me her initial. He next informed me that promotion was coming my way, and in answer to the question uppermost in my mind, he said I would return home in 1944. As far as money was concerned I would never be very well off; being a Methodist Minister, again I knew this; and I should achieve success in the profession that I have chosen. Then followed something that interested me very much. He told me to draw the following diagram:

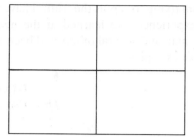

While I was drawing this, he gave me a piece of paper wrapped up very carefully and asked me to put this in my pocket; this I did. He next told me to give the name of a star. I said "Jupiter" and in the top right-hand square he put the letter "J"; next he asked me to say a number, I gave him No. 8 which he wrote down in the square below "J". Next he asked me for the name of another star. I said "Mars" and he wrote down "M" in the bottom left-hand square, and on giving him No. 7 he placed that in the vacant square; so that the diagram now read:

7	J
M	8

Next he said "Cross out any pair you like." I crossed out J8 which left M7. "Now", he said, "look on the piece of paper in your pocket." When I did, I saw on it M7. I suppose there is some answer to all this but I was completely mystified. This was my lucky star and my lucky number. Within seven days or seven weeks I should receive a long-looked-for letter. It was all done so very confidently and made so very interesting that I hardly noticed that half an hour had passed. With this he left me.

I wonder if there is anything in what he says, or have I been a fool. Maybe it will be ten rupees well spent, maybe it will be wasted.

The story should end there and leave me in my world of fantasy and dreams, but as I am trying to report the truth, I have to add that, a day or so after this experience, we learned at the headquarters of the regiment that this man and several others had been arrested and were to be tried as Japanese spies.

GEORGE BASSETT
This Also Happened (1947)

WAR AND FREEDOM

Trust me, To-day's Most Indispensables,
Five hundred men can take your place or mine.

RUDYARD KIPLING
The Last Department (1886)

Towards the Front Line

In the autumn of 1942 General Wavell organised an unsuccess-
ful attack against Arakan in Japanese-held Burma in a bid to
bolster British prestige. Leonard Marslund Gander went along
as a war correspondent and in this letter to his wife he describes
conditions on the India-Burma border, so far as the censor
would permit.

Nov. 1942

We are on our way back from Chittagong to Calcutta and, believe it or
not, the city of carrion birds and cripples seems a most desirable
place, somewhere we can have hot baths, good regular cooked meals,
tennis, etc. For we have been doing a certain amount of roughing it,
and finished up by being well and truly marooned by cyclonic floods
on the Burma border for four days. After that we walked back for
more than twenty miles – I should say walked, waded, canoed and
finally limped, for I have never felt so stiff in my life. . . .

You will understand that for security reasons I cannot tell you
precisely where we were nor exactly what companionship we had, but
I can say that we were not lonely. Also we were never at any time
short of food, if frequently short of temper. The Old Etonian staff
officer who acted as our guide was one of the most unpractical men I
have ever met. As you know I am not gifted that way either, Stanford
if anything is worse and certainly more abstracted . . . The fourth
member of the party was the conducting officer slightly more willing
to get down to the job than the O.E. but twerpish and Lancashire.
The scene when we attempted to put up or take down the four tents
was an unbelievable shambles. O.E. was so ignorant of the country
and language that he almost wanted to look for chota mallets to drive
in the chota pegs. I offered a lot of sage advice to which nobody paid
any heed and got all the canvas wrapped round me till I looked like
the Sheik of Cox's Bazaar. The only man who knew what he was
doing was Stanford's bearer Mahomed who was worth his weight in
gold.

However, I give myself full marks for having brought tins of fruit, plates, knives, forks, maps, and a large number of other useful things – including nailed boots and anklets. Stanford had practically nothing of use except a fine sense of humour and powerful physique. He is amusing because he can never foresee any difficulties. . . .

I forgot to say that we only pitched the tents once, afterwards deciding that it was much less trouble to scrounge a roof of some sort. And our first camping site was on a seashore where we had an early morning swim then a breakfast of sardines on buttered biscuits. We were usually close enough to an army kitchen to get tea, and later part of the time fed in an officers mess. When we started off towards the front line southwards we had two lorries. Fortunately Stanford and I were in the first one driven by a Colonel whom we picked up who knew the way and was in a hurry. He proved a most invaluable help, for not only did he push on regardless of obstacles and difficulties but also he took back a story for us. As I write I still don't know whether this or any other story has passed the censor. However, continuing my yarn, at a particularly difficult river crossing where there was no bridge but a sort of ford made of bamboo poles our lorry got across with a rush but the O.E. got his badly stuck in the river. The Colonel said he must rush on as he had an urgent conference. We went on with the Colonel, after suitable commiseration, thinking perhaps wishfully that we had seen the last of our boy friends. However, they turned up later. Our next trouble was several damaged bridges where we had to abandon the lorry altogether and walk. Eventually the Colonel went on alone on the back of a motor cycle while we created a first class sensation by taking out our typewriters in a primitive jungle village and sitting down at a sort of wayside cafe to write our despatches. The inhabitants were all straight down from the trees. About a hundred of them gathered round watching us intently and seriously, including a large proportion of naked boys – no girls or women, for some reason, I suppose they were doing the domestic work. They craned over one anothers shoulders anxious to miss no part of the performance, wide eyed with astonishment. Two eskimoes landing by balloon on Hampstead Heath could hardly have created a greater stir. . . .

They were very friendly. For some incredibly small sum they produced Russian tea – with limes – bananas, and a large fruit like a cross between a grape fruit and an orange called a pomela (I don't know if that's the right spelling). Then presently a lorry came along and we bundled our stuff in and were off again, stories completed for the Colonel to take.

All this time, by the way, I had raging neuralgia. We reached our first destination and were debating whether we should immediately push on into Burma proper when we noticed some black clouds rolling up on the horizon. I never dreamed that it would rain at that time of year but thought that just in case perhaps we'd better stop where we were. Just as well that we did. We had the brilliant idea of putting our tents in a little valley till Mahomed pointed out that the water would probably run down hill and flood us out. Eventually we never put the tents up at all but crawled like hermit crabs into a forest officer's bamboo hut situated on the flat top of a little hillock. And there we stuck for four days with brief excursions to the bog and the mess. I have never seen such rain. It fell in solid chunks making everything damp and if you ventured outside it was equivalent to jumping into a river for wetness. Of course we had no mackintoshes with us. . . . We improved the time by writing despatches, which we unsuccessfully tried to send by runners, and by having occasional quarrels. Stanford much resented the way in which O.E. ordered his bearer about and finally told him so. I was much amused at the exchange of pleasantries, but myself had an argument with the conducting officer who accused us of trying to evade censorship. It was all most depressing. And we knew the Japs weren't far off.

Still, at last the rain stopped and then began our trek with twenty-six indefatigable coolies. But I have written so much about that I can't bring myself to repeat it all for the umpteenth time. . . .

Well, dearest, there has been a lot of myself and my experiences in this letter but every day I am thinking of you all, wondering what you are doing in this fourth grim winter of war, longing to be back. Speed on steamer, back to Calcutta where I expect there will be letters waiting for me.

L.M. GANDER
Manuscript Letter

The Philosopher

Corporal Parlow of the Intelligence Corps was on the staff of the Wireless Experimental Centre located about four miles from Delhi. The Centre was India's equivalent of Bletchley Park, and their task was to intercept Japanese wireless signals. (1943)

Sunday 2 May

Holdsworth is back from hospital looking very fit & pleased with himself – he thinks dysentery a good "line." I was up early & had a good shower – water more plentiful lately. B——, the fulsome arse-licking Cpl in charge of the office greeted us with threats that if we didn't keep better time, myself in particular, he'd put us all on a charge – he thought that I, as senior N.C.O., shd "set a better example" (the usual platitude). B.O.R.s, he declared, are forbidden to talk to C.W.O.s in office hours – in some units you'd be put on a charge for talking to an Indian – long live fraternity! long live the glorious British Empire, which has to employ wogs to help preserve itself from the Japanese, but doesn't care to lower its prestige by speaking to them. B—— was obviously again referring to my talking with 2 of the C.W.O.s for about an hour yesterday p.m., out of sheer boredom – true the conversation was not always respectful towards everything B—— stands for, but it did contribute a tiny fraction towards Anglo Indian understanding. According to B—— he is merely transmitting the commands of the new officer, C——, the ex-C.S.M. who bristles with bullshit – this cretin walks in and out of the office as if on parade, sits down & stands up by numbers & occasionally bursts into a sort of raucous song . . . only officers of course are permitted to croon during office hours – all this only goes to show that we're in the Army first & in India second, if at all. . . .

Temperatures lately have been in the 100's – 107 the other day – today is dry & scorching – 100° at least. I told one of the C.W.O.s that the sahibs call them "wogs" & he said they call us "monkeys" – he thought we called all coloured people niggers or "darkies". . . .

256

Mon 3 May

Got truck to New Delhi about 9.15 with F, both thankful that LC had spent so much on himself last night that he couldn't afford to come out. Got 50 cigs each at —— & thence to India Coffee House for coffee upstairs, cooled by an electric fan & later renewal of acquaintance with Mr Shanks. Tonga to Chandni Chowk in old Delhi, said to be richest street in Asia – my first visit – the tonga wallah tried to overcharge us but a passing policeman persuaded him to accept the regulation fare (1/8). CC is nothing sensational – a warren of shops, selling everything from boots & shoes to camphor balls & brass locks – pavements narrow & seething, a beggar or two, professional letter writers squatting on the curb, a couple of inches from the passing trams, busily inditing messages for illiterates – any amount of queer looking sweets and queerer smells . . . Debouching from CC we got to the Wavell Canteen, after searching in vain for the railway station buffet, said to have a good cuisine – had a meal of salad & ice cream & spent an hour or so reading old "Picture Posts" in the Rest Room. Even here there was no peace, the room being suddenly invaded by a swarm of bearers who started to remove all the chairs, on the pretext that the roof had to be repaired – its just the same at the camp, there's hardly an hour of the day when the bearer doesn't come in our room on some errand or other – no privacy, no peace, lousy wogs & lousier compatriots, dust heat & stench, that's army life in India.

From there we walked to the Cecil Hotel wh. lies in the "Civil Lines" outside the walls of old Delhi. The Civil Lines are the most salubrious & English spot in all Delhi, a sort of Delhi garden suburb – spacious commons, tree-lined avenues, brownish-green grass, a patch of water here & there & hardly a sign of Indians, except the hotel servants, who are so decorously attired, respectable & well disciplined that they cd easily be mistaken for portly English butlers or scraggy Soho waiters, (according to type) at a Servants' Fancy Dress Ball.

I had thought of bathing (there's a swimming pool too) but as it wd have cost about 2R. with hire of towel & costume, I decided against it on grounds of economy. We had tea in a sort of forecourt, tolerably cool & with a view of the garden – good tea out of a pot, sandwiches, cake etc for a chip each. Sitting about were one or two raddled looking sahibs & memsahibs, of hardbitten, parasitic, nouveau riche aspect & out of an inner room came pleasant piano music, played, we discovered, by an officer from C Section – lingered awhile talking & got a lift back to New Delhi where we went to the Plaza to see Rita Hayworth in "My Gal Sal" . . . Rita H. dancing is a dream of delight –

the cinema itself isn't quite so well aired as the Rivoli, but we got quite good seats for R.1, the place being only half full. At the end you stand up, not very stiffly, for God Save the King & the Royal Family appear on thc screen in a touching domestic flash, mother & father & the 2 princesses, the younger one acting playfully with a henpecked-looking terrier – calculated to bring a lump in the most unpatriotic throat. Home by tonga after a very enjoyable day, costing altogether 8-14 – not exorbitant. Found a telegram from parents awaiting me giving Easter greetings & the glad news that all are well . . .

Tues 4 May

. . . More tightening up – W.A.C.I.s now have to be in by 10.30 every night except Wed & Sat – looks as if the more promiscuous are going to be out of pocket.

The new officer C——— reminds me more & more of a window-dresser at the 50/- Tailors or a shopwalker at Burton's . . . The 2 or 3 C.W.O.s with whom I'm on friendly terms call me "the philosopher", probably because my views coincide with theirs on the issue most fundamental to them & educated Indians in particular. . . .

Rao, one of C.W.O.s, explained the workings of a hookah during the p.m. – very hygienic, because the tobacco fumes pass through water which purifies them of nicotine & causes the bubbly sound a hookah emits. Not so hygienic is the practice of passing the hookah round from mouth to mouth, pyorrhoea & halitosis notwithstanding. . . .

Stopped work at 5.30 because of another M.O.'s lecture in the cookhouse, which dragged on till 7.30. We must take 2 teaspoonfuls of salt per day – take such & such precautions against snakebite – a series of "useful", "interesting" lectures will be given on First Aid – voluntary, but anyone "interested" shd attend – best book on the subject is St. John's Ambulance manual, unfortunately unobtainable in India – lectures will be given by all the nursing staff, unfortunately there's no blackboard, but still they'll do their best – V.D. also shd be notified immediately – B.O.R.s if they suspect contamination shd apply to the M.I. room for an E.T. packet – these can't be publicly displayed as this is a mixed station – as regards prostitution the position is better in Calcutta, where there are large no's of licensed, supervised brothels – but not in Delhi . . .

Bach rather alarmed us, saying that a punkah wallah . . . had installed himself in their cell, which stands in a corner like ours. What worries us is the possibility of having to take in some odoriferous untouchable as an unpaying guest for the summer months.

Wed 5 May

Up about 6.15 & got a shower with chattee water – disturbed 3 or 4 large grey rats swarming up the iron bars outside the latrine windows & playing hide & seek around the "jerries". A nice atmosphere in the office today, conducive to correspondence & even to buffoonery . . . killed at least a dozen flies. On duty again as office stooge but it didn't amount to much. . . . As I left the office at lunch time I was amazed to be stopped by C——— the new officer, who asked "How are you feeling now?" He must be taking me for someone else.

CPL. L.K. PARLOW
Manuscript Diary

Military abbreviations

C.W.O.   *Civilian Wireless Operator*
B.O.R.   *British Other Ranks*
C.S.M.   *Company Sergeant Major*
W.A.C.I.   *Women's Army Corps of India*
M.O.   *Medical Officer*
M.I.   *Medical Inspection*
E.T.   *Early Treatment*

One Sweltering Night

*Along the India-Burma border the impassable terrain kept the
main British and Japanese forces well apart between major
offensives. But in the coastal border area south of Cox's
Bazaar, small scale skirmishes were a regular feature of life –
encouraged not least by Churchill's call for the offensive spirit
to be maintained at all times. John Handley recalls one
successful night's work undertaken in this spirit. (1943)*

When the Japs were in Budhidaung and there was even talk that they
might try to infiltrate to Chittagong, I was Intelligence Officer with a
Brigade Headquarters at Cox's Bazaar, the little old-time port and
trading post of Arakan. There was no "front" then, but just a great
wide no-man's-land of mud and mangrove and tidal creeks and
islands. Save for the mosquitos and the sweaty heat, it might have
been a bit of Essex coast at home.

It was the malaria season and the European war was going full blast
so we had just to hang on for better days, shake down our drafts, get
some long service men away on leave, and keep our tails up with what
the Brigade Commander called "minor enterprises". So, every night,
our fighting patrols were out hunting the enemy in no-man's-land,
getting to grips whenever possible. And for every Jap brought in, alive
or dead, they scored one leave ticket.

We had a company of Scotties there, a battalion of Gurkhas, the
usual odds and ends and a few Royal Indian Navy to work our "fleet"
of native boats. . . .

One sweltering night an hour after dark, Maungdin, my Arakan
shikarri, brought in news. Standing up to his neck in water and hidden
by the mangrove bushes, he had, he said, watched a raiding party of
Japs cross Main Creek five miles down from our camp in native
"sampans" and set off inland towards his own village, the only place
worth looting hereabouts. . . .

I knew the spot exactly, having bathed and fished there with the
Gurkhas before the Jap got into these parts. At a turn of the creek

. . . a sandy spit juts out, rising above the mangrove swamp and forming a backwater and a little beach, ideal for the enemy's purpose except that it is on the exposed side of the spit. . . . No place that for him to load his boats and get away with prisoners and booty. But it might serve our turn.

A word to the B.M. and things started humming. In fifteen minutes a platoon moved off inshore to find and attack the raiders. . . . And a minute later we slipped our moorings and paddled silently down to Main Creek, looking like a very innocent native fishing boat.

The night was dark and the glimmer of light from the camp soon faded astern. We kept in mid-stream, two hundred yards from cither bank . . . At three or four hundred yards we might just be spotted as a dark shadow moving on the water. We dared not start the engine till we had flushed the Jap.

We had on board six Gurkhas with a havildar, picked swimmers all, stripped to their loin cloths and with kukris slung. In the bows, tucked in behind some bits of armour camouflaged with native fishing gear, were Tiny, the six foot subaltern commanding the patrol, and a couple of Scotties with their rifles cocked. The remaining eight of them were amidships with the Gurkhas, taking a turn at the paddles, while, aft, two R.I.N. ratings took the tiller and fondled the engine which they had sworn to start the moment it was called for. . . .

Our plan was one quick gamble. First we must locate the Jap and then go in bald headed, banking on speed and darkness to render his fire innocuous. But we had a card up our sleeves for him too.

The shikarri suddenly half rose and pointed forward eagerly, signing for absolute silence. There was the sand-spit: I could faintly see the line of it against the sky, perhaps half a mile ahead. We were charging down on it at five knots. Tiny signalled "Easy all," then raised his glasses. . . . The Gurkha havildar was with him, peering ahead. "Boats", he whispered; for Gurkhas can see in the dark. Tiny nodded and made a gesture like a left hook. The havildar grinned. They had it all fixed up together.

For an instant I had forgotten Maungdin. He suddenly let go a mighty sneeze. I leaped on him with a blanket and as I did so there came six spurts of fire from the ridge and then the crack of rifles and bullets humming wide and high.

"Get going", said Tiny, quietly, to the havildar, and watched him move aft. And then he yelled at the top of his voice "Engine", and "Helm hard aport."

The engine roared like a charging tank as we swung in towards the bank, and the Japs stopped firing for ten precious seconds. I think the engine shook 'em and they suspected some secret weapon. But our only secret now was the Gurkhas who had slipped silently into the water and shot away down stream like eels.

We charged the bank and beached in mud and mangrove at a tiny inlet a few hundred yards upstream from where the Japs were still firing. The Scotties tumbled out like a pack of hounds, Tiny with them, yelling orders. They vanished into the scrub, extended, started firing. By the row they made they might have been a company attacking. That was the idea: secrecy had, most literally, gone by the board. . . .

Drawing the cover off my luminous watch, I counted the minutes since the Gurkhas had gone overboard. Eight, eight and a half, nine. Had they got ashore? Where were they? I pictured them creeping up behind the enemy with kukris drawn.

At the tenth minute, to the tick, our firing stopped. I watched and listened intently. The flash and crack of the enemy rifles still came intermittently, strung out along the ridge, and behind them now the moon was rising. Suddenly, silhouetted against the sky, there hove up a thick squat figure with arms flung out like a charging bear. Something flashed blue and there came a long blood curdling scream . The blue steel swooped again and the scream stopped.

Then the Japs broke and ran squealing, all ways, more of them than had been firing. Some were cut down by the Gurkhas as they ran and some, crashing like wild pig through the mangrove, met the bayonets of the Scots who had pressed on after ceasing fire to be in at the kill. In ten swift bloody seconds it was over. And then the moon broke out and we could see.

The crew brought round the flagship to the bay where the enemy sampans were beached. We floated them, piled in the enemy dead, and made ready for towing. There were no prisoners. . . .

There was a bit of an argument next day about the score as some of the heads would not fit. But Brigade Headquarters were in generous mood and handed out leave tickets for the whole patrol.

JOHN HANDLEY
"A Minor Enterprise"
The Indian Annual 1946

Military abbreviations

B.M.   *Brigade Major*
R.I.N.   *Royal Indian Navy*

The Real Calcutta

Army sergeant Louis Hagen lived in India for over a year and sketched an observant portrait of Calcutta as it was then, just after the end of the War in the East. (1945/1946)

The European part of Calcutta occupies less than a tenth of the city. Here the English live, work and play. The buildings look European and so do the hotels, large shops, government and other offices. It *looks* European enough until you leave your car or taxi and begin to walk along the main streets. Chowringhee is Calcutta's Oxford Street, but for colour and excitement, the former makes the latter look like a wet Sunday afternoon. Here you don't have to walk into shops and ask for goods, anything and everything is sold on the buzzing street. You can buy parrots, diamonds, Bibles or pornographic literature, tiger skins, musical instruments, Leicas and monkey nuts, puppies and children's toys. Everything you want is there, but you don't have to ask for it; they pelt you with it. Crowds of Indians, from little toddlers to bearded old men accompany you wherever you go, offering their goods, cajolling, making prices and reducing them every ten yards. . . . And while you walk along, rickshaws, gharries and taxis follow you in case you feel tired . . . "Want to buy a pair of sandals or gloves?" "Carpets, pottery?" "Dirty pictures, proud college girls?" "Backsheesh, Sahib, no father, no mother." "Rajah Sahib!" "Shoe shine, Sahib!" "Parker fountain pens, Ronson lighters?" "Longines watches, gold cigarette cases, rubies, diamonds . . . ?" You can trust them to cheat you and make a sucker out of you. They will even sell you a cut price murder. The Goonas or thugs, whose job it is to do the dirty work, can fix you a bumping off for as little as twenty rupees. . . .

Around the doors of the big hotels and restaurants, the crowd of vendors and naked beggars is thickest. . . .

Most of the prosperous-looking white people one sees in these restaurants are quite unconscious of the teeming life outside in the street. It just doesn't interest them, nor does Calcutta, neither does

263

India. The real Calcutta, for them, does not exist at all; except when it is forced to their notice by the smell of filth wafting in through the windows of their cars. All these people are kept busy devising means of escape; escape from their empty, boring lives. . . . They have built up a completely artificial existence of their own and as far as they are concerned, this *is* life in Calcutta. Their hunting grounds are the country clubs, swimming clubs and night clubs, the bars and the racecourse. A great deal of gin and whisky are consumed and much time and ingenuity are expended running after the few white, or nearly white, women who are outnumbered by the men by about ten to one. The general idea is to get drunk pretty regularly, keep oneself occupied and, if possible, vaguely amused. But it really couldn't matter less anyway.

These people are not the pukkah sahib type, most of whom are terribly busy nowadays. They are a mixed and floating population. One might call them the South East Asia Café Society. Many of them are in the services, at H.Q. perhaps, or on long leave waiting about to be demobbed. Some of them are English business men with "all sorts

Grand Hotel, Calcutta

of interests," just what, one never really finds out. There are people on missions, engineers, representatives, French officers and civil servants connected with the trouble in French Indo China, Polish officers and civilians (homeless and wandering like the Jews are said to be), or civilians freed from internment in Malaya, vaguely trying to decide what to do. There are war correspondents with lots of time, and Americans with time, money and usually a girl. . . .

In the evening, they move into the fantastically expensive night clubs for more drinks, more talk and women, if they are lucky. The shortage of women is chronic, especially the kind one can take to the pukkah joints. If standards were high, there wouldn't be any women at all. They cost you a packet, for they drink plenty of whisky which is as scarce and black market as they are. The higher class clubs, apart from the big hotels, are mostly a poor imitation of Hollywood. On the whole they are pretty drab and their floor shows are third rate. But wherever you go, "The 300," the "British-American," the "Hawaiian" or the "Winter Garden," you will always meet the same people who will always be saying the same things. There is always talk about other joints in places all over the East; everyone seems to have been to the same places and done the same things. It doesn't matter if it is Singapore, Hongkong, Saigon, Kunming, Penang, Batavia or Shanghai; they can tell you where to get hooch, who lives where and who is doing what. They know all about their little world, wherever it happens to be. To sit and listen to them talking in their phoney-childish jargon, it is hard to realise that these people are in reality quite sane and normal, human beings. They are expatriates, suffering from the effects of a confined and unnatural life. This is what the East has done to them. There is rather too much reality in the East for their European taste, so they have run away from it altogether. . . .

If I were ever to be submitted to another of those free-association psychology tests or I.Q.s, which crop up at regular intervals in a soldier's career (I think I went through about six) and were given the word "Calcutta," my snap association would unquestionably be "Garbage," with "Stink" as a possible second choice. Under no circumstances would the words: "Second City of the Empire" occur to me in this context. . . .

If the noise one associates with Calcutta is that of hawking and spitting and the smell is that of garbage, the sight is certainly gharries. Those ramshackle contraptions that crawl about the streets throughout the day and night. A gharry can be anything, a Victoria, a phaeton, a growler, a landau, a barouche, a fiacre or something that looks like a Wild West stage coach. One thing they all look, is old. The whole turn-out looks old; the gharry, the driver and most of all the horse. It is inconceivable that the horses could ever have been young. . . .

When they are off duty, the gharries go to a part of the town called Entally. I have been there; it is typical Calcutta squalor and Busteeland. There are merely rows and rows of broken-down stables with leaking roofs and tumbled down walls, a smell to knock you down and thousands of flies. This is where men and beasts live, sleep and eat. The horses stand drooping and apathetic or lie motionless; they do not appear to be alive and they certainly have no will to live. Entally has been the home of the stable owners for well over a hundred years and for well over a hundred years it has been the scene of unbelievable suffering. I wondered with a sick feeling how much longer this would go on. The methods used on these horses to treat their ailments are appalling. Flesh is simply burned away with acid; and diseased bone is removed with a hammer and chisel. These animals are driven until they die on the roads, or are unable to get up in the morning. A C.S.P.C.A. (Calcutta Society for the Prevention of Cruelty to Animals) does exist, but its funds are so limited and its powers so leisurely applied that nothing much is ever done. If any of these horses were seen on a road in England, it would be instantly surrounded by an indignant crowd who would probably start by lynching the driver. Here, a gharry wallah may lose his licence for drunkenness or careless driving, but cruelty only carries a small fine. There is, of course, no reason why these men should regard pain, starvation and overwork as anything to make a fuss about when their own lives are very largely a combination of all three.

LOUIS HAGEN
Indian Route March (1946)

Back to Work

Mahomed Ali Jinnah, the Moslem leader, became convinced that when independence arrived Moslems would need to have their own separate state if they were to avoid Hindu domination. His call for Direct Action in support of this view led to serious disturbances. In Calcutta there was a weekend of communal rioting in August 1946 after which the official death toll, Hindu and Moslem together, was 4,700. As soon as the city was quiet again the British had to get it cleaned up. Major Livermore's diary tells what this was like.

. . . the stench was becoming unbearable and at about 9 p.m. that night we received orders that the main streets at least must be clear of bodies by the time the curfew lifted at 4 a.m. next morning. Stench masks and gas capes would be sent to aid us in lifting the decomposing corpses; the location of Muslim burial grounds and Hindu burning ghats would reach us as soon as possible; otherwise, it was just improvise as far as we could see. I well remember the "awful 'ush" that fell upon the "O" Group as the C.O. passed on the order. We looked at each other in silence for a moment, then realising that the sooner we started the better, everyone began to talk at once. . . . The prospect of spending the night picking up the ghastly objects which we had seen enough of during the day was not pleasant and the assembly were looking a bit wry until a plaintive voice from somewhere in the room chirped up with, "How the hell do I tell a Muslim from a Hindu when they've all been dead three days?" Admittedly the subject was not in the least humorous but that remark, shrewd though it was, caused a burst of laughter and we were back on form again. It was at this moment that our senior police liaison officer, who up to now had ruminated silently in a corner, began to prove his worth. The Corporation Engineer, he said, lived in the district and would provide transport in the shape of refuse lorries to reinforce the few trucks we could spare. There was also a caste of Hindu called Doms, who would handle dead bodies. Eight of these were attached to the police station in which we sat and more could be obtained from the Carmichael

267

Hospital. This would ease the task considerably, and, we hoped, get it done sooner. . . .

At last we were started. With one other officer, a British police sergeant and four Doms, I drove my truck to our first place. All went well for the first fifteen minutes; the sweepers got three bodies completely in the truck then stopped work and chattered wildly. I could not understand them and at last discovered through the police sergeant that they thought the smell too bad to work in and would not continue unless they were provided with stench masks like the military. I thought this a fair request and issued them with one each. They tied them round their heads with the pad on their foreheads and quite happily went back to work. In spite of the fact that they could see our pads over mouth and nostrils they continued in this way for the next two days. Their faith must have been tremendous!

Luckily we found that the sweepers could distinguish between Hindu and Muslim bodies. I was loading Muslims and in the early hours of the morning made my way to a nominated cemetery on the eastern outskirts of the city. Arrived at the gate I was told that a truck had stuck between two trees on the track inside (it was half a mile from the gate to the actual graves, which had been bulldozed in the waterlogged ground), and that there were already many vehicles queued up and unable to turn about. I was advised to wait outside. It needed no persuasion as the noisome atmosphere was overpowering even at that distance. Upon enquiring I found that there were, in open graves and trucks, about seven hundred bodies in the vicinity of the cemetery. I draw a veil over the next hour or so: suffice to say that at 3.30 a.m. we had had enough, so leaving one officer to look after the convoy until relief arrived, we returned to continue the clearing of the streets. The other Company areas were almost clear of bodies but it took two more days and nights to finish my own area – a total of five hundred and seven corpses in the one Company sector, most of which came from a locality less than four hundred yards square. Apart from the dead the streets were in a frightful condition. Refuse was piled high and already there was a threat of a cholera epidemic. The environments of my Company H.Q. were particularly bad, so a talk was given to several of the local leading citizens along with a demonstration by the troops in one of the lanes. As part of the demonstration we used lime. This appeared to be a new idea for the locals, because after sweeping and shovelling with unabated vigour until the roads were clear, they descended upon my C.Q.M.S. with containers of all shapes, sizes and descriptions demanding lime, which they used liberally on the surrounding district, including the animals. This relieved us of our entire stock for the time being, but the difference in the streets and atmosphere was well worth it. This was not, however, the end of the matter for, bright and early the next morning, another and larger queue was fighting for places to get more lime. It transpired that they thought that daily treatment was the order of the day; they took much convincing that they were perhaps a little over-enthusiastic.

Another big task in this third week of August was to get the shops open and working; particularly the food shops and markets. Many were on the verge of collapse through lack of food, so we toured the area with local officials and prominent citizens trying to restore the morale and confidence of both the shopkeepers and the public. It was unfortunate that one of the first men who responded to our appeal was shot by hooligans as he went to open his store. This meant redoubling our efforts. Strangely enough the next person to be almost shot was myself, and that by troops into the bargain. Early one morning I was outside the Shambazar fruit and vegetable market arguing with the superintendent and some of the stall-holders, trying to persuade them to resume trade as soon as possible. After a few minutes there quite a crowd foregathered. The Indian participants as Indians will, became excited in the argument and there was a great deal of arm waving, general shouting and gesticulating, which must have looked like the makings of a frenzied mob to the patrol leader. I was engrossed, and it was a police officer with me who pointed out a military patrol down the Cornwallis Road. I noticed that one of the troops was waving his hands and shouting something, but beyond waving back to reassure him I took no notice, not realising that I was hidden by the crowd. He must have thought that his first impressions were correct and as the crowd made no attempt to disperse he took action. The next thing I realised, very forcibly, was the crack and thump of a rifle bullet. The thump sent splinters flying from the wall a few feet away. The Indians disappeared as if by magic and disclosed me in a most undignified attitude on the pavement. My Indian friends had a good laugh at my expense, but it was some time before my sense of humour got the better of my indignation.

MAJOR L.A. LIVERMORE
Extracts from his Diary quoted in
While Memory Serves (1950)
by Lieut-General Sir Francis Tuker

The Midnight Hour

The moment of Independence arrived at last on the night of 14th August 1947, skilfully engineered by the Viceroy, Lord Louis Mountbatten. Once the transfer of power was formally completed at midnight, Jawaharlal Nehru and Dr Rajendra Prasad came to see Mountbatten with an invitation. Alan Campbell-Johnson, Mountbatten's Press Attaché, was a witness of this informal but moving occasion.

As midnight struck Mountbatten was sitting quietly at his desk. I have known him in most moods; to-night there was an air about him of serenity, almost detachment. The scale of his personal achievement was too great for elation, rather his sense of history and the fitness of things at this dramatic moment, when the old and the new order were reconciled in himself, called forth composure.

Quite deliberately he took off his reading-glasses, turned the keys on his dispatch boxes and summoned me to help tidy the room and stow away these outward and visible signs of Viceregal activity. Although there was a whole army of servants outside, it never occurred to either of us to call them. Only when all the papers had been put away and his desk cleared were they called in to move some of the furniture and provide room for members of the Press who had been invited to witness the event.

Correspondents who had been at the solemn ceremony at the Legislative Assembly began to dribble in. They reported that immense crowds had gathered on the route and that we could expect Prasad and Nehru to be somewhat delayed. The proceedings in the Assembly had apparently been most impressive. With moving eloquence Nehru had said, "Long years ago we made a tryst with destiny, and now the time comes when we shall redeem our pledge, not wholly or in full measure, but substantially. At the stroke of the midnight hour, when the world sleeps, India will awake to life and freedom."

Weary but happy, having escaped from the greetings of tremendous

270

throngs, Prasad and Nehru finally arrived. In the little scene that ensued, friendship completely burst the bounds of formality. The Press correspondents flanked the room, photographers stood on the circular table. Although Nehru had given approval that the Press should be there, I think he must have forgotten that he had done so. Whether it was the presence of an audience, or just the normal reaction after the great scenes in the Assembly, neither of them seemed to know quite what to do.

Finally Mountbatten and Prasad stood facing each other, with Nehru half sitting on Mountbatten's desk between them. Prasad began murmuring a formal invitation. However, he forgot his lines, and Nehru played the role of benign prompter. Between them they explained that the Constituent Assembly had just taken over and had endorsed the request of the leaders that Mountbatten should become the first Governor-General. To this message he smilingly replied, "I am proud of the honour, and I will do my best to carry out your advice in a constitutional manner."

Thereupon Nehru, handing over a large and carefully addressed envelope, said in ceremonious terms, "May I submit to you the portfolios of the new Cabinet?" The ceremony was all over in less than ten minutes, but there was more humanity and hope in this unrehearsed encounter than in most of our Te Deums and victory parades.

I was once more alone with Mountbatten. Just to satisfy his curiosity and remind himself of the exact names of the Government to which he had previously agreed and which he would be swearing-in in a few hours' time, he opened the large envelope, but he was not to see his Prime Minister's submission that night, for by sublime oversight Nehru's envelope was empty.

ALAN CAMPBELL-JOHNSON
Mission with Mountbatten (1951)

GLOSSARY

*These definitions of Anglo-Indian usage have been taken
from contemporary dictionaries published in the 1880s; the
spelling of the headwords is as shown in those dictionaries
and not as given by individual authors.*

Afridi – a large Pathan tribe . . . The Afridis are the best armed and
the most warlike of all the border tribes.

Amir – a commander, chief, or lord . . . It is the title affected by many
Musulman sovereigns of various calibres, as the Amir of Kabul,
the Amir of Bokhara, &c.

Anglo-Indian – a term applied to an Englishman residing in India, or
anything pertaining to the English in India. [From about the
turn of the century 'Anglo-Indian' gradually came to be used to
mean 'Eurasian'.]

Anna – the sixteenth part of a rupee, nominally equivalent to three
half-pence.

Ashram – hermitage; place of religious retreat.

Ayah – a native lady's-maid or nurse-maid.

Ba – *lit.* 'mother'.

Baboo (Babu) – properly a term of respect attached to a name, like
Master or *Mr.*, . . . among Anglo-Indians it is often used with a
slight savour of disparagement . . . the word has come to signify
'a native clerk who writes English'.

Banchoot, Beteechoot – terms of abuse, which we should hesitate to
print if their odious meaning were not obscure 'to the general'.
If it were known to the Englishmen who sometimes use the
words, we believe there are few who would not shrink from such
brutality.

Banyan (Bunya) – a Hindu trader.

Bapu – *lit.* 'father'.

Bazaar – a permanent market or street of shops.

Bearer – a domestic servant who has charge of his master's clothes,
household furniture, and (often) of his ready money.

Bela – a block of forest.

Bengal – the region of the Ganges Delta and the districts immediately above it.

Betel-nut – the leaf of the *sirih* or betelpepper smeared with chunam, or lime, and tobacco, and the nut of the areca palm, chewed together.

Bheesty – the universal word in the Anglo-Indian households of N. India for the domestic . . . who supplies the family with water, carrying it in a mussuck or goatskin, slung on his back.

Bhoot – the common term for the multitudinous ghosts and demons of various kinds by whom the Indian peasant is so constantly beset.

Brahma – the supreme being, the first cause of all things.

Brahman (Brahmin) – the name of the first of the four castes into which . . . Hindus were originally divided . . . Besides acting as priests to almost every caste of Hindus, the Brahmans now fill a large part of every profession requiring education.

Brandypawnee – brandy and water.

British India, British Territory – these names are applied in India to that part of the country which is not under the jurisdiction of any native chief, but is directly administered by British officials. It contains about three-quarters of the area and four-fifths of the population of the whole country.

Bucksheesh (Backshish) – we don't seem to have in England any exact equivalent for the word . . . *tip* is accurate, but is slang; gratuity is official or dictionary English.

Buggy – in India this is a (two-wheeled) gig with a hood.

Bund – any artificial embankment, a dam, dyke or causeway.

Bundobust – arrangement, settlement . . . The word is often used by Anglo-Indians to express the planning, preparation or arrangement of any undertaking great or small.

Bungalow – the most usual class of house occupied by Europeans in the interior of India; being on one story, and covered by a pyramidal roof, which in the normal bungalow is of thatch.

Bungalow, Dawk – a resthouse for the accommodation of travellers, formerly maintained (and still to a reduced extent) by the paternal care of the Government of India.

Bustee – an inhabited quarter, a village. . . . The word is applied in Calcutta to the separate groups of huts in the humbler native quarters, the sanitary state of which has often been held up to reprobation.

Cantonment – it is applied to military stations in India, built usually on a plan which is originally that of a standing camp or 'cantonment'.

Caravan seray – a building for the accommodation of travellers with their pack animals; consisting of an enclosed yard with chambers round it.

Caste – the various classes into which Hindus are by birth divided . . . A Hindu can never change his caste, but he may, for offending against its rules, be excommunicated by his caste-fellows, and become an outcaste.

Chapati – a thin flat cake; especially one of flour and water, without leaven, baked on a griddle.

Charpoy – a bedstead consisting of a plain frame of wood set on four short legs; broad tapes are folded along and across the frame to form the bed.

Chatty – an earthen pot, spheroidal in shape.

Cheechee – a disparaging term applied to half-castes . . . and also to their manner of speech.

Chi – short for chiranjivi ('of long life'); a mode of affectionate address from an elder to a junior.

Chik – a hanging screen or curtain made of narrow thin strips of bamboo . . . The chik serves to moderate the glare of the sun and exclude the view from outside.

Chokidar – a watchman.

Chota – little, small. The word is often used in English with an Indian noun; as chota haziri, a light early breakfast; chota saheb, the younger gentleman.

Chudder – a sheet, or square piece of cloth of any kind; the ample sheet commonly worn as a mantle by women in N. India.

Chuprassy – the bearer of a *chapras*, i.e. a badge-plate inscribed with the name of the office to which the bearer is attached. . . . an office-messenger.

Cinghalese – *see* Singalese.

Collector – the chief administrative official of an Indian . . . District.

Compound – the ground enclosed round about a house and pertaining to it.

Cooly – a hired labourer, or burden-carrier.

Curry – a dish made originally of sour milk, with salt, pepper, turmeric, and other spices, and eaten with rice or pulse; as now prepared for Anglo-Indians, meat or vegetables are used instead of the sour milk.

Cuscuss – the roots of a grass . . . which abounds in the drier parts of

India . . . used in India during the hot dry winds to make screens, which are kept constantly wet in the window openings and the fragrant evaporation from which greatly cools the house (*see* Tatty).

Dacoit – a robber belonging to an armed gang.

Dandy – a kind of vehicle used in the Himalaya, consisting of a strong cloth slung like a hammock to a bamboo staff, and carried by two (or more) men.

Dawk – transport by relays of men and horses, and thence 'the mail' or letter-post, as well as any arrangement for travelling, or for transmitting articles by such relays (*see* Bungalow, Dawk).

Deccan – the south of India, the peninsula south of the Vindhya range.

Dhall – a kind of pulse much used in India, both by natives as a kind of porridge, and by Europeans as an ingredient in kedgeree, or to mix with rice as a breakfast dish.

Dhoby (Dobie) – a washerman.

Dhooly (Doolie) – a covered litter. It consists of a cot *or frame*, suspended by the four corners from a bamboo pole, and is carried by two or four men.

Dhoty – the loin cloth worn by all the respectable Hindu castes of Upper India, wrapt round the body, the end being then passed between the legs and tucked in at the waist, so that a festoon of calico hangs down to either knee.

Dirzee – a tailor.

Dom – the name of a low caste, apparently one of the aboriginal races. . . . in some places [they] perform the lowest offices, as carrying dead bodies and skeletons.

Doob – a very nutritious creeping grass spread very generally in India. . . . it is eagerly sought for horses by their 'grass-cutters'.

Doray (Durai) – this is a South Indian equivalent of Sahib.

Doraisanny – 'Lady' or 'Madam'.

Durbar – a Court or Levee. Also the Executive Government of a Native State.

Ekka – a small light two-wheeled carriage made chiefly of bamboo; it is drawn by a single horse or pony, the shafts meeting on the animal's back; it has no seat in the European sense, and is used only by natives.

Eurasian – a modern name for persons of mixt European and Indian blood, devised as being more euphemistic than Half-caste and more precise than East-Indian.

Fakeer – properly an indigent person, but specially 'one poor in the sight of God,' applied to a Mahommedan religious mendicant, and then, loosely and inaccurately, to Hindu devotees and naked ascetics.

Firinghee – this term for a European is very old in Asia, but when now employed by natives in India is either applied (especially in the South) specifically to the Indian-born Portuguese, or, when used more generally for 'Europeans', implies something of hostility or disparagement.

Gharry – a cart or carriage. The word is used by Anglo-Indians, at least on the Bengal side, in both senses.

Ghat (Ghaut) – a landing place, steps on the bank of a river for bathing on . . . Also a mountain pass; or mountains themselves, especially the ranges of southern India known as the Western and Eastern Ghats.

Gingelly – the common trade name for the seed and oil of *Sesamum indicum*, v. *orientale*.

Goanese – a resident of Goa, but used especially to designate the community, originally the offspring of Portuguese fathers and Indian mothers . . . They are much employed as domestic servants, and also as clerks.

Goorka (Gurkha) – the name of the race now dominant in Nepal . . . They are probably the best soldiers of modern India.

Gorawallah – a groom or horsekeeper; used at Bombay. On the Bengal side *syce* is always used.

Gram – that kind of vetch which is the most general . . . food of horses all over India.

Gram-fed – properly the distinctive description of mutton and beef fattened upon gram, which used to be the pride of Bengal. But applied figuratively to any 'pampered creature'.

Guicowar – the title of the Mahratta kings . . . The word means 'Cowherd'.

Guru – a religious teacher, a spiritual guide.

Gyaul – a large animal of the ox tribe, found wild in various forest tracts to the east of India.

Gymkhana – a gymkhana in western India is a club for all kinds of sports . . . in northern India the name is given rather to a particular celebration of sports than to a permanent club.

Hakim – a sage, a physician.

Harijan – 'people of God'; the name coined by Gandhi for the Untouchables.

Havildar – an officer in native regiments corresponding to a sergeant.

Hindee – by Europeans it is most commonly used for those dialects of Hindustani speech which . . . are spoken by the rural population of the N.W.Provinces and its outskirts.

Hindoo – a person of Indian religion and race. This is a term derived from the use of the Mahommedan conquerors.

Hooly (Holi) – the spring festival, held at the approach of the vernal equinox, during the 10 days preceding the full moon . . . It is a sort of carnival . . . Passers-by are chaffed, and pelted with red powder, or drenched with yellow liquids from squirts. Songs, mostly obscene, are sung in praise of Krishna.

Hooka – the Indian pipe for smoking through water, the elaborated hubble-bubble. That which is smoked in the *hooka* is a curious compound of tobacco, spice, molasses, fruit, &c.

Howdah – a great chair or framed seat carried by an elephant.

Jain – the non-Brahmanical sect so called; believed to represent the earliest heretics of Buddhism, at present chiefly to be found in the Bombay Presidency.

Jemadar – technically, in the Indian army, it is the title of the second rank of native officer in a company of sepoys. . . . And in larger domestic establishments there is often a *jemadar*, who is over the servants generally, or over the stables, camp service and orderlies.

Jinricksha (Rickshaw) – a small gig invented about 1872 and constructed to carry one or more persons, drawn by a coolie in shafts and sometimes pushed by another from behind.

Jompon – a kind of sedan, or portable chair used chiefly by the ladies at the Hill Sanitaria of Upper India. It is carried by two pairs of men.

Jungle – the native word means in strictness only waste, uncultivated ground . . . the Anglo-Indian application is to forest, or other wild growth.

Karbari (Karbhari) – a minister, an agent; particularly a native ruler's ministers.

Kedgeree, Kitchery – a mess of rice, cooked with butter and *dal*, and flavoured with a little spice, shred onion, and the like; a common dish all over India, and often served at Anglo-Indian breakfast tables.

Khakee – dusty or dust-coloured . . . applied to a light drab or chocolat-coloured cloth. This was the colour of the uniform worn by some of the Punjab regiments at the siege of Delhi, and became very popular in the army generally during the campaigns of 1857-58.

Khalasi – a tent-pitcher.

Khansama – in Anglo-Indian households in the Bengal Presidency, this is the title of the chief table servant and provider, now always a Mahommedan.

Khudd – this is a term chiefly employed in the Himalaya, *Khadd*, meaning a precipitous hill-side, also a deep valley. . . . The word is in constant Anglo-Indian colloquial use at Simla and other Himalayan stations.

Kitmutgar – the Anglo-Indian use is peculiar to the Bengal Presidency, where the word is habitually applied to a Mussulman servant, whose duties are connected with serving meals and waiting at table.

Koran – the sacred book of the Muhammadans, and considered by them to be the fountain-head of all science, knowledge, and law.

Krishna – the name Vishnu took in his eighth or full incarnation. . . . Krishna is the most popular of the Hindu gods.

Kus-kus – *see* Cuscuss.

Lakh – one hundred thousand, and especially in the Anglo-Indian colloquial 100,000 Rupees, in the days of better exchange the equivalent of £10,000.

Lingam – the phallus or emblematic representation of Siwa in his character as the reproductive power . . . The symbol, made of stone and of double form to represent the blending of the male and female principles in creation, is set up in temples dedicated to Siwa.

Loot – plunder. It has . . . long been a familiar item in the Anglo-Indian colloquial. But between the Chinese War of 1841, the Crimean War (1854-5), and the Indian Mutiny (1857-8), it gradually found acceptance in England also, and is now a recognised constituent of the English *Slang Dictionary*.

Lota – the small spheroidal brass pot which Hindus use for drinking, and sometimes for cooking.

Lushai – the name of a powerful and independent people touching upon the borders of the Chittagong hill tracts.

Mahar – the name of the low caste of the Deccan.

Maharaja – a supreme king; applied in courtesy to every raja, or to any person of high rank or deemed holy.

Mahatma – Great Soul.

Mahout – an elephant driver. The mahout sits on the neck of the elephant; he bids it move forward by applying the pointed end of his goad, stops it by the butt end, and turns it by pressing his leg on the neck.

Mahratta – the name of a famous Hindu race.

Maidan – a plain, a level tract; any large open space, especially one covered with grass and maintained as a place for recreation or for the parade of troops.

Marwarree – properly a man of Marwar, or Jodhpur country in Rajputana, is used in many parts of India as synonymous with Banyan (q.v.)

Mate (Maty) – an assistant under a head servant . . . The word is in use almost all over India. . . . in Madras the *maty* is an under-servant, whose business it is to clean crockery, knives, &c., to attend to lamps, and so forth.

Memsahib – the appellation among Indian servants of an English married lady.

Mofussil – the country stations and districts, as contra-distinguished from 'the Presidency' . . . Thus if, in Calcutta, one talks of the Mofussil, he means anywhere in Bengal out of Calcutta.

Mohur – the official name of the chief gold coin of British India [equivalent to 15 or 16 silver rupees depending on location].

Monsoon – a division of the year according to the prevailing wind; but applied more particularly to the period of the south-west wind which blows from June to September, and brings the heavy rains.

Moonshee – it is commonly applied by Europeans specifically to a native teacher of languages.

Muhammadan – a follower of Muhammad, a Musalman.

Murghi – a fowl, a hen.

Musalman (Mussulman, Muslim) – *see* Muhammadan.

Mussuck – the leathern water-bag, consisting of the entire skin of a large goat, stript of the hair and dressed, which is carried by a *bhishti* (*see* Bheesty).

Must – it is applied . . . to male animals, such as elephants and camels, in a state of periodical excitement.

Native State – politically India is divided into two parts, commonly known as British territory and the native states. . . . The native states are sometimes called feudatory – a convenient term to express their vague relation to the British crown.

Paddy – rice in the husk, but the word is also . . . applied to growing rice.

Pagoda – the European designation of a Hindu temple in the south of India.

Pakka (Pukka) – a Hindi word meaning (1) ripe, cooked, and (2) genuine, proper. . . . It is generally understood in the sense of 'real'.

Palankeen (Palanquin) – a box-litter for travelling in, with a pole projecting before and behind, which is borne on the shoulders of 4 or 6 men.

Panjab – the country of the five rivers, the Jhelam, Chenab, Ravi, Bias, and Satluj. It is now one of the eight provinces of British India.

Pariah-dog – the common ownerless yellow dog, that frequents all inhabited places in the East, is universally so called by Europeans.

Parsee – this name, which distinguishes the descendants of . . . emigrants of the old Persian stock . . . is only the old form of the word for a Persian.

Pathan – a name commonly applied to Afghans, and especially to people in India of Afghan descent.

Peer – a Mahommedan Saint or *Beatus*. But the word is used elliptically for the tombs of such personages.

Peg – a popular name in English for a glass of spirit and soda-water.

Pice – a copper coin of the value of three pies or the quarter of an anna. . . . Pice is sometimes used as a name for money generally.

Pie – a copper coin, the twelfth part of an anna, or about the value of half a farthing.

Pilau (Pilow, Pilaf) – a dish, in origin purely Mahommedan, consisting of meat, or fowl, boiled along with rice and spices.

Polo – the game of hockey on horseback, introduced of late years into England, under this name, which comes from Balti; *polo* being properly in the language of that region the ball used in the game.

Puggry (Puggerie) – the term being often used in colloquial for a scarf of cotton or silk wound round the hat in turban-form, to protect the head from the sun.

Pukka – *see* Pakka.

Punkah – a) in its original sense a portable fan; b) but the specific application in Anglo-Indian colloquial is to the large fixed and swinging fan, formed of cloth stretched on a rectangular frame, and suspended from the ceiling, which is used to agitate the air in hot weather.

Purdah – a curtain screening women from the sight of men.

Purdesee – 'one from a foreign country'. In the Bombay army the term is universally applied to a sepoy from N. India.

Puttee – a piece or strip of cloth . . . round the lower part of the leg used in lieu of a gaiter, originally introduced from the Himalaya, and now commonly used by sportsmen and soldiers.

Raja – a king, a prince; a common title for any Hindu ruler, and bestowed sometimes on private persons of high rank.

Rampoor Chudder – when made with figured ends is probably the best representation of the old shawl . . . from 6 to 8 feet long, by about half that breadth (*see* Chudder).

Ram Ram – the commonest salutation between two Hindus meeting on the road; an invocation of the divinity [i.e. Rama, the seventh incarnation of Vishnu].

Rickshaw – *see* Jinricksha.

Rupee – a silver coin, the unit of the standard of value in India. . . . The rupee is divided for purposes of account into annas and pies, twelve pies making one anna and sixteen annas one rupee.

Sadhu – one who is perfect, a saint, a sage . . . It is commonly used of all Hindu religious mendicants.

Sahib – the title by which, all over India, European gentlemen, and it may be said Europeans generally, are addressed, and spoken of, when no disrespect is intended, by natives.

Salam – peace; the common word of salutation among Musalmans, and now in general use by all classes of persons; uttering the exclamation salam, bowing and raising the right hand to the forehead.

Sanskrit – the sacred language of the Hindus, so called as being perfectly constructed, polished, and refined.

Sari – a Hindu woman's principal garment. It is a long piece of silk or cotton cloth which is wrapped round the middle of the body with one end falling nearly to the feet and the other thrown over the head.

Sarkar – the government, the supreme authority in the state.

Sepoy – in Anglo-Indian use a native soldier, disciplined and dressed in the European style.

Shameeana – an awning or flat tent-roof . . . sometimes pitched like a porch before a large tent.

Shikar – sport (in the sense of shooting and hunting); game.

Shikaree – a sportsman. The word is used . . .

    a. As applied to a native expert, who either brings in game on his own account, or accompanies European sportsmen as guide and aid.

    b. As applied to the European sportsman himself.

Sikh – the distinctive name of the disciples of Namak Shah who in the 16th century established that sect, which eventually rose to warlike predominance in the Punjab.

Singalese (Cinghalese) – native of Ceylon.

Siva (Siwa) – the third person of the Hindu triad [with Brahma and Vishnu] . . . He has several distinct characters. In the first place . . . he is the destroying and dissolving power of nature . . . Secondly . . . he is the eternally blessed one or the causer of blessings, the eternal reproductive power of nature.

Sodhi – the name of the subdivision of the Khatri caste to which belonged Ram Das, the fourth guru of the Sikhs, in whose family succession to the office of guru became hereditary.

Sola Topee – *see* Topee, Sola.

Soor – a pig; a vulgar term of abuse.

Station – a word of constant recurrence in Anglo-Indian colloquial. It is the usual designation of the place where the English officials of a district, or the officers of a garrison (not in a fortress) reside. Also the aggregate society of such a place.

Sudra – the name of the last of the four classes into which . . . Hindus were originally divided. The Sudra is described as the feet of the creator, and his office was to serve the three others.

Syce – a groom.

Tamasha – a spectacle, a show, an entertainment; any occurrence that attracts and amuses spectators.

Tattoo (and abbreviated, **Tat**) – a native-bred pony.

Tatty – a screen or mat made of the roots of fragrant grass (*see* cuscuss) with which door or window openings are filled up in the season of hot winds.

Ticca – this is applied to any person or thing engaged by the job, or on contract. Thus a *ticca garry* is a hired carriage.

Tiffin – a light repast of fruit, etc., eaten at midday; but the word is used in English as equivalent to luncheon.

Tonga – a two-wheeled, four-seated, low carriage of strong construction for use in country where there are no made roads; it is drawn by a pair of ponies abreast, one in each of the ruts made by the wheels of country carts.

Tope – a clump or cluster of trees.

Topee, Sola – a pith helmet, worn as a precaution against sunstroke. From the Hindi *shola*, a pithy reed, and *topee* a hat. Occasionally wrongly written *solar*, because supposed to have some connexion with the sun.

Trichies – the familiar name of the cheroots made at Trichinopoly; long and rudely made, with a straw inserted at the end for the mouth. They are (or were) cheap and coarse, but much liked by those used to them.

Tulwah – 'a sabre' . . . a general term applied to shorter or more or less curved side-arms.

Tussah (Tusser) – a kind of inferior silk.

Urdu – the Hindustani language as spoken . . . by the Muhammadans of India generally.

Vakeel – an attorney.

Verandah – the gallery or terrace . . . which runs (wholly or partially) round an Indian house, both to protect it from the sun and to serve as a cooler resort than the house proper when the sun is down.

Vishnu – the second person of the Hindu triad [with Brahma and Siva] – the preserver.

Wala – this is a word of very common use in the vernaculars of India; it may be affixed to almost any noun or verb, and the word so formed then denotes a person connected . . . with the thing expressed by the first word; thus *gari-wala* means cart-man . . . Wala is often spelt *wallah* in English.

Yataghan – a sword without guard and often with a double-curved blade.

Zebu – this whimsical name, applied in zoological books . . . to the humped domestic ox (or Brahminy bull) of India, was taken by Buffon [French naturalist, d.1788] from the exhibitors of such a beast at a French fair, who perhaps invented the word.

Zenana – the apartments of a house in which the women of the family are secluded. This Mahommedan custom has been largely adopted by the Hindus of Bengal and the Mahrattas.

GEORGE CLIFFORD WHITWORTH
An Anglo-Indian Dictionary (1885)

COL. HENRY YULE and A.C. BURNELL
Hobson-Jobson (1886)

BACKGROUND EVENTS

1857 Outbreak of the Sepoy Mutiny (1857-58)
      300 miles of railway are open in India
1858 Government of India transferred from East India Company to
      British Crown
      Lord Canning becomes first Viceroy (1858-62)
1859 The "White Mutiny" of European troops transferred from
      Company to Crown service
      The "Blue Mutiny" (1859-60) of coolies against conditions on
      the indigo plantations
1861 Severe famine in North-West Provinces
      American Civil War (1861–65) boosts exports of cotton from
      Bombay: boom (1863-66) leads to over-speculation
      Order of the Star of India instituted
1864 Great cyclone strikes Calcutta (4th & 5th October)
      Simla becomes the regular summer capital of India
1865 Start of severe famine in Orissa (1865-67)
      Telegraph established between India and London
1867 Straits Settlements no longer administered from Calcutta
1868 Regular weekly postal service started India/Britain
1869 Birth of Mahatma Gandhi
      Opening of the Suez Canal
      5,000 miles of railway are now open in India
      India exports 10 million pounds of tea to Britain (China sends
      Britain 100 million pounds)
      Lord Mayo becomes Viceroy (1869-72)
      Visit of the Duke of Edinburgh (1869-70)
1870 Calcutta and Bombay linked by rail (via Allahabad)
      Value of the rupee approximately two shillings
1872 Lord Mayo assassinated

Results of first census show a total population of 206 million

1873 Famine affects Bihar (1873-74)
Parcel post service established between India and Britain
Value of the rupee begins a twenty year decline

1874 Calcutta-Howrah bridge link completed
The East India Company formally dissolved
Start of rapid expansion of Bengal Jute industry (1874-80)

1875 Visit of the Prince of Wales (1875-76)
Start of rapid expansion of Bombay cotton industry (1875-77)

1876 Persistent famine in southern India (1876-78): 5 million die
Queen Victoria proclaimed Empress of India

1877 Delhi Durbar held to celebrate India's new Empress

1879 Jinrickshas first introduced into Simla

1880 Improved weekly mail service London-Bombay has transit time of 17½ days

1881 The first Factory Act in India

1882 Post Office Savings Banks are opened throughout India

1883 Robert Koch identifies the cause of cholera
Quetta formally annexed by Britain

1885 Foundation of the Indian National Congress
Foundation of the Countess of Dufferin Fund to provide medical aid to Indian women
Lord Roberts becomes Commander-in-Chief India (until 1893)
Louis Pasteur develops an effective vaccine against rabies
Collapse of the Indian coffee industry due to pests

1886 Hindu-Muslim riots in Delhi
The Indian and Colonial Exhibition held in London

1887 Golden Jubilee celebrations for the Queen–Empress
Tata's Empress Cotton Mill is opened at Nagpur

1888 Publication of Rudyard Kipling's "Plain Tales from the Hills"

1889 Visit of the Duke of Clarence (1889–90)

1890 Visit of Russian Tsarevich (later Emperor Nicholas II)

1891 17,500 miles of railway are now open in India

1893 Value of the rupee falls to low point of one shilling and a penny
Queen Victoria opens the Imperial Institute in London
Hindu-Muslim riots in Bombay

1895 Military campaign to relieve the British force in Chitral

1896 Plague breaks out at Bombay (1896–1900)
Widespread famine affects 70 million people (1896–97): ¾ million die

1897 The Great Shillong Earthquake (Assam)

Ronald Ross identifies the cause of malaria ("junglefever")
Punitive expeditions mounted against rebel tribes on the
North-West frontier
Indigo industry declines as new chemical dyes compete

1898   Plague spreads to Calcutta

1899   Introduction of the Imperial Penny Postage scheme

1900   25,000 miles of railway are now open in India
India exports 134 million pounds of tea to Britain (China sends
Britain only 24 million pounds)

1901   Death of Queen Victoria
Census shows a total population of 294 million

1902   Lord Kitchener becomes Commander-in-Chief India (until
1909)

1903   Delhi Durbar held to celebrate coronation of King-Emperor
Edward VII
The railway is extended to Simla
Plague widespread in India

1905   The Great Dharmsala Earthquake – 100 miles from Simla
Visit of the new Prince of Wales (1905-06)
Lord Minto becomes Viceroy (1905–10)
Partition of Bengal leads to Hindu unrest

1906   Foundation of the Muslim League
State visit of the Amir of Afghanistan (1906–07)

1907   Attempt on the life of the Lieutenant-Governor of Bengal
Tata Iron and Steel Company founded in Bihar
Rudyard Kipling wins Nobel Prize for Literature

1910   Lord Hardinge becomes Viceroy (1910–16)
Death of King Edward VII

1911   Coronation Durbar held at Delhi by King-Emperor George V
Transfer of the capital from Calcutta to Delhi announced
Partition of Bengal revoked

1912   Attempted assassination of the Viceroy at Delhi

1913   Rabindranath Tagore wins Nobel Prize for Literature
3,000 motor cars imported into India this year

1914   Outbreak of the Great War in Europe (1914–18): Indian troops
serve in France
Mahatma Gandhi returns from South Africa
35,000 miles of railway are now open in India

1915   Home Rule League formed

1917   Britain announces policy to increase Indian self-determination

1918   Influenza epidemic kills an estimated 6 million people in India

1919 Amritsar massacre: at least 379 killed and 1,500 wounded
India becomes a member of the new League of Nations
1920 Beginning of the Non-Cooperation Movement
1921 Visit of the Prince of Wales
Census shows a total population of 319 million
1922 Mahatma Gandhi jailed for sedition (1922–24)
1924 Publication of E.M. Forster's "A Passage to India"
1926 Devaluation of the rupee
1929 Start of the Great Depression (1929-33)
First Air-Mail service from Britain (to Karachi)
1930 Indian scientist Sir C.V. Raman wins Nobel Prize for Physics
Mahatma Gandhi leads the Salt March
Civil Disobedience movement starts
Airship R101 crashes on inaugural flight to India
1931 100,000 Indian patriots are imprisoned
Inauguration of New Delhi
Gandhi visits Britain for talks with the Government and King
1932 Second Civil Disobedience movement: Gandhi again jailed
1935 Severe earthquake destroys Quetta: well over 20,000 killed
1936 Death of King George V
Death of Rudyard Kipling
1939 Start of World War II in Europe (1939–45)
1940 Muslim League demands a separate Muslim State (Pakistan)
In London a survivor of the Amritsar massacre murders Sir
Michael O'Dwyer (Lieut-Governor of the Punjab in 1919)
1941 Census shows a total population of 388 million
1942 India is threatened by Japanese forces in Burma: Japanese
occupy the Andaman Islands
"Quit India" movement is started
1943 Famine in Bengal: 3 million die
1944 Japanese invasion of Assam
1945 Japanese forces defeated in Burma
End of World War II
British Government announces intention to grant India
independence
1946 Mutiny of the Royal Indian Navy at Bombay and Karachi
6,000 die in 3 days of communal violence in Calcutta
Communal riots occur in many parts of India
1947 Lord Mountbatten appointed Viceroy
Serious unrest widespread throughout the country
India and Pakistan gain their Independence (15th August)

Acknowledgements

Grateful acknowledgements are due to the following publishers, authors and others:

Mrs Laura Huxley and Chatto & Windus Ltd: *Jesting Pilate* by Aldous Huxley.
Curtis Brown: *My Early Life* by Winston S. Churchill. Reproduced with permission of Curtis Brown Ltd, London. Copyright the Estate of Sir Winston S. Churchill.
W. & G. Foyle Ltd: *Foreign Devil* by Gordon Enders.
Eric Glass Ltd: *Verdict on India* by Beverley Nichols.
Robert Hale Ltd: *Born to Trouble* by Patrick Alexander.
William Heinemann Ltd: *Indian Patchwork* by Edward and Mary Charles.
Random Century Group: *Big Game, Boers and Boches* by Lt-Col V. Prescott-Westcar and *Khyber Caravan* by Gordon Sinclair.
The Duchess of Manchester: *My Candid Recollections* by The 9th Duke of Manchester.
The Viscount Scarsdale for permission to quote from Lady Mary Curzon's correspondence.
Mr Alan Campbell-Johnson: *Mission with Mountbatten*.
The Department of Documents, Imperial War Museum, together with the following: Nigel R. Gander and Julian M. Gander for permission to quote from the manuscript letter of Leonard Marsland Gander; Mr L.K. Parlow for permission to quote from his manuscript Diary.
The Royal Pavillion, Art Gallery and Museums, Brighton, for permission to use the cover illustration *Elephant with Trappings* by C.M. and E.J. Detmold

Every effort has been made to trace the owners of copyright material; however, if any other acknowledgements are due but have been omitted the Compiler offers his sincere apologies.

Index

Illustrations are indicated in italics

In Print

New and Forthcoming Books

Traveller's Literary Companion to the Indian Subcontinent *edited by Simon Weightman (School of Oriental and African Studies, London).* With a literature stretching back thousands of years and a vibrant modern literary culture, the Indian subcontinent is an ideal subject for the Literary Companion series. The volume ranges from the *Ramayana* to contemporary novelists such as Salman Rushdie and R.K. Narayan. The colonial experience provided many British writers with an exotic locale and the works of Rudyard Kipling, E.M. Forster and travel writers such as Richard Burton are fully covered. As with all books in the series, extracts are specially selected to convey a sense of place, making the book ideal holiday reading. ISBN 1 873047 25 8 *(hb), 1 873047 35 5 (pb), 350pp (approx), hb £34.95 (approx), pb £12.95 (approx).* Publication 1993.

Traveller's Literary Companion series
Africa, Oona Strathern (forthcoming 1993)
Eastern Europe, James Naughton, ed (forthcoming 1993)
Indian Subcontinent, Simon Weightman, ed (forthcoming 1993)
True Tales of British India, Michael Wise, ed
Japan, Harry Guest (forthcoming 1993)
South and Central America, Jason Wilson (forthcoming 1993)
South-east Asia (forthcoming 1993)

Books on Japan and South-east Asia
Alone in this World, Yoshio Markino
A British Artist in Meiji Japan, Sir Alfred East
Companion to Japanese Britain and Ireland, Bowen Pearse
A Japanese Artist in London, Yoshio Markino
Teaching English in Japan, Jerry O'Sullivan
The Tower of London, Natsume Soseki

The Puppeteer's Wayang: A Selection of Modern Malaysian Poetry edited by Muhammad Haji Salleh

All the above titles are available from In Print Publishing Ltd, 9 Beaufort Terrace, Brighton, UK. Tel: +44 (0)273 682 836. Fax: +44 (0)273 620 958.

Michael Wise was born in London in 1937 and is a graduate of Oxford University where he obtained an MA in Philosophy, Politics, and Economics. His subsequent business career took him overseas, particularly to the East, where he lived and worked for several years. His historical and literary interests led him to pursue the travel literature of the countries he came to know best, and in the 1980s he had three collections published by Times Books International. With *True Tales of British India* Michael Wise has again focused on an area where he has worked, and is contributing the first volume in a new series of Traveller's Companions being issued by In Print.